Using Microsoft Internet Explorer

Quick Start to

Internet Explorer Basics

When clouds are moving across the background, Internet Explorer is transferring a document or file.

Click here to return to your home (start) page.

Click here to go to the favorites list.

The title bar shows the current document's name.

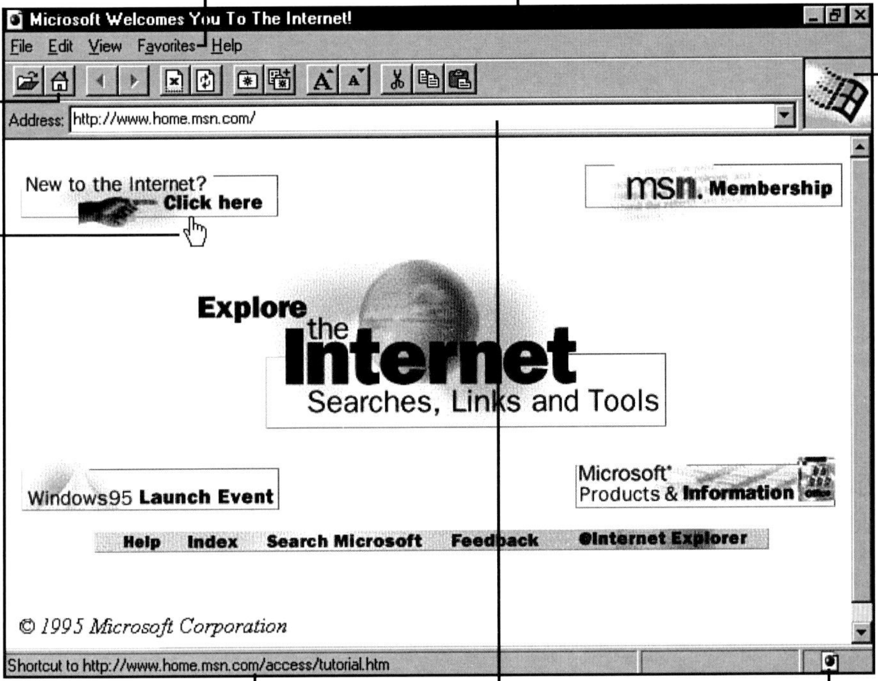

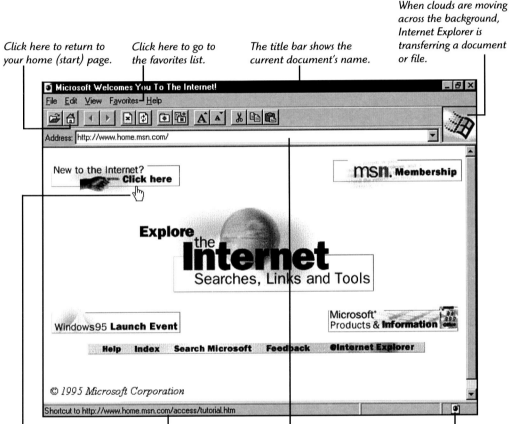

When the mouse pointer changes to a hand, you're over a link. Click on the link to jump to another page. (Links may be on pictures, or may be underlined, colored text.)

While the mouse pointer is over a link, the status bar shows the URL (the address of the referenced document).

Type an address (a URL) here, then press Enter; you'll go to that Web page.

This little icon indicates the current procedure. Hold the pointer over it to see the URL of the current document.

QUE® 201 W. 103rd Street • Indianapolis, IN 46290 • (317) 581-3500

Toolbar Buttons

Click here to open a Web document on your hard disk.

Click here to return to your home (start) page.

The Back button returns you to the previous document.

This button takes you to the next page (the one you were viewing before clicking on the Back button)

To stop transferring a document or file, click here.

To get a fresh copy of the document from the Web, click on the Refresh button.

Click here to open the Favorites folder.

Click here to add a Web document to the Favorites folder.

This button increases the size of the text in the document window.

This button reduces the text size.

Select text from the Address text box or in a text box in a form, and click on this button to remove the text to the Clipboard.

Click on this button to copy highlighted text to the Clipboard. (Including text within the document itself.)

Click on this button to paste text from the Clipboard into the Address text box or a text box in a form.

Using
Microsoft Internet Explorer

Using Microsoft Internet Explorer

Peter Kent

QUE®

Using Microsoft Internet Explorer

Library of Congress Catalog No.: 95-71462

ISBN: 0-7897-0551-6

97 96 95 6 5 4 3 2 1

Interpretation of the printing code: the rightmost double-digit number is the year of the book's printing; the rightmost single-digit number, the number of the book's printing. For example, a printing code of 95-1 shows that the first printing of the book occurred in 1995.

Screen reproductions in this book were created using Collage Plus from Inner Media, Inc., Hollis, NH.

Composed in *ITC Century*, *ITC Highlander*, and *MCPdigital* by Que Corporation.

Credits

President
Roland Elgey

Publisher
Stacy Hiquet

Publishing Director
Brad R. Koch

Editorial Services Director
Elizabeth Keaffaber

Managing Editor
Sandy Doell

Director of Marketing
Lynn E. Zingraf

Senior Series Editor
Chris Nelson

Publishing Manager
Brad Koch

Acquisitions Editor
Beverly M. Eppink

Product Director
Benjamin Milstead

Production Editor
Ruth Slates

Editor
Heather Kaufman Urschel

Assistant Product Marketing Manager
Kim Margolius

Technical Editor
Gregory Newmann

Technical Specialist
Cari Skaggs

Acquisitions Coordinator
Ruth Slates

Operations Coordinator
Patty Brooks

Editorial Assistant
Andrea Duvall

Book Designers
Ruth Harvey
Sandra Stevenson

Cover Designer
Dan Armstrong

Production Team
Angela D. Bannan
Jason Carr
Chad Dressler
Damon Jordan
Daryl Kessler
Michelle Lee
Bobbi Satterfield
Andrew W. Stone
Scott Tullis
Kelly Warner
Colleen Williams
Jody York

Indexer
Kathy Venable

This one's for Mum.

About the Author

Peter Kent lives in Lakewood, Colorado. He's spent the last fourteen years training users, documenting software, and designing user interfaces. Working as an independent consultant for the last nine years, Peter has worked for companies such as MasterCard, Amgen, Data General, and Dvorak Development and Publishing. Much of his consulting work has been in the telecommunications business.

Peter is the author of *Using Microsoft Network* (Que) and the best-selling *Complete Idiot's Guide to the Internet* (Que). He's also written another six Internet-related books—including *The Complete Idiot's Guide to the World Wide Web*—and a variety of other works, such as *The Technical Writer's Freelancing Guide* and books on Windows NT and Windows 3.1. His articles have appeared in many periodicals, including *Internet World*, *Windows Magazine*, *Windows User*, *The Dallas Times Herald*, and *Computerworld*. Peter can be reached electronically at Microsoft Network/PeterKent, CompuServe/71601,1266, or Internet/pkent@lab-press.com.

We'd Like to Hear from You!

As part of our continuing effort to produce books of the highest possible quality, Que would like to hear your comments. To stay competitive, we *really* want you, as a computer book reader and user, to let us know what you like or dislike most about this book or other Que products.

You can mail comments, ideas, or suggestions for improving future editions to the address below, or send us a fax at (317) 581-4663. For the online inclined, Macmillan Computer Publishing has a forum on CompuServe (type **GO MACMILLAN** at any prompt) through which our staff and authors are available for questions and comments. The address of our Internet site is **http://www.mcp.com** (World Wide Web).

In addition to exploring our forum, please feel free to contact me personally to discuss your opinions of this book: I'm **PDS CIS #102121,1324** on CompuServe, and I'm **bmilstead@que.mcp.com** on the Internet.

Thanks in advance—your comments will help us to continue publishing the best books available on computer topics in today's market.

Benjamin Milstead
Product Development Specialist
Que Corporation
201 W. 103rd Street
Indianapolis, Indiana 46290
USA

Contents at a Glance

Table of Contents

Introduction

Part I: The First Steps

1 What is the Internet?

Finding a service provider

see page 19

2 Introducing the Web

Where is all this? The Web server

see page 25

Tools to simplify life

see page 29

3 Installing Internet Explorer

Where Do I Get Internet Explorer?

see page 35

Part II: Caught in the Web

4 The Opening Moves

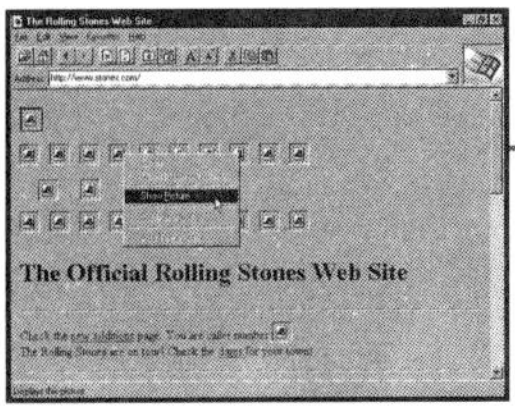

And now... the cache

see page 78

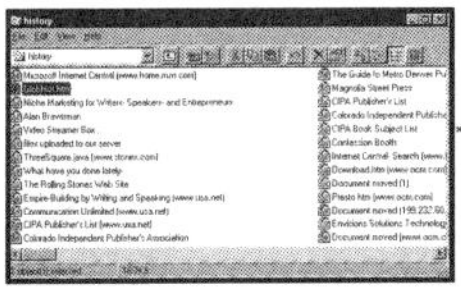

7 Customizing Internet Explorer

Changing program options

see page 102

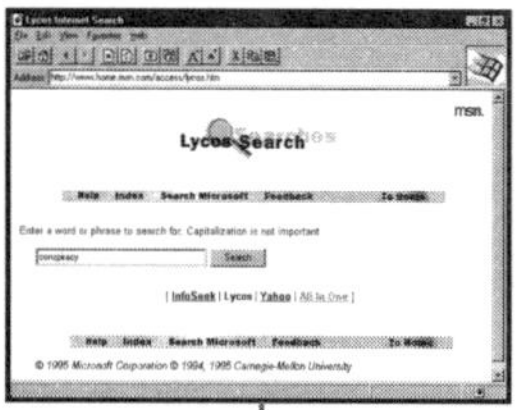

8 Searching for Information on the Web

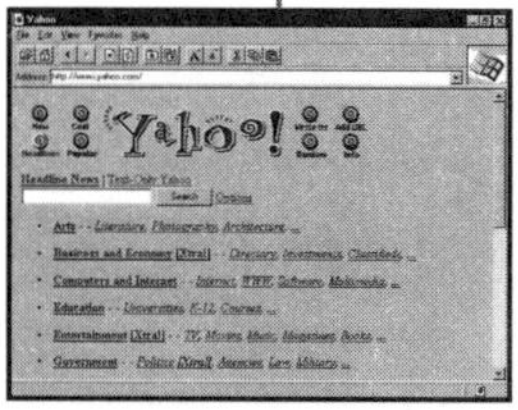

Virtual Libraries

see page 122

Interesting Business Sites on the Web

see page 124

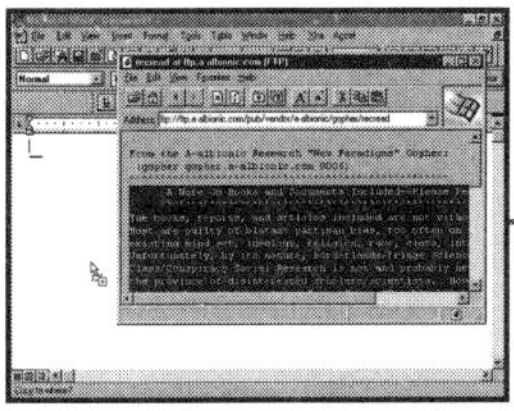

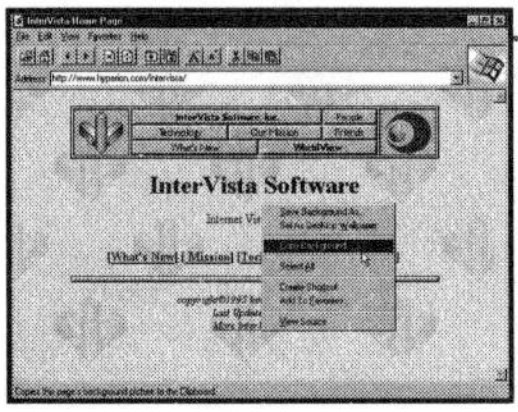

What happens when Explorer transfers a file?

see page 144

Part III: Traveling the Internet

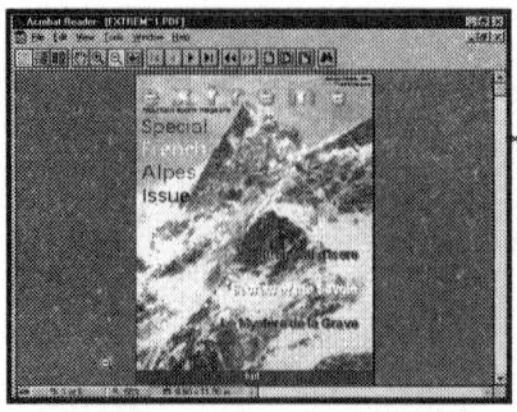

Finding Internet resources

see page 173

How can I find anything?

see page 188

Working in a Telnet session

see page 199

15 Reading Newsgroups From the Web

What's this got to do with Internet Explorer?

see page 204

Part IV: At Work on the Web

16 E-mail, Finger, Chat, and More

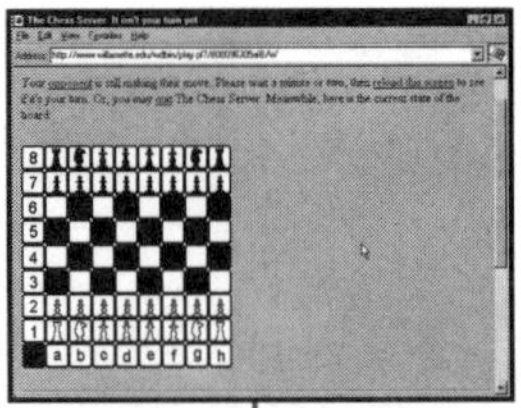

17 Create Your Own Home Page

Why bother with Web publishing?

see page 232

Creating your web page

see page 243

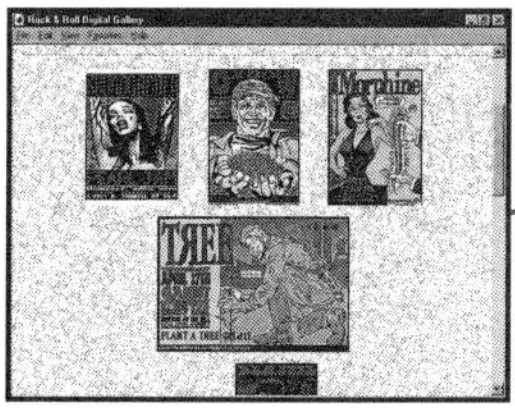

Part V: Appendixes

A Installing Explorer on Non-MSN Systems

Creating an Internet connection "from scratch"

see page 299

Action Index

Saving what you find

see page 310

Introduction

Poor old Bill Gates. Criticized from all sides for trying to take over the world, all he really wants to do is sell a lot of software. More software than anyone else, yes, but still, isn't that what being in business is all about, coming out on top?

As no doubt you've noticed by now (or you wouldn't be reading this book), Mr. Gates' Microsoft recently released Windows 95. When Microsoft began developing Windows 95 (or Windows 4.0, or Chicago, or whatever else it was called during development), nobody had heard of the Internet. Well, no *real* people, anyway. Only a few cybergeeks here and there. *The Internet* was not a term you'd see on the front cover of Time or Newsweek, or one that you'd hear on the ten o'clock news.

Things have changed a lot over the last couple of years. Everyone's heard of the Internet (though most still don't really understand what it's all about), and almost everyone with a computer seems to want to get onto it (though many aren't sure why). So in the middle of the development of Windows 95, Microsoft realized something important; their new operating system had better have built-in Internet tools, if only to compete with OS/2. Not only that, but Microsoft had plans to launch a new online service, **The Microsoft Network** (MSN). So to keep up with ever other online service, this one had better have full Internet access.

We've got to have the Web

But Windows 95 and MSN had to have more; not simply full Internet access and Internet tools, in particular they needed a Web browser, a program that would allow users to "surf" the World Wide Web. Now, there's a little confusion here, in the real world, about the relationship between the Web and the Internet. Many people seem to think they're synonymous. Nothing's farther from the truth. The Internet is an enormous network of computer networks, computers all over the world connected together. The Web is simply one of a number of software systems operating over that network.

Perhaps not "simply" one of a number of systems. Right now it's the most popular and the most exciting way to find information on the Internet. It's the system that gets most press (perhaps because it can provide so many pretty pictures), and it's the one that all new users want. They may not have heard of FTP, or Telnet, or Gopher. In fact they may not even know the term *The World Wide Web*; but they know what they want, and what they want is what they've seen on TV and in the press, and that's the Web. (I'll explain all these terms in chapters 1 and 2, by the way.)

Enter *Internet Explorer*

That's where **Internet Explorer** comes in. First, a little genealogy. You may have heard of **Mosaic**. "Born" at NCSA (the National Center for Supercomputing Applications—that is, paid for with tax dollars), Mosaic was the first widely available graphical World Wide Web browser. Text browsers had been around for some time. These were programs that could display World Wide Web documents, but only the text portion; no pictures, no sounds, no video, not much at all. They worked, and they worked well, but they were as exciting as reading a Telex. That didn't matter too much, because there wasn't much more than text on the Web; why have anything else, when there were no browsers to display it?

But Mosaic broke the "wow, cool" barrier. With Mosaic you could move around on the Web by clicking on links in documents with a mouse. And if any of the documents contained pictures, you could see them on your screen. And if any of the documents contained links to other forms of media, you could work with those, too. Mosaic not only made the Web easy to use, but it made it fun.

Along came a company called Spyglass, which licensed Mosaic from NCSA, and created Enhanced NCSA Mosaic, an excellent Web browser, easier to work with than Mosaic, and more stable too. And along came Microsoft, which licensed Enhanced NCSA Mosaic from Spyglass, made some changes to it to integrate it with Windows 95, and called it Internet Explorer.

Internet Explorer is available for free to MSN users who want full Internet access. And it's part of Microsoft Plus!, a Windows 95 add-on that contains a few neat toys and some Internet software. (Microsoft Plus!'s "street price" is around $45.)

What makes this book different?

This book explains how to work with Internet Explorer, from the basics (installing it and moving around in Webspace), to more advanced stuff (running FTP sessions, using finger, even creating your own Web pages).

Many Internet Explorer users will start working with Internet Explorer without any help. They'll quickly figure out how to click on links to move around, and probably figure out how to enter URLs (Web addresses) to go directly to pages. But will they figure out how to run multiple Web sessions, why pages they've seen before seem to pop up very quickly, or why links in pages they looked at a few weeks ago don't seem to work anymore? Will they find out how to use finger to get earthquake information, what the news: and mailto: URLs can do for them, or how to create a cascading Favorites menu?

Using Microsoft Internet Explorer will explain all this and plenty more. By the time you've finished this book, you'll know more about working on the World Wide Web than 99% of all Web users. You'll be able to use Internet Explorer quickly and efficiently, and find what you need when you need it.

You don't have to be a power user to work with this book. I'm assuming that you have a few Windows basics down—how to use a mouse, how to open menus and work in dialog boxes—but I won't give you abbreviated instructions that only a computer geek could understand. I'll tell you clearly what you need to do to get the job done. This is a book for people who want to understand how to user Explorer right now, with a minimum of fuss, but a maximum of benefit.

How do I use this book?

You can dip into this book at the point you need help—you don't have to read from page one to the end if you don't want to. I've put plenty of cross references in, so if you reach a point where you need some background information that I've covered earlier, you'll know where to go.

There are a number of ways for you to find information, too. There's a detailed Table Of Contents—in most cases you'll be able to skim through this and find exactly where to go. There's an index at the back of course, to help you jump directly to a page. The problem with indexes, though, is that they refer to words, rather than procedures. That's why we've also included an Action Index, just before the normal index. Quickly read through the Action Index sometime—you'll find that it's essentially a list of procedures, things you want to do with MSN, with the number of the page you need to go to for the instructions.

It's a good idea to spend a few minutes just leafing through the book, finding out what's there. That way, when you run into a problem, you'll have an idea of where to go to find the directions you need.

How this book is put together

I've divided this book into several parts, according to the different functions and procedures. Part I explains how to get started with Internet Explorer, Part II describes working on the World Wide Web, and Part III explains how to use Internet Explorer to work with non-Web Internet systems (FTP, Telnet, and so on). In Part IV I've explained how to create your own home page, and provided a short "sampler" of interesting and useful sites on the Web. (In fact you'll find information about useful sites scattered throughout the book at appropriate points.)

Part I: The First Steps

In chapter 1, I've explained what the Internet actually is, to make sure we start off with a clear understanding. I've described how to find a service provider (if you don't want to use MSN), and what all the different Internet services can do for you.

In chapter 2, I describe the World Wide Web itself, and how it works—the different components that function together. And chapter 3 talks about the different ways to install Internet Explorer.

Part II: Caught in the Web

Part II of this book is dedicated to the Web proper. Chapter 4 describes the first basic procedures you must understand to move around on the Web. Chapter 5 describes more advanced "navigation" techniques, and in chapter 6 I show you how to use the history list, Favorites list, and desktop shortcuts to make getting around easier.

In chapter 7 I'll show you how to customize Internet Explorer in a number of ways, some minor, some very important. Chapter 8 explains a critical skill, searching for information on the Web. (The Web is an enormous mess of strange and diverse stuff; without understanding how to search for what you need you'll quickly get lost.) In chapter 9 you'll learn how to save things you find on the Web—the text itself, pictures, sounds, backgrounds, program files, and so on.

Chapters 10 and 11 explain how to work with the "multimedia" aspect of the Web. How to play sound and video of various formats, view Adobe Acrobat hypertext files, "fly through" 3-D objects, and more. You often have to install special **viewers** to use these forms of media; I explain where to find them and how to install them.

Part III: Traveling the Internet

There's plenty more on the Internet *outside* the Web, and in this part of the book I explain how you can use Internet Explorer to work with other parts of the Internet. In chapter 12 I've explained the different types of addresses that point out of the Web, and how to work with Gopher (a menu system that leads you to Internet resources all over the world).

In chapter 13 you'll find out about the Internet's software libraries, the FTP sites, and how you can copy files from these libraries back to your computers; you can grab programs, sounds, clip art, documents, and more. Chapter 14 discusses Telnet, a system that allows you to log onto other computers around the world, to play chess, search databases, and so on. Internet Explorer can't run a Telnet session directly, but it can launch Microsoft Telnet.

Chapter 15 describes what happens when you click on a news: link, a link to an Internet newsgroup. And chapter 16 explains a few more non-Web systems that you can access through Internet Explorer: e-mail, finger, chat, games, WAIS, and so on.

Part IV: At Work on the Web

In this part of the book I'll explain an advanced topic: Web authoring. In chapters 17 and 18 you'll learn how to create your own home page (it's really quite easy), and even how to set up your own Web site so other people can view your words of wisdom.

Finally, in chapter 19, you'll find a small Web Sampler, a number of sites you may find useful or interesting, and which should give you an idea of the wide range of "stuff" out there on the Web.

Part V: Appendixes

In Part V you'll find an appendix explaining how to install Internet Explorer if you are converting from an MSN account to another service provider, or if you've never had an MSN account and don't want one. Initially most users will probably use Explorer through MSN, and installing the software with MSN is explained in chapter 3. But installing the program for another service provider takes a bit more effort (okay, maybe a lot more effort). You'll find instructions in the Appendix.

At the end of this book, you find a normal index. But back up a few pages and you find another index—an Action Index. If you're looking for a particular procedure or action, look in here; this index will point you to the page that helps you find the information you need.

Information that's easy to understand

This book uses a number of special elements and conventions to help you find information quickly—or to skip things you don't want to read.

Web addresses (URLs) and newsgroups are all in **bold type**, like this: **rec.food.sourdough**, as is text that I'm instructing you to type, and new terminology. Messages that appear in message boxes and status bars are in *italic*, as is link text (that is, the text in a Web document which, when clicked on, takes you to another document or file). Items that can be selected from dropdown list boxes are also in *italic*. Program or login script text is in this special font.

Throughout this book, we use a comma to separate the parts of a menu command. For example, to start a new document, you choose File, New. That means "Open the File menu, and choose New from the list."

And if you see two keys separated by a plus sign, such as Ctrl+X, that means to press and hold the first key, press the second key, and then release both keys.

TIP

Tips either point out information easily overlooked or help you use your software more efficiently, such as through a shortcut. Tips may help you solve or avoid problems.

CAUTION

Cautions warn you about potentially dangerous results. If you don't heed them, you could unknowingly do something harmful.

Q&A

What are Q&A notes?

Q&A notes appear as questions and answers. We try to anticipate user questions that might come up and provide answers to you here.

“ ***Plain English, please!***

These notes define technical terms or computer jargon. ”

Sidebars are interesting nuggets of information

Sidebars include information that's relevant to the topic at hand, but not essential. You might want to read them when you're not online. Here you may find more technical details, or interesting background information.

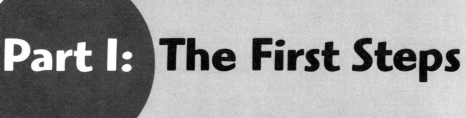

Part I: The First Steps

1

What is the Internet?

In this chapter:

- **What is this thing called *the Internet*?**
- **Nobody owns the Internet**
- **What services are available?**
- **The four different forms of Internet access**
- **Using Microsoft Network**
- **Finding a service provider**

You've heard about the Internet a thousand times. But what exactly is the Internet?. . . . .

Even now, two years after the Internet became big news, there's still much confusion about what kind of animal it really is. So in this chapter I'm going to explain just that. I'll also explain the different ways to get connected to the Internet, and how to find an Internet **service provider**.

What's it all about?

The Internet is a network of networks. A computer network is a group of computers that are connected so they can communicate with each other. The computers send messages to each other, and share information in the form of computer files. The Internet connects tens of thousands of these networks, with more being added constantly. And on those networks are millions of computers.

No doubt you've noticed all the Information Superhighway hype over the last couple of years. Thanks to heavy media coverage, the Internet is growing rapidly. Though few people had even heard of it three years ago, now almost everyone's heard of the Internet (even if they don't really know what it is).

Lots of different networks have been joined together to produce the world's largest group of connected computers. The networks which make up the Internet belong to government bodies, universities, businesses, local-community library systems, and even some schools. Most are in the United States but many are overseas —from Australia to Zimbabwe.

What makes the Internet so special is the fact that Internet users can **log in** to a host computer and use the computer's resources, or even get to the resources without logging in. When you connect to the Internet, you can connect to thousands of different computer systems containing a wealth of information. The information available includes government archives, university databases, local community computing resources, library catalogs, messages about any subject you can imagine, and millions of computer files—photographs, documents, sound clips, video, and anything else you can put into digital form.

> **Plain English, please!**
>
> To **log on** or **log in** to a computer system means you tell it who you are, and the computer decides if it wants to let you use its services. A log-on (or logon) procedure usually entails providing some kind of account name and a password.

Who owns the Internet?...

When I'm asked who owns the Internet, I use this analogy: it's like a phone system. A phone system has lots of different "switches," owned by different organizations, all connected together. When someone in Denver tries to phone someone in New York, he doesn't need to know how the call gets through—which states and cities the call passes through. The telephone network handles it all for him. These private companies have decided the mechanics—the electronics—of the process, and it doesn't matter one whit to the average caller how it's done. The Internet works in much the same way. Just as there's no single telephone company, there's no single Internet company.

...Nobody!

Nobody "owns" the Internet. Who owns the world's telephone network? Nobody. Each component is owned by someone, but the network as a whole is not owned by anyone. The Internet is a system that hangs together through mutual interest. The world's telephone companies get together and decide the best way the "network" should function. They decide which country gets what country code, how to bill for international calls, who pays for transoceanic cables, and the technical details of how one country's lines connect to another.

The Internet is very similar. It began in the early '70s, with various government computer networks, and it has grown as different organizations realized the advantages of being connected. Its origins can be traced back to ARPANET, a Department of Defense computer system that was used to link a variety of research centers together. (ARPANET was not originally, as is popularly reported, a way to test how computer networks can survive war, though the military research was undertaken later.)

The NSF (National Science Foundation) gave the Internet a real boost when it realized that it could save money by creating a network of several supercomputer centers, and researchers—such as in major universities—could connect to them. In the past decade the Internet has grown tremendously. All sorts of organizations connected their networks, each with its own particular configuration of hardware and software.

In the past it was a non-commercial system; business was even frowned upon. In spite of that, the largest growth of the Internet has been in the last two years as the system has become commercialized. This has brought millions of dollars into the Internet, allowing development of new software, new connections, online businesses, and so on.

Just a little confusing...

If you've spent some time online with one of the large commercial online systems—CompuServe, Prodigy, America Online, or whatever—you'll find the Internet very different. It's not as organized. There's a wealth of information, entertainment, and software...but it's often difficult to figure out how to get to all this stuff. (Don't worry, I won't just teach you how to use Internet Explorer. I'll also show you where you can search for stuff that interests you.)

What's the point?

Why would you want to use the Internet? More specifically, why would you want to use Internet Explorer? Let's get a little more specific, and look at the services available to you on the Internet:

Service	Description
E-Mail and Mailing Lists	Send e-mail messages to anyone in the world (well, assuming that person has an Internet e-mail account). You can also subscribe to e-mail-based discussion groups.
Newsgroups	Thousands of discussion groups, on almost any subject you can think of.

Service	Description
The World Wide Web	This is a giant **hypertext** system—while you are viewing a document, you can click a link, and another document appears. Travel around the world by pointing and clicking. Sound, pictures, video, even 3-D images enrich the World Wide Web and make it the hot Internet tool. And the primary concern of this book, of course, as Internet Explorer is a Web **browser**, a program used to view Web documents.
Gopher	A menu system that lets you wander through computers on the Internet, searching for documents. Up to the beginning of 1994, it really seemed like the Gopher system would play a critical role in the future of the Internet. Now you hardly hear about Gopher; everyone's more interested in the World Wide Web.
FTP	File Transfer Protocol; a system that lets you transfer files from computers all over the world back to your computer. It's like a giant software library—millions of files — that contains programs, sound clips, music, pictures, video, and documents.
Telnet	A system that lets you log in to someone else's computer and run programs on it. Some people actually invite the public into their computers; you might get to play chess, view a government job listing, or search a NASA database.
WAIS	Wide Area Information Servers. You don't hear a lot about these right now; again, the Web is all that seems to interest people. Still, WAIS provides a handy system for searching databases for information, and you can often use it from the World Wide Web.
finger	A service originally based on the UNIX finger command, this lets you request information about a particular user's account. You may get basic stuff—like the user's name and the last time he was logged onto his account. Or you might get some information that the user wants to distribute—weather or earthquake reports, book reviews, sports results, or whatever.
Internet Relay Chat	A giant, world-wide chat system. You type messages that other people can read and respond to immediately. It's a real time form of messaging.

Plain English, please!

Hypertext is the term given to electronic documents that have links to other documents. As you are reading the document you'll see some form of link; a picture or underlined text. Clicking on the link takes you to a different document.

If you already know a little about the Internet, you may be surprised to hear that we'll be covering several of these services in this book. No, this isn't a book about the Internet—it's a book about Internet Explorer, which runs on the World Wide Web. But Internet Explorer can also run FTP and Gopher sessions and launch Telnet sessions. In Part III of this book, "Traveling the Internet," we're going to jump from the World Wide Web proper into some of the other Internet services you can use from Internet Explorer.

The different sorts of Internet connections

There are several different ways to hook up to the Internet and work online:

Connection Type	Description
Permanent	A connection directly from a computer to the Internet. These are generally quite expensive to set up and run; mostly businesses have such connections. In fact, only recently have any businesses except large companies and organizations installed such connections; prices have dropped dramatically in the last couple of years.
Dial-In Direct	A connection from a computer through a modem to the Internet. Once connected, the computer becomes a **host** on the Internet. The connection uses a special communications protocol called TCP/IP. Such connections are often known as SLIP, CSLIP, and PPP.
Dial-In Terminal	Also a connection from a computer through a modem, but a much simpler form. In this system, the computer becomes a terminal of another computer that is connected to the Internet. The connection uses simple serial communications software—Windows Terminal, HyperACCESS, CrossTalk, ProComm, or any other such program.
E-Mail	A connection to the Internet that lets you send and receive e-mail, and nothing more.

> ### *Plain English, please!*
>
> A **host** computer is one that other computers on the Internet can communicate with directly. Just because your computer can receive e-mail doesn't mean that it's a host—the e-mail is sent to the host computer to which a terminal is connected, for instance, and the terminal then gets it from the host. Host computers have special IP (Internet Protocol) numbers that identify them on the Internet.

The best of these connections is the permanent connection. Due to its expense, we can forget it (unless you are employed by a company or organization that has such a connection; in that case you may be able to connect through the system's network—talk to the system administrator). Let's forget the e-mail connection, since all you can do with e-mail is send text messages to and fro. We want the World Wide Web, which is more complicated.

We're not interested in the dial-in terminal connection, either. The problem with such a connection is that it's basically a text-based connection. Once connected, you'll find yourself typing commands or choosing from a text-based menu. These connections don't display pictures or play sounds, and will not run Internet Explorer.

That leaves us with the dial-in direct connection—a form of **TCP/IP connection**. TCP/IP means Transmission Control Protocol/Internet Protocol. It's the basic communications "language" used by the Internet, and once you have a TCP/IP connection you can work on the Internet proper. You need a special version of TCP/IP, however; one that's designed to run through modems and telephone lines.

> ### *Plain English, please!*
>
> A **protocol** defines how computers should talk to each other. It's like a language—if a group of different people all agree to speak French (or English, or Spanish), they can all understand each other. Communication protocols provide a set of rules that define how different modems, computers, and programs communicate.

The TCP/IP stack

In order to use software designed for TCP/IP, you need what's become known as a **TCP/IP stack**. This is a special program that interfaces between your software and the Internet.

Perhaps you could think of it like this. The Internet uses a special protocol—a special language—called TCP/IP. Your software doesn't really understand this language, so it uses a translator—the TCP/IP stack. You can also think of the stack as a TCP/IP **driver**. For instance, your Windows word processor doesn't know how to print a document on your printer. When you want to print something, you have to select a print driver. The word processor sends the document to the print driver, and the print driver translates it and sends it on to the printer.

So, when you use an Internet program—such as Internet Explorer—the program has to send information to the stack, which translates it and sends it out onto the Internet. If information is sent back to the program, the stack translates from TCP/IP into something that the program can understand.

Why should I use the Windows 95 stack?

At the risk of confusing you, let me get more specific...TCP/IP software combines two elements, a file called WINSOCK.DLL (which may be regarded as the actual stack), and a dialer, the program that dials into your service provider. Internet Explorer is designed to work with the Dial-Up Networking program, and a WINSOCK.DLL that is installed when you install the Internet connection.

You *may* actually be able to replace the Windows 95 WINSOCK.DLL file with one provided by another company—the CompuServe WINSOCK.DLL, for instance. So to be quite precise, you *can* use a different stack. (Dial-Up Networking works with the current CompuServe WINSOCK.DLL file.)

So while you could, in theory, replace the Windows 95 WINSOCK.DLL with the CompuServe WINSOCK.DLL, you still couldn't use the CompuServe Internet Dialer—you'd still need to use the Dial-Up Networking (or MSN) software to use Internet Explorer. So forget other stacks, and use Dial-Up Networking—and the WINSOCK.DLL file—that comes with Windows 95

What's PPP and SLIP?

There are two types of TCP/IP connection that can be made through a modem—**PPP** (Point to Point Protocol) and **SLIP** (Serial Line Interface Protocol). Some stacks can only use SLIP, some only use PPP, but some can use both. What does this mean? Quite simply, when you set up an Internet account, you must make sure that the stack you are using will work with the type of account being set up on the service provider's computer. (A service provider is a company or organization that provides Internet service—we'll get to that in a moment.)

The basic Windows 95 stack can only run on PPP connections. However, if you have Microsoft Plus!, a suite of programs sold in conjunction with Windows 95, you have additional software that will allow the stack to use SLIP connections. If possible, though, you should use PPP, as in most cases it is faster and more stable.

One more thing before we leave stacks. There are many different stacks. For instance, I used to run Trumpet Winsock, a shareware stack. I've also had stacks that came with commercial products, such as Internet Chameleon and SuperHighway Access. Internet Explorer is designed to run with the Windows 95 stack, though, and you'll find that it probably won't run with another stack. To run Internet Explorer, you'll need to install the Windows 95 stack. See chapter 3, "Installing Internet Explorer," for details.

Finding a service provider

Before you can use the Internet, you need to find a **service provider**, a company that provides access to the Internet. Microsoft has made this easy for you, if you choose Microsoft Network (MSN) as your service provider. MSN is Microsoft's new online service, and is similar in some ways to CompuServe, America Online, Prodigy, and so on. (Of course Microsoft would say it's *better*, and there are some important differences, as you can discover from my book, *Using Microsoft Network*, by Que.)

MSN has two levels of service. The first level provides the basic services; you can log on and use the MSN computers, work in the MSN BBSes, meet people in the MSN chat rooms, use e-mail, and so on. The second level provides full Internet access; you get a real PPP connection to the Internet, so you can run Internet Explorer (or any other software designed for TCP/IP connections). For information about MSN, see chapter 3, "Installing Internet Explorer."

Of course you may not want to use MSN. MSN may not have any TCP/IP telephone numbers in your area. If it doesn't, you'd have to pay long-distance charges to use the Internet through MSN. If MSN is more expensive than other service providers in your area, you may want to work with another service provider.

Let someone else pay

The best way to connect to Internet is to use OPM—Other People's Money. Most Internet users are connected through an organization that has a dedicated connection to Internet. Many large companies have their own computers connected directly to Internet and allow their employees access to it.

Talk with the person in your organization in charge of the Internet connection, if there is one. You may be able connect your Windows 95 computer through the network to the Internet.

Another way to get a free Internet connection is through a college. If you are a student (in some cases, even a part-time student), you can often get an Internet connection. However, many colleges still only provide dial-in terminal connections, and you need a dial-in direct connection.

Another free connection—Free-Nets

The next step is to look for a **Free-Net**. These are community computing systems. They may be based at a local library or college. You may be able to use Internet from a terminal at the library, or perhaps even dial into the system from your home computer. And, as the name implies, they don't cost anything. (Well, some may have a small registration fee—$5, perhaps—but if not actually free, they are pretty close to it.)

Free-Nets offer a variety of local services, as well as access to Internet. You may be able to find information about jobs in the area, local events, and recreation. You may be able to search the local library's database, find course schedules for local colleges, or ask someone questions about Social Security and Medicare.

> ***Plain English, please!***
>
> You'll see the terms Free-Net, freenet, FreeNet, and maybe other variations. All these terms are service marks of NPTN (National Public Telecommuting Network), who prefer to use the term Free-Net.

Again, the problem with Free-Nets is that they usually won't provide TCP/IP connections; most, at least currently, only have dial-in terminal connections. To find a Free-Net, e-mail **info@nptn.org**, or call the NPTN (National Public Telecommuting Network) at 216-247-5800. If you can't find a Free-Net, maybe you should start one in your town. NPTN can tell you how.

More freebies

To find more free sites, take a look in *Boardwatch Magazine*, *ComputerShopper*, *Online Access*, and other such magazines. (You can find these in many bookstores these days.) Also, check your city's local computer publications, and ask other Internet users you meet. You'll find bulletin board systems advertising Internet access, but you may also find listings of free BBSes with Internet access. For instance, in Denver there's NYX, a system at a local university. You can get a free account on NYX, and access the Internet. Again, however, you may find that most such systems do not have TCP/IP connections, only plain old dial-in terminal connections.

Paying for the connection

If you can't figure out where to find a free or almost-free Internet connection, you're on your own—you're going to have to pay.

How do I find a good service provider?

The standard of service you'll get can vary widely. Some service providers are very helpful, with responsive technical support, good documentation, and even setup programs that will lead you through installing a dial-in direct connection. Others will set up an account for you on their end, and then let you figure out the rest. Also, some services are currently overused—complaints of busy signals when trying to connect are common. If you know other Internet users, ask for a recommendation. Otherwise you'll just have to pick one and see what it's like.

Look in your city's local computer publication for ads. Talk to everyone you know who works with computers. Maybe someone will have an idea. The business pages in local newspapers often carry ads, too. If you already have access to Internet e-mail, or know someone who does, send a message to **info-deli-server@netcom.com**. In the body of the message type **Send PDIAL**. The recipient will automatically return a message that includes a large list of service providers in the United States, some with international access.

Also, you may want to get *Internet Access Providers* (Mecklermedia, $30). It's an international directory of service providers, regional networks, and bulletin boards, all with Internet access. (You can order it through your local bookstore, call 800-632-5537, call 203-226-6967, call 071-976-0405 in the UK, or e-mail **info@mecklermedia.com**.)

2

Introducing the Web

In this chapter:

- **What HTML and HTTP do for you**
- **The two meanings of the term *home page***
- **Using Web servers and Web clients (browsers)**
- **Understanding URLs**
- **Using browser features**
- **The history list and Favorites**

The World Wide Web is a software system that uses the Internet to create a giant web of interrelated documents. Here are a few Web basics you should know . . . .

This book is about a World Wide Web browser, not the Internet in its entirety. It's probably a good idea to understand a few basics about the Web before we jump straight in. What *is* the Web? How's it all fit together?

As you've already heard (in chapter 1), the Web is a hypertext system of documents linked together electronically. The Web lets you "navigate" between documents by clicking on links between those documents—and lets you go directly to a document by providing your *browser* (your Web program, Internet Explorer) with the document's address.

In order to understand the workings of the World Wide Web, let's start with its basic building blocks.

HTML—Web bricks

The primary building material on the Web is the *HTML* document. HTML means *Hypertext Markup Language*. HTML documents are computer files containing ASCII text—just plain 'ole text.

But the text contains special codes or **tags**; the codes are created using the normal ASCII-text characters, but they are codes nonetheless. They are not there for *you* to read, they are there for recognition by web browsers.

A **browser** is a program that helps you read HTML documents. When your browser opens an HTML document, it looks closely at the codes. The codes, or tags, tell the browser what to do with each part of the text—"these few words are a link to another document, this line is a heading, this is the document title," and so on.

After it has read the codes (this happens very quickly, by the way) the browser then displays the text on your computer screen. It strips out the codes and formats the text according to the code's instructions. (You can tell Internet Explorer to interpret the codes to some degree, as we'll see in a moment.)

You really don't need to know what these HTML codes are, unless you want to publish your own Web documents. You'll learn more about the codes in chapters 17 and 18, but for now take a quick look at figures 2.1 and 2.2. The first is a document displayed in Internet Explorer, after the browser has formatted the HTML document. The second is the same document displayed in Notepad, which shows you what the actual HTML document looks like, codes and all.

Fig. 2.1
Here's what the CIPA (http://usa.net/cipa) document looks like in Internet Explorer

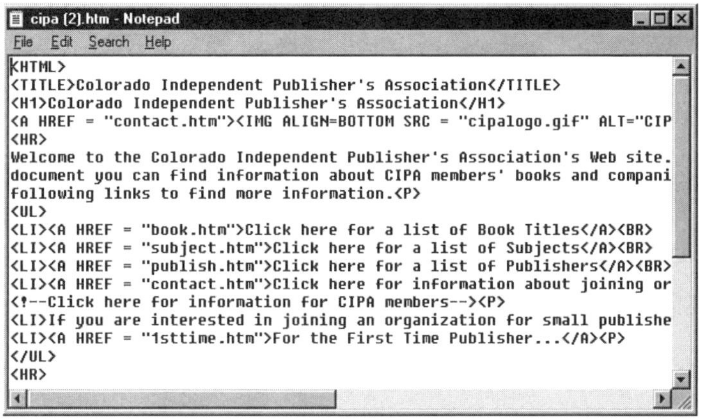


```
<HTML>
<TITLE>Colorado Independent Publisher's Association</TITLE>
<H1>Colorado Independent Publisher's Association</H1>
<A HREF = "contact.htm"><IMG ALIGN=BOTTOM SRC = "cipalogo.gif" ALT="CIP
<HR>
Welcome to the Colorado Independent Publisher's Association's Web site.
document you can find information about CIPA members' books and compani
following links to find more information.<P>
<UL>
<LI><A HREF = "book.htm">Click here for a list of Book Titles</A><BR>
<LI><A HREF = "subject.htm">Click here for a list of Subjects</A><BR>
<LI><A HREF = "publish.htm">Click here for a list of Publishers</A><BR>
<LI><A HREF = "contact.htm">Click here for information about joining or
<!--Click here for information for CIPA members--><P>
<LI>If you are interested in joining an organization for small publishe
<LI><A HREF = "1sttime.htm">For the First Time Publisher...</A><P>
</UL>
<HR>
```

Fig. 2.2
Here's the document from figure 2.1, shown in Notepad.

Where is all this? The Web server

So where, physically, are these documents stored? On computer systems throughout the world. How do you get to them? A Web **server** makes them available. This is a program that receives requests from your browser, and transmits the Web documents back to you. What term should we use for the actual information stored on the computer? Each individual HTML file is known as a **document** or **page**. You'll also often hear the term **site**, to mean a collection of documents about a particular subject, stored on a particular computer. It is also used to refer to a computer that contains a number of documents or pages.

Smaller bricks—other media

The Web is based on text, but there's plenty more out there too. Just about any form of Internet tool or computer file can be linked to the Web. You'll find pictures, sounds, video, FTP sites, Gopher sites, WAIS database searches, Finger sites, 3D images, and more.

You'll usually find that you start by reading a document, then jump from that document to something else. However, these days *many* documents have **inline graphics**—pictures that are linked into the documents and appear when you display the document (you can see a picture in figure 2.1, for instance). How can these pictures be linked to an ASCII document? A special HTML tag tells the browser where the picture is (generally in the same directory as the HTML document), and the browser grabs the picture and inserts it in the correct position.

Your HTML "player"—the browser

If you want to listen to a music CD, you need a CD player. If you want to listen to an LP, you need a record player. If you want to see a video, you need a videocassette player. And if you want to see an HTML file, you need a **browser**, such as Internet Explorer.

> **"Plain English, please!"**
>
> Browsers are sometimes also known as Web **clients**. A Web **server** is a system that contains Web documents, and lets people in to view those documents. A **client** is the program that is serviced by the server—it's the program that displays the Web documents. The term *browser*, however, is more commonly used. "

Browsers can be very simple, letting you view nothing but the text in Web documents, letting you move between documents, but little else. Or they can be very sophisticated, letting you save information, play sounds and video, and create bookmarks so you can find your way back. Internet Explorer is near the top end, providing lots of neat features.

You've got a say, too

Some of the more sophisticated browsers also let *you* decide how to display HTML files. You don't get to view each file's HTML codes and decide what to do with them. Rather, you give the browser a set of rules. Internet Explorer is a little limited in this respect, though it still lets you define the font sizes used for the document text, and modify the text and background colors.

But how does the browser get the data?

When you want to view a Web document, Internet Explorer has to transfer the document from a site—in Albania, Albany, or Australia—back to your computer. How is that done?

The Internet has all sorts of **Transfer Protocols**, systems used for transferring different forms of data across the Internet. These include SMTP, the Simple Mail Transfer Protocol (used for sending e-mail); NNTP, Network News Transfer Protocol (used for transmitting newsgroup messages all over the place), and HTTP, HyperText Transfer Protocol.

HTTP is the system used by the Web to transfer data to and fro. That's really all you need to know, and the only reason I'm telling you is that you'll run across the term HTTP now and again. If you really want to know how HTTP *works*, you're out of luck in this book!

By the way, like many writers and Web users, I refer to the Web as if you were traveling around on it. I (and others) say "go to the such and such site," "navigate to something or other," and so on. Strictly speaking, of course, you are not going anywhere. (Your chair will remain firmly attached to your floor.) Rather, documents are being sent from the Web server computers to your computer. But in many ways the "travel" analogy works well. You are getting documents, pictures, and sounds from all over the world. While you physically remain in one spot, intellectually you are on a journey.

URL—the Web address

Everything on the Internet needs some kind of address—otherwise, how would you find anything? The Web's no different. Each resource on the Web has an address, a URL—*Universal Resource Locator*. Here's one, for instance:

http://www.iuma.com/IUMA-2.0/pages/registration/registration.html

The URL starts with **http://**. This indicates the site is a normal HTTP (HyperText Transfer Protocol) site; you are going to an HTML document. Sometimes the URL starts with something different. If it starts with **ftp://**, for instance, it means you are on you way to an FTP site. As you'll see in chapters 12 to 16, Web browsers can access other Internet systems, not just HTTP.

Next comes the address of the host computer (the address of the computer that has the Web server you are contacting), in this case **www.iuma.com**. Following that is the address of the file directory containing the resource—**/IUMA-2.0/pages/registration/**. You probably are aware that in the world of Windows and DOS, directories are indicated with backslashes (\ ). In the UNIX world, however, they are indicated with forward slashes (/). Most Internet Web sites are running on UNIX computers (though that may change, Windows NT seems to be taking off), and the forward slash has become the standard for URLs, whatever type of computer the document is found on.

Finally, you have the resource itself—**registration.html**. In this case you can tell that it's an HTML document. The .html extension makes that clear. (If the document is on a Windows computer it may have an .HTM extension instead.)

Sometimes the URL won't have a filename at the end. That's not necessarily a mistake. For instance, if you are going to the Ziff-Davis Publishing Web document, you'll use the **http://www.ziff.com/** URL. This specifies the host, but no directory or document. That's okay, their Web server is set up to show you the document they want you to see.

What can you do with it?

What are you going to do with a URL? Well, you can get almost anywhere on the Web by simply following links in documents. But you may spend several weeks trying to get where you want to go! The URL is a short cut. Web browsers have a way that you can tell them to go to a particular URL. I'll show you how to get Internet Explorer to go where you want it to go in chapter 5.

TIP **You may hear or read something like "point your Web browser** to . . ." This simply means use your browser's URL command to go directly to the document.

You'll find URLs all over the place. In *Newsweek*'s regular Cyberscope column, in various directories of resources on the net, and throughout this book (in particular Chapter 19, which will give you all sorts of places to point your browser).

Tools to simplify life

We've pretty much covered the basics of the Web itself, but before we move on, let's consider some of the ways that Internet Explorer can make traveling the Web easier for you.

First, it's nice to be able to save the document you are viewing. Internet Explorer lets you do so in a number of ways; you can save a text file directly to disk, copy text to the Clipboard, even drag text from the browser to another program. And you can let Explorer save documents in its **cache**, so the next time you want to view the document you'll be able to retrieve it very quickly (without even logging onto the Internet to get it—the cache is on your hard disk).

Then how about downloading files? There are lots of files on the Web that are "pointed to" by links in text documents. Internet Explorer will let you transfer those files back to your computer. In fact you'll even be able to carry out FTP sessions, to grab files not just from Web sites but from File Transfer Protocol sites, libraries of programs, sounds, documents, and plenty more.

The home page (or is it start page?)

Here's an argument I'm not going to win—"What is a **home page**?" It's a greatly misused term, that's what it is! You'll often hear the term used to refer to a particular Web site's main page. "Hey, dude, check out the Rolling Stones' home page," you might hear someone say (it's not a home page, dude, but nonetheless it's at **http://www.stones.com/**). It would be more correct to call it the Rolling Stones **Web site** or **page** or **document**.

Home page is actually a browser term, not a Web site term. It's the page that appears when you first open your Web browser. A company could set up a document for all of its employees. When they start their browsers they see this home page, with all the links they'd normally need. A service provider could set up a home page so that when any subscriber started a browser it displayed that page. And you can even create your own home page, with links to all the sites you commonly use (see chapter 17).

The home page is a sort of starting point, and most browsers have a command or button that will take you directly back to the home page, wherever you happen to be on the Web. (If every document on the Web is a home page, what sense does having a Home Page button make? *Which* home page should it take you to?)

Anyway, I've pretty much lost this argument. Many HTML authors are creating what they are terming "home pages," so the term now has, in effect, two meanings. The programmers who created Internet Explorer decided to use the term **start page** instead of home page, to avoid the ambiguity, I guess. Explorer is probably the only browser you'll find to have done this, and in fact they only partially made the switch; the Open Start Page toolbar button shows a picture of a house, like almost every other browser around.

Where've I been? The History list

Some kind of **History list** is useful. This is simply a list of all the documents you've viewed in the current session. A history list lets you quickly select a document and return to that document. Internet Explorer has an excellent History list, based on the familiar Windows Explorer program. (Windows Explorer is Windows 95's new "file manager" type program. When you open the History list you are actually opening a Windows Explorer window, displaying the directory—the folder—that holds the history entries.) It provides plenty of flexibility, as you'll see in chapter 6. But unlike most browsers, it doesn't just list the documents you've viewed in the current session. It lists documents you've seen in earlier sessions, too. How far back will it go? How much disk space do you have available to list URLs?

Where did I go yesterday? Bookmarks and Favorites

A bookmark system lets you save the URLs and the titles of documents to which you think you'll want to return. It's easy to get lost on the Web. Spend an hour online, close your browser, then try to repeat your path through the Web—impossible. Just remember poor old Hansel and Gretel trying to find their way through the woods. And you are traveling across the world!

Bookmarks, though, let you create a list of this useful stuff, then use the list to go directly back to one of the sites. Explorer's bookmarks system is known as the **Favorites list**, and it's excellent. You can add as many bookmarks as you want, then organize them into folders; again, this list is based on the Windows Explorer. The list is available two ways—in the Favorites folder (opened by clicking on a button in the toolbar) and in the Favorites menu. You'll learn more about the Favorites in chapter 6.

What was that again?

We've covered the basics, but as you'll soon find out, there's plenty more. Before we go on, here's a quick summary of a few Web and Explorer terms:

Term	Definition
HTML	Hypertext Markup Language, the "coding" system used to create a Web text document.
Web Server	A Web server is a computer running a program that provides information to a Web browser. Web documents are managed by the server.
Web Site	I generally use the term **Web site** to mean a group of related Web documents on one computer—with this definition, a computer may contain several Web sites. Some people use it to mean a computer containing Web documents, though I prefer to think of that as a Web server.
Browser	A program that can read HTML documents, and lets you navigate through the Web. Sometimes known as a Web **client.**
HTTP	Hypertext Transfer Protocol, the system used to transfer Web data between the Web site and your browser.
URL	Universal Resource Locator, a Web "address," used to tell a browser where to find a document or other resource on the Web.

continues

Term	Definition
Home page	Not a Web site's main page. Rather, it's the first page that appears when the browser starts. (Okay, use the term to mean a Web site's main page if you want, see if I care!)
Start page	Internet Explorer's term for the home page—the one that opens when you start Explorer.
History list	A list of all the places you've been on the Web, in the current session and previous sessions. Lets you jump directly back to a particular document.
Bookmarks	A URL that has been saved in some kind of system from which you can quickly select it, so you can jump back to a useful or interesting site.
Favorite list	What Explorer calls its list of bookmarks.

Just how big is the Web?

One more thing before we go. How big is the Web? Well, read the Web document at **http://www.mit.edu:8001/afs/sipb/user/mkgray/ht/wow-its-big.html** (you'll find out how to use this URL later in the book) for a really good idea of how big it is (or was, the last time the author updated the document). The author claims that each day about 50 Gigabytes of data crosses the Web—that's the equivalent to tens of millions of pages of text! (The number's out of date, though; it's probably *much* higher by now.) And the Web is growing 1%... per day!

3

Installing Internet Explorer

In this chapter:

- Finding Internet Explorer
- Setting up an MSN account
- Downloading Explorer from MSN
- Installing from Microsoft Plus!
- Converting from another service provider to MSN
- Installation bugs
- What to do if you're not an MSN member

Installing Internet Explorer can be easy, or it can be hard. Take your pick . . . .

Before you can run Internet Explorer, you've got to install it. There are two ways to do so; the easy way, and the hard way. Ah, I can hear you say, I'll take the easy way. But before you do that, you have to decide which Internet service provider you want to use.

You see, the easiest way to install Internet Explorer is to configure it to run through Microsoft Network (MSN). This is the new online service you've probably heard about; the basic software comes with Windows 95, so you can quickly and easily install the MSN software and sign up for the MSN service. (For detailed information about MSN, read *Using Microsoft Network*, from Que).

Internet Explorer is *not* part of the basic MSN software, though. If you want full Internet access through MSN—including the Internet Explorer program—you can sign up for this service online. MSN will then download the Internet software to your computer's hard disk for you. Or you can obtain Microsoft Plus!, an accessory pack for Windows 95; this contains the Internet Explorer software. When installing the Internet software from Microsoft Plus! the setup program will ask you if you want to use Internet Explorer with MSN. If you answer Yes, the setup program will make all the necessary settings for you. Quick and easy.

TIP **Microsoft has priced its service to be very competitive with the** other major online services–CompuServe, America Online, Prodigy, and the like. These services generally charge more than an independent Internet service provider, though. It's possible to find service providers charging, for instance, $1.25 an hour or even less; some charge a flat rate–$20 a month for unlimited use, for example.

MSN is currently charging a monthly rate of from $3.33 to $19.95, which provides from 3 to 20 hours a month–an effective hourly rate of between $1 and 1.65, which is competitive with many service providers. Additional hours range from $2 to $2.50 an hour, which is a bit higher than most service providers. Note, however, that MSN has announced that it may split charges, having one set of charges for MSN proper, with additional charges for Internet access.

But you may not want to use MSN. Perhaps you already have an Internet service provider, and want to continue using that company. Or maybe you've decided that MSN is too expensive, and you want to find a cheaper service provider. Or maybe MSN doesn't have Internet-access telephone numbers in your area.

The other way to use Internet Explorer, then, is to install it to run with another Internet service provider. This may be hard; setting up the software to connect to a system other than MSN takes more time and effort. On the other hand, many service providers will soon start providing detailed information on how to do this, or perhaps even create setup programs that will enter the correct settings for you.

Where do I get Internet Explorer?

Where, then, do you get the Internet Explorer program? You have several choices:

- Obtain Microsoft Plus!; this software is a Windows 95 add-on, with a "street price" of around $45. Microsoft Plus! contains the Internet Explorer software.
- Join Microsoft Network. Once you are a member, you can request full Internet access, and the Internet Explorer software will be transferred to your computer.
- Join Microsoft Network and get the Internet Explorer software. Later you can close your Microsoft Network account and set up an account with another Internet service provider; you'll be able to continue using Internet Explorer with that new service provider. But if you don't have Microsoft Plus!, you won't have the Dial-Up Scripting Tool (this tool makes connecting to your service provider easier).
- Get the software from an online service or the Internet. You can download Explorer from a variety of sources (see appendix A). The software comes with the Internet Setup Wizard, to lead you through installing an Internet connection.

- Buy a new computer. Most new PCs will come with Windows 95 installed. They will also contain the Internet software, probably preconfigured to work with Microsoft Network, including Internet Explorer. If you've done this, you can skip to the next chapter and get started.

Installing the software if you're an MSN member

If you are a member of the MSN online service, you have two ways to install the software. At some point you'll probably see an e-mail message asking if you want to have full Internet access through MSN. (At the time of writing exactly how or when this message or announcement will appear or what it will say is not clear.) If you follow the instructions in the message, the software will be transferred to your computer and installed. You won't have to worry about setting up any complicated networking stuff, because the setup program will do it all for you.

If the setup program can't find any Internet-access telephone numbers in your area, though, you will be asked to pick numbers in another area. Of course in that case you may decide that you don't want to pay long-distance charges to use MSN's Internet service, and look elsewhere for a local service provider. See Appendix A for information about setting up an account with another service provider.

The other way to install the software is directly from Microsoft Plus!. Run Setup, and select the Internet Jumpstart Kit. Follow the instructions; at some point you'll be asked if you want to use the Internet software with MSN. Respond Yes, and the setup program will make all the settings for you.

TIP **If your computer is set up to share files with other network users,** the Internet Setup program will display a message box recommending that you change this setting. Choose Yes and the Wizard will turn off file sharing. It's not a good idea to have file sharing on a computer connected to the Internet, as other Internet users could access those files. (It's not likely, but it is possible.) Talk to your network administrator about what you should do.

Installing the MSN software

You quite likely have the MSN software installed already. Minimize all your programs and look on the desktop—if you see an icon labeled *The Microsoft Network*, it's installed. Or open the Start menu and choose Programs. If the MSN software is installed, you'll see The Microsoft Network near the end of the Programs menu. If you don't have the MSN software installed, you can quickly install it. Follow this procedure:

1. Click the taskbar's Start button to open the Start menu.
2. Choose Settings (near the bottom of the Start menu); a cascading menu appears.
3. Choose Control Panel. The Control Panel window opens.
4. Double-click the Add/Remove Programs icon in the Control Panel (or click it once and press Enter). The Add Remove/Programs Properties dialog box appears.
5. Click the Windows Setup tab near the top of the window. After a few moments a list box appears.
6. Scroll down the list until you see an entry labeled "The Microsoft Network."
7. Click the little check box on the left side of the line. You may see a message box telling you that you have Schedule+ 1.0 installed, and that once you install MS Exchange (an essential part of Microsoft Network), group scheduling will be disabled. Schedule+ is the Windows 3.11 scheduling program; there's a free replacement that you can order from Microsoft. Close the message box.
8. Choose OK. Windows 95 now copies the files from your installation CD or disks to your hard drive. It tries to do so without your intervention, by scanning your drives for the appropriate installation files. If it can't find the files (for instance, if they are on a floppy disk), it requires your assistance—follow the instructions.
9. When the procedure finishes, click the X button in the top right of the Control Panel to close the window.

Setting up your account

Now, to set up your MSN account, double-click the Microsoft Network icon on your desktop (minimize your applications so you can see the icon), or click the taskbar's Start button, and then choose Programs, The Microsoft Network. After a few moments you see the Microsoft Network dialog box. Follow this procedure to set up your account:

1 Choose OK. You'll see a dialog box asking for your area or city code and the first three digits of your phone number. (Your area code may already be filled in, depending on the information you provided during Windows 95 setup.) See figure 3.1.

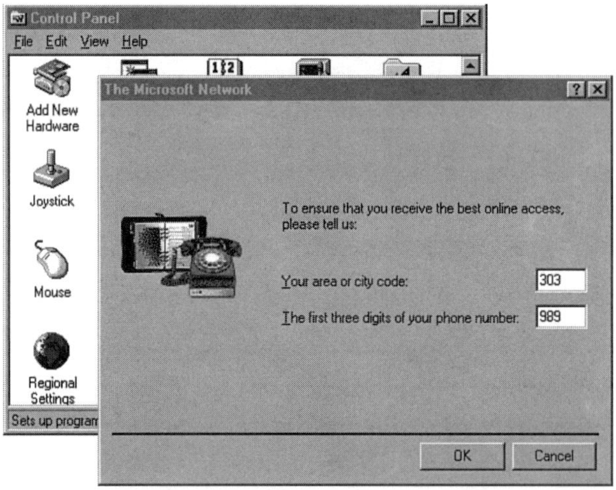

Fig. 3.1
Tell MSN where you are.

2 Enter the area code and the first three digits of your phone number and then choose OK. A message box appears.

3 Choose Connect and the program dials into the Microsoft Network.

4 After a short while, the program logs off MSN, and you see a dialog box with three large buttons in the middle, and several at the bottom.

5 Choose Price to see information about the current MSN pricing and, perhaps, free trials. Choose Close to return to the previous dialog box.

6 Choose Details to read a short description of MSN. Choose Close to return to the previous dialog box.

7 Now choose the Tell Us Your Name And Address button, and the dialog box you can see in figure 3.2 opens.

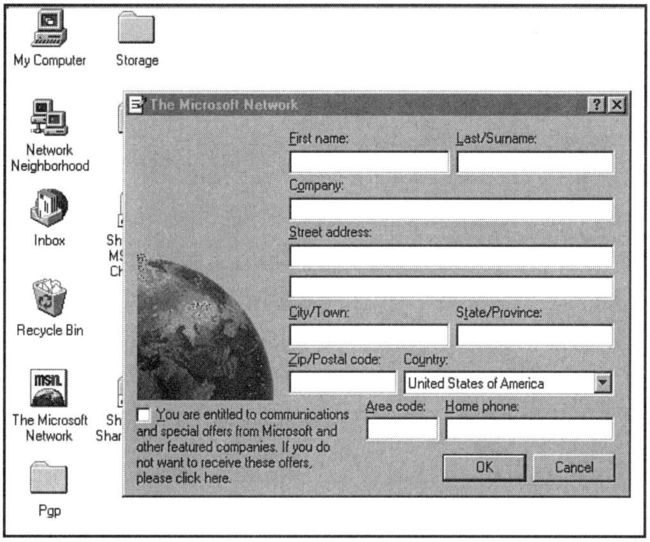

Fig. 3.2
Enter all your address information.

8 Enter your name and address. At a minimum, you must enter your first and last names, street address, city, and zip code. Notice the check box in the bottom left corner. Click this if you don't want Microsoft sending you junk mail or selling your address! Choose OK to return to the previous box.

9 Now click the Next, Select a Way To Pay button. This time you see the dialog box in figure 3.3; you must select a credit card and enter your bank name, card number (you can include dashes in the number if you wish), and expiration date. You should also modify the Name on card text box if necessary. Choose OK to return to the previous box.

At the time of writing the only way to get an account was with a credit card. If you don't have one, you may be out of luck!

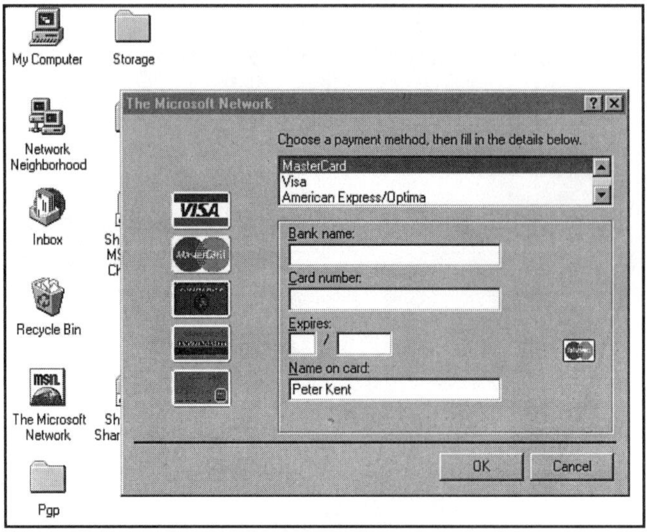

Fig. 3.3
Enter your credit-card information. If you don't have one—you may be out of luck!

10 Now choose the Then, Please Read the Rules button. (You may be tempted to skip this, but MSN won't let you proceed until you've gone into this dialog box.) Read the rules and then choose the I Agree button (assuming you do agree, of course).

11 Choose Join Now. You see a dialog box with two telephone numbers, Primary and Backup numbers; the backup number is used automatically if the primary is busy (see fig. 3.4). Take a quick look at the numbers. If you need to change a number for some reason, choose Change.

If MSN couldn't find a number in your area code, it won't fill in these fields—choose Change, and list of numbers you can select from appears. (Note that long distance calls between states are often cheaper than within states. Call your phone company for rates.)

Once you have the numbers you want, choose OK.

Fig. 3.4
Here's your chance to change phone numbers.

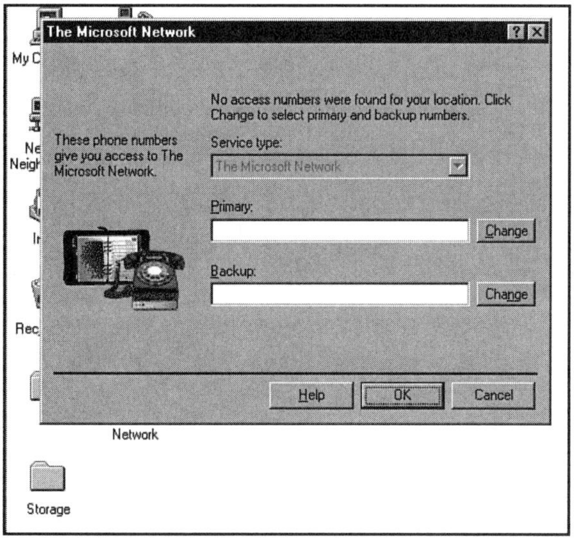

12 Another message box appears. Choose Connect to dial into MSN again and transfer the information you have entered.

TIP **Want to enter an advanced dialing procedure—using a credit card** from a hotel, for instance? Or is the MSN number selected for you a long distance number, even though it's in your area code? You can choose the Settings button in this message box to modify the way you dial into MSN. See "Setting up your dialing properties," later in this chapter.

13 After a minute or two, you see a box asking you for a Membership ID and Password (see fig. 3.5). The Membership ID is your MSN e-mail address, and the name by which you are shown online (in the MSN BBSes, for instance). You must type at least 3 characters, but as many as 64. (You can use numbers, letters, hyphens, and underscores, though no spaces.) Enter a password that is at least 8 characters—as many as 16. You can use any letter or number, and hyphens. You can't type the same text for both Membership ID and password, though, or even something that is very similar.

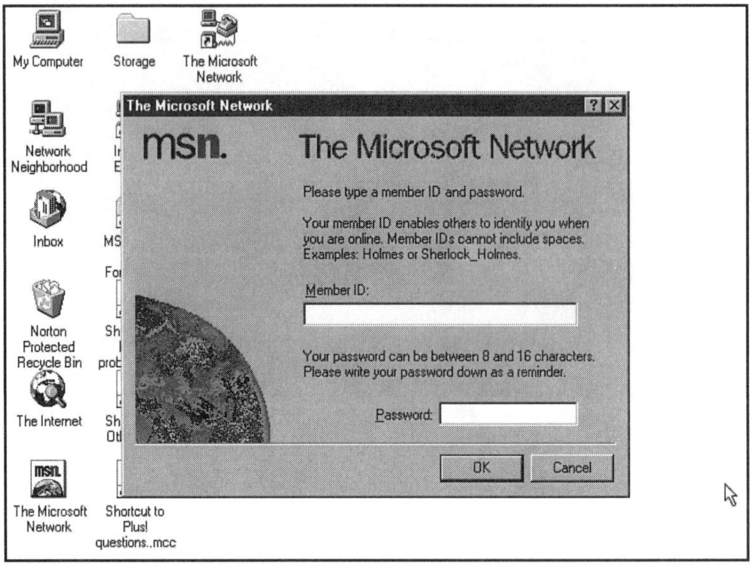

Fig. 3.5
Choose the Membership ID and password you want to use.

14 Write down your Membership ID and password, and then choose OK. A message box appears.

15 Choose Finish. That's it, you've set up your account, and logged out.

Q&A ***I've already set up an MSN account. How can I set up another, for a family member or colleague?***

Open the Start menu and choose Run. Type signup, and press Enter.

Getting the Internet software

You've installed the MSN software, but not the Internet-access software. You can download that directly from MSN. Start by going to the Internet forum; use the INTERNET Go word. (That is, choose Edit, Go to, Other Location in MSN Central, type **internet**, and press Enter.) When the The Internet Center folder opens, look for an icon that seems like it may lead to the software you need. The icon is currently titled *Getting on the Internet*, though the title could change.

Double-click on this icon, and an online document will open. Click on the Upgrade Instructions icon to display another document.

Inside the document that is now displayed you'll find a line that says *Click here to download*, or something similar. Click on the little icon on that line, and MSN will begin transferring the software to your computer.

When the download has finished, you'll be disconnected from MSN. Then the Setup program will begin. Follow this procedure:

1. You'll see the large Welcome to Microsoft Network dialog box. Click on OK.
2. You'll now be prompted to enter the first three digits of your phone number; type these digits, then click on OK.
3. Now you'll see a message box telling you that Setup will connect to MSN and get new numbers. Click on Connect.
4. You'll see the MSN Sign In dialog box. Enter your Member ID and password, if they are not already there, and click on Connect.
5. The program connects, gets the new numbers, and logs off. You'll see a dialog box showing the new TCP/IP numbers that it found for you.

   If it didn't find TCP/IP numbers in your area, you have two options. Don't use the MSN Internet access, or use a long distance number to connect. To select new telephone numbers, click on the Change button. To return to using the normal, non-TCP/IP numbers, choose *The Microsoft Network* from the Service Type drop-down list box.
6. When you've finished selecting numbers, click on OK.
7. You'll now see a dialog box telling you to restart. Close your applications, then click on OK.

That's it; you've installed your Internet software. The next time you connect to MSN, you'll automatically use the TCP/IP telephone numbers.

By the way, Microsoft says that you'll also be able to find the Internet Explorer software in MSN's Microsoft Windows 95 forum (GO WINDOWS), though at the time of writing it wasn't there.

The Internet-access numbers

Note that when you install the Internet software, the Setup program will provide the MSN software with different phone numbers. To use Internet access your MSN software has to dial numbers that will provide a TCP/IP connection. By default your MSN software will be set up to automatically use these new numbers, with no action required on your part; the next time you connect to MSN, you'll be connecting to the TCP/IP lines.

If you ever want to stop using the Internet access service, all you need to do is select different telephone numbers; in the MSN Sign In dialog box (the box that appears when you double-click on the MSN icon), click on the Settings button to open the Connection Settings dialog box. Then click on the Access Numbers button, and select *The Microsoft Network* from the Service Type dropdown list box. The old, non-Internet access numbers will be placed into the Primary and Backup text boxes.

Installing from Microsoft Plus!

If you have Microsoft Plus!, you can install all the software directly from there (and save some online time). Run the Setup program, and select the Internet Jumpstart Kit. Then follow the instructions; at some point you'll be asked if you want to use the Internet software with MSN. Respond Yes, and the setup program will make all the settings for you. You'll be taken through a procedure that is similar to the ones we've just looked at, to set up your account and select the correct access numbers.

Going the other way—becoming an MSN member

Maybe you want to go the other way—you had another service provider, now you want to become an MSN member. First, you would install the MSN software in the normal way. When you start MSN for the first time, though, you may see the message box in figure 3.6. What's this all about? When you set up your connection to the first service provider, you entered DNS (Dynamic Name Service) server IP (Internet Protocol) addresses. DNS servers are computers that provide addressing information to your software, to help your programs "navigate" around the Internet. When you installed your first Internet connection you entered the addresses of these servers. But the MSN service wants to provide those addresses for you; it doesn't want the Network software to be configured for these addresses.

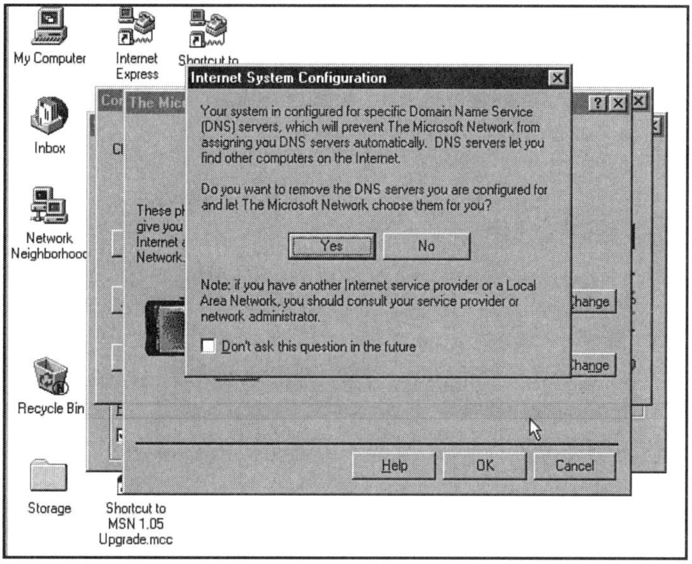

Fig. 3.6
This message box asks if MSN can remove your DNS server addresses.

If you are no longer using your other service provider, click on Yes and allow MSN to go ahead and make its changes. If you plan to use both service providers, though, you can probably shift the DNS numbers from the Network settings.

There are two places that these DNS numbers may be stored. You can place them in the Dial-Up Networking properties for a particular service provider, or in the Network settings (opened from the Control Panel—see Appendix A for more information about these). If the numbers are in the Dial-Up Networking properties, they are used only for that connection. If they are in the Network settings, though, they are used for all TCP/IP connections for which DNS numbers have not been defined in Dial-Up Networking.

So you should open the Dial-Up Networking folder (Start, Programs, Accessories, Dial-Up Networking); right-click on the connection icon and choose Properties; click on the Server Type button; click on the TCP/IP Settings button; click on the Specify Name Server Addresses option button; and enter the DNS numbers given to you by your service provider. Then you can start MSN again, and when you see the message click on the Yes button to remove the DNS numbers from the Network settings—they'll remain in the Dial-Up Networking properties.

It's also possible to *keep* the DNS numbers in the Network settings; MSN will then use those numbers. However, this may mean that the MSN Internet service is not as reliable as it would be otherwise, and may be just a little slower.

Installation bugs

There are some bugs with the installation programs in Windows 95 and the Plus! package. If you've tried out a variety of different configurations—installing software for both MSN and another service provider, removing one or the other, adding one or the other, or whatever—strange things may start happening. For instance, you may not be able to view the URL of a Favorites or History item (see chapter 6). Or perhaps you have connected to the Internet via your service provider, but when you try to use Internet Explorer the MSN Connect dialog box opens.

Windows 95 doesn't keep track of what it's removed and added quite correctly. If you run into these problems I suggest that you remove MSN and the Internet Jumpstart Kit and reinstall the software.

Installing the software if you're not an MSN member

If you are *not* an MSN member, you may want to consider at least trying the service for the duration of the free-trial period. The MSN software is already on the Windows 95 installation disk or disk set, so you can quickly install it and become a member—and you may find you like it. (Of course you should rush out and buy my *Using Microsoft Network*, also from Que.) Once you've become a member, you can sign up for Internet access to get the software. Later, you can switch to another service provider if you prefer. (I explain how to make that switch in "Converting from MSN to another service provider," in Appendix A.)

You can also install Internet Explorer from Microsoft Plus!, and configure it for another service provider. When you do so, you have a little more work than the MSN member, because you have to set up the TCP/IP software correctly. In fact so much work, that the editors and I decided to shift the information about this into an appendix at the back of the book. This original chapter was *huge*, and it seems likely that most users will be working with Internet Explorer through Microsoft Network, at least initially. So, if you want to install Internet Explorer for another service provider, or if you've been using Internet Explorer with MSN and now want to configure it for another service provider, see Appendix A.

(Now, I don't want to make it sound too difficult, as though it's some unmanageable task. You can install a connection for another service provider, though there may be a lot of steps you must take. It just takes a little time and effort.)

TIP **Internet Explorer is designed to run using Microsoft's TCP/IP** stack—the Windows 95 Dial-Up Networking program. If you've already been connecting to your service provider and using TCP/IP software—perhaps you installed another Internet program that has its own TCP/IP "stack" or interface—you won't be able to run Internet Explorer through that software. You'll have to install the TCP/IP software that comes with Windows 95 or Microsoft Plus!

Part II: Caught in the Web

4

The Opening Moves

In this chapter:

- **Starting Internet Explorer**
- **Loading HTML files into Explorer**
- **What's the home page (the start page)?**
- **The Explorer window and its components**
- **Moving around the Web**
- **How do I find my way back?**

Let's get started with Internet Explorer . . . . >

It's time to get started working with Internet Explorer. I'm assuming that by now you have your TCP/IP connection to the Internet, and you have Internet Explorer installed. (If you haven't, see chapter 3.) In this chapter I'm going to explain how to start Internet Explorer and get it running on the Internet (there are several ways), and show you what to do once you are online—how to move around on the Web.

Starting Internet Explorer

Depending on how you have configured your software, there are several ways to start Internet Explorer. Remember, in order to use Internet Explorer to move around on the Web, the program has to be open (of course) and you have to be connected, through a TCP/IP line, to the Internet.

- Double-click on The Internet icon. Internet Explorer opens. Start moving around on the Web (you'll see how later in this chapter, under "How Do I Use The Browser?"), and the program will open the Dial-Up Networking Connect To dialog box, so you can connect to your service provider.
- Open the Dial-Up Networking Connect To dialog box, and then click on Connect to start your TCP/IP connection. Then start Internet Explorer.
- If you're an MSN member, start MSN in the normal way, but connect through one of the TCP/IP numbers. Then start Internet Explorer.
- Double-click on a desktop shortcut that references an Internet resource, or a History-list entry, or a Favorites-list entry. Internet Explorer will open, and the Connect To dialog box appears. (Unless the item referenced by the shortcut happens to be in Internet Explorer's cache.)
- If you are working on MSN, select a link to a Web site. You'll find them scattered throughout MSN. Internet Explorer will open and display the referenced Web document.
- Open an .HTM or .HTML file by double-clicking on it in Windows Explorer, Windows 95's file-management program, or by "running" it from the Start menu's Run command; Internet Explorer will open and load the file so you can read it.

Each of these items needs a bit more explanation, so let's look at each in turn.

Start Internet Explorer first

You don't have to connect to the Internet before you start Internet Explorer. As you'll learn later, in chapter 5, Internet Explorer stores documents you've already viewed in the **cache** directory. So if you want to view one of these documents again, there's no need to log onto the Internet (spending online dollars and valuable time); you can display the document directly from the cache.

But what happens when you begin navigating around the Internet—when you click on a link, for instance, to a document that is *not* in the cache, but has to be retrieved from the Internet? At that point Internet Explorer "calls" Dial-Up Networking or the MSN program (depending on which method you are using to connect to the Internet) and tells it to log onto the Internet. You'll see the Connect To dialog box, or, if connecting through Microsoft Network, you'll see the MSN Sign In dialog box (see fig. 4.1 for an example). Click on the Connect button, and Dial-Up Networking or the MSN program logs on so Internet Explorer can find the document you've requested.

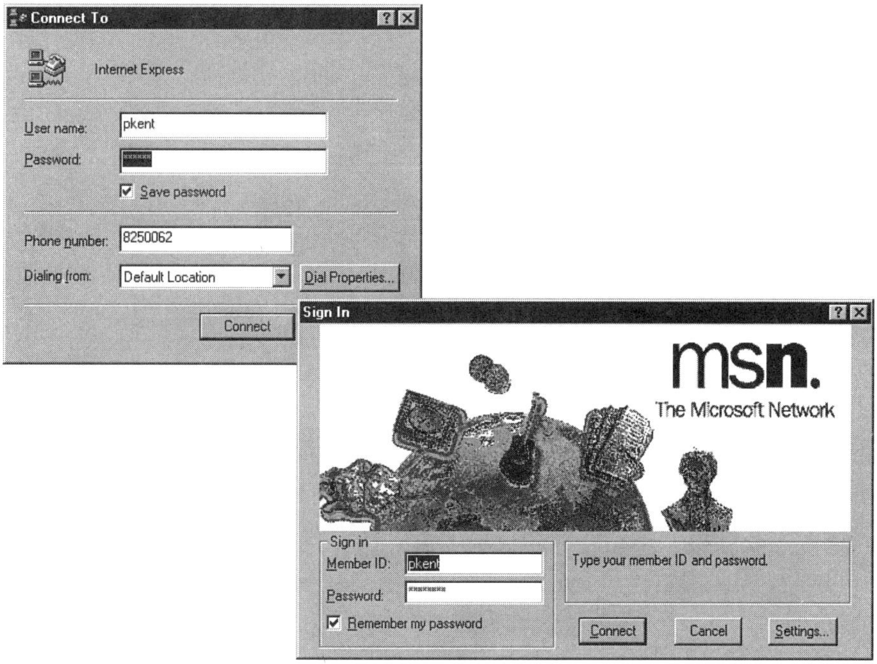

Fig. 4.1
The Connect To or Sign In dialog box appears when Internet Explorer calls Dial-Up Networking or MSN.

So, to use this procedure, simply double-click on The Internet icon on your desktop. Internet Explorer will open. Start working with Internet Explorer; when it needs to get something from the World Wide Web, it will call Dial-Up Networking for you.

Q&A ***When I start Internet Explorer it "calls" Dial-Up Networking immediately. What's going on?***

The first time you open Internet Explorer this will happen, because it needs to get the Start page (the home page) for the first time (the Start page won't be in the cache). But Internet Explorer may call Dial-Up Networking as soon as you start subsequent sessions, too, depending on the cache update setting.

There are two settings for updating the cache. There's Once Per Session, which means that the first time you request a Web document during a session Internet Explorer will retrieve it from the Web, even if it has a copy in the cache. Then there's Never, which means that if there's a copy in the cache, Explorer will always use that copy. If you have the first setting selected, Internet Explorer will call Dial-Up Networking as soon as you start the program, because it needs to update the home page.

Finally, another reason—if the document is no longer in the cache (because in an earlier session you ran out of hard disk space and Explorer deleted the document), Explorer will have to retrieve the document from the Web. See chapter 5 for more information about the cache.

Setting up the auto-dial feature

When you installed Internet Explorer, the Setup program set up the auto-dial feature for you, telling Explorer which Dial-Up Networking connection you want to use to connect to the Internet. What if you have created several connections, though, or have just swapped from using Microsoft Network to some other Internet service provider? You need to modify the auto-dial setting. Here's how.

1 Open the Start menu and choose Settings, Control Panel. The Control Panel folder opens.

2 Double-click on the Internet icon. The Internet Properties dialog box opens (see fig. 4.2).

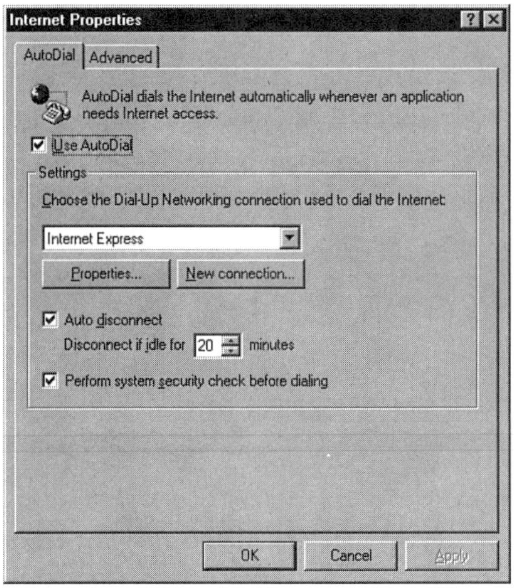

Fig. 4.2
The Internet Properties dialog box lets you select a Dial-Up Networking connection, and set the auto-disconnect and security options.

3. Make sure that the Use AutoDial check box is selected. If it *isn't*, you'll have to start your TCP/IP connection before you use Internet Explorer to retrieve documents from the Internet.

4. Select the Dial-Up Network connection you want to use.

5. Notice the Auto Disconnect check box. This helps you save online dollars by automatically logging off your Internet connection if your Internet programs are inactive for the time specified in the Disconnect if Idle For incrementer box. For instance, if you have this set you can leave Internet Explorer downloading a file from the Web, and Dial-Up Networking will log off automatically for you a few minutes after the download has finished (the number of minutes in the incrementer).

6. Notice the Perform System Security Check Before Dialing check box. If you are the only person using your computer, you'll probably want to leave this turned off. It's useful if others use your computer, though, because this feature will check to make sure file sharing is not turned on before you connect to the Internet.

   Windows 95's networking features allow you to share the files on your hard disk with other network users. If you have file sharing turned on when you install the Internet software, the Setup program warns you. But what happens if you or someone else turns on file sharing later, after the Internet software's installed? If you connect to the Internet with file sharing turned on, other people on the Internet may be able to get to your files. (Unlikely, it's true, but possible.)

Selecting this check box, though, tells Dial-Up Networking to check to see if file sharing is turned on before it connects to the Internet. (If you start your connection directly from Dial-Up Networking—which we'll look at next—it won't check for file sharing.) If Dial-Up Networking finds that your computer has file sharing turned *on*, you'll see the warning dialog box shown in figure 4.3. You can then click on No to continue with your connection to the Internet, or Yes to turn off file sharing and reboot your computer.

7 Finally, notice the Advanced tab. This area enables you to set up a Proxy Server. This is a special network connection to the Internet through a local area network. If you are connecting to the Internet through your company's Internet connection, for example, your system administrator may have set up a Proxy Server.

8 When you've finished with this dialog box, click on the OK button to save your settings.

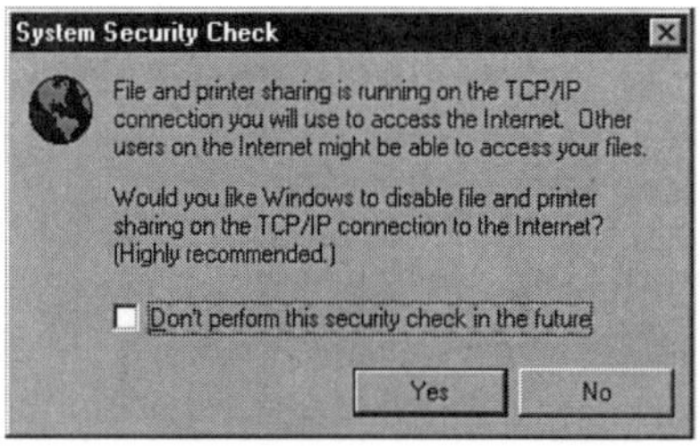

Fig. 4.3
This message box appears if you have turned on the Perform System Security Check Before Dialing option and if Dial-Up Networking has discovered you have file sharing turned on.

Start the TCP/IP connection first

Another way to start Internet Explorer is to start your TCP/IP Dial-Up Networking connection *first*, by following these steps:

1 Open the Start menu, and choose Programs, Accessories, Dial-Up Networking. The Dial-Up Networking folder opens.

2 Double-click on the icon representing the connection you want to use, and the Connect To dialog box opens.

3 Click on Connect and Dial-Up Networking dials into your service provider's system.

4 Double-click on The Internet icon on your desktop to start Internet Explorer.

TIP **You can speed things up by creating a desktop icon for your Dial-**Up Networking connection. Right-click on the icon in the Dial-Up Networking folder and choose Create Shortcut. A message will ask if you want to create a shortcut on the desktop. Click on Yes.

Or simply drag the icon from the Dial-Up Networking folder and drop it onto your desktop, and click on Yes in the message box that appears.

You can also add the icon to your Start menu. Simply drag the icon from the folder, or the shortcut from your desktop, onto the taskbar's Start button.

Connect to MSN

If you are an MSN member and have installed the full-Internet-access software, you now have four ways to connect to MSN.

- Use the original, non-Internet telephone numbers. You won't be able to run Internet Explorer, though, because you won't be running the TCP/IP software necessary for full Internet access.
- Open Internet Explorer. When Explorer needs to connect to the MSN Internet telephone number the Sign In dialog box will open (as we saw under "Start Internet Explorer First"). When you click on the Connect button you will be connected to the Internet. You will be able to use Internet Explorer, and can use all the normal MSN services, too.

TIP **When you connect to MSN using this second method, you won't** see the MSN Central window. Right-click on the MSN icon in the taskbar "tray" (the area with the small icons on the right side of the bar; there's a modem icon there, too). Then choose from several commands that display MSN Central, take you to an area of MSN using a Go word, and so on.

- Dial into the MSN Internet access number using Dial-Up Networking, as we've just seen (under "Start the TCP/IP Connection First"). You can now use Internet Explorer, but you won't yet be connected to the MSN services. When you start MSN, by double-clicking on the MSN icon for instance, you will be connected to MSN services (the BBSs, chat rooms, and so on) through the TCP/IP connection. You'll now be able to use Internet Explorer *and* all the MSN services.

- Dial into MSN using the Internet access numbers (I'll show you how next). Once connected, you'll be able to use all the MSN services *and* start Internet Explorer, so you can use the Internet services, too.

Starting MSN using the Internet-access numbers

If you'd like to start MSN through the TCP/IP connection—so that you can run the standard MSN services and use Internet Explorer at the same time—follow this procedure:

1. Start your MSN program in the normal way; double-click on the MSN icon or open the Start menu and choose Programs, The Microsoft Network, for example.

2. The Internet-access numbers are probably selected by default, but let's check to make sure. When the Sign In dialog box appears, click on the Settings button.

3. In the Connection Settings dialog box, look above and to the right of the Access Numbers button. You should see a line that reads `Service Type: Internet and MSN` (see fig. 4.4). This means that the software will be dialing into the TCP/IP number. If it doesn't say this, click on the Access Numbers button, select Internet and the Microsoft Network from the drop-down list box in the dialog box that opens, and then click on OK.

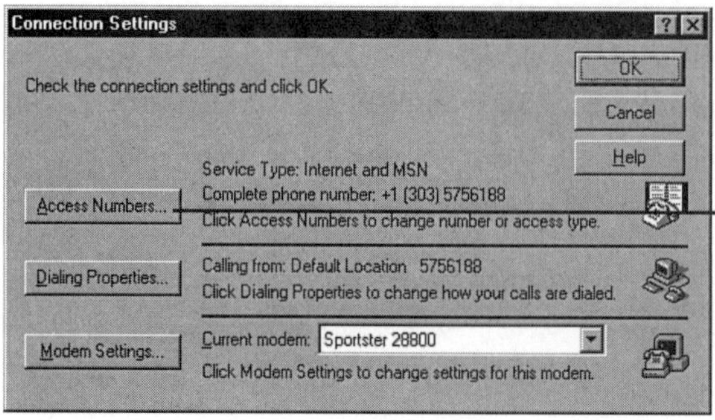

Fig. 4.4
The Connection Settings dialog box shows you which type of telephone number you are about to dial.

Here's where you can see the type of number you'll use to dial into MSN.

4. Click on OK to close the Connection Settings dialog box.

5. Click on Connect to dial into MSN. The software dials into MSN and logs on. You'll see MSN Central.

6 You are now connected to both MSN and the Internet, and can start Internet Explorer. Double-click on The Internet icon.

Using the shortcuts and MSN links

In chapter 6 you learn how to create shortcuts to Web documents. There are three types: desktop shortcuts, Favorites, and the history list. Double-clicking on any of these while Internet Explorer is closed will automatically open Internet Explorer. If the referenced document is in the cache it may be pulled from there (depending on how you've configured the cache). If the document is not pulled from the cache, as soon as Internet Explorer opens it will try to log onto the Internet using Dial-Up Networking or the MSN program.

You'll also find shortcuts and links already created for you in MSN. For instance, if someone sends a message to a BBS discussion group on MSN, and wants to tell people about a Web site they've found, they can place shortcuts in the message. When you read this message you can double-click on the shortcut to open Internet Explorer and go to the Web site. (You must have connected to MSN through the Internet-access telephone number.) You'll also find links to the Web elsewhere, such as in the MSN Today window.

Opening HTML documents

Finally, there is one more way to open Internet Explorer. If you have an .HTM or .HTML document on your hard disk—remember, these are the basic building blocks of the World Wide Web—you can "run" it and Internet Explorer will open. Just as .TXT files are associated with Notepad and .WAV files are associated with Sound Recorder, .HTM and .HTML are associated with Internet Explorer.

For instance, if you have a .HTM or .HTML file on your hard disk you can open Windows Explorer (the Windows 95 file-management program) and double-click on the file; Internet Explorer will open and display the file. Many of the files in the cache are .HTM and .HTML files; double-clicking on these will display them in Internet Explorer.

Let's get started: The home (start) page

Well, we've just spent a couple of thousand words explaining how to start Internet Explorer. It's not difficult, really, it's just that there are several ways to do it.

Now I'm going to assume that Internet Explorer is open and the home page is displayed. Sorry, make that the **start page**. In Internet Explorer lingo it's known as the start page, though the term home page is more common on the Web—if you've used another Web browser you're probably already familiar with the term.

The start page is simply the page that Explorer opens when you first start the program. What does the start page look like? At the time of writing it looked like the page shown in figure 4.5. This may not be what it looks like by the time you get there, though; it's changed a number of times already. In chapter 7, I'll show you how to specify a different start page.

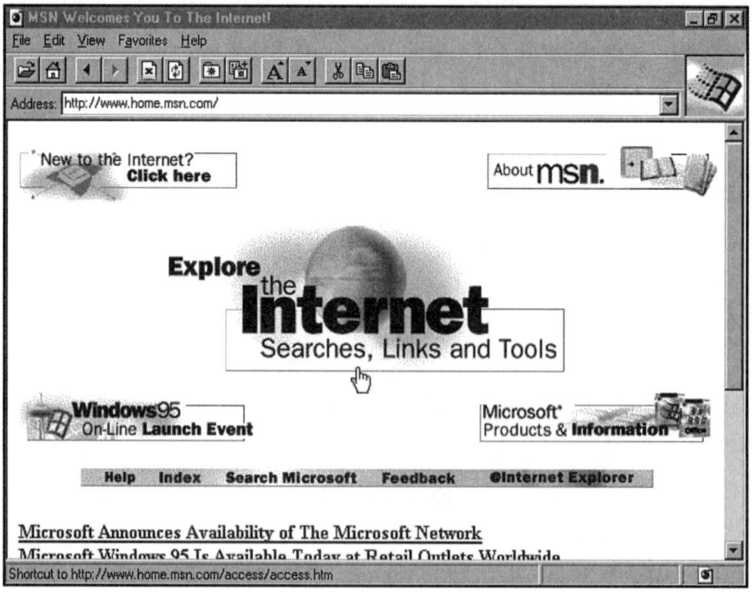

Fig. 4.5
Here's what the Internet Explorer home (or start) page looked like last time I checked. It may change, though.

Let's consider what you'll find in this Web document:

- A background—The background may be the default color of gray. But Web authors can create special background textures, patterns, and colors that are used instead of the browser's default color. In this case, the background is white. The default Internet Explorer background color is gray, but the Web author has added his own background.

- Text—Of course a Web document can contain text. Not all the text you can see is true text, though. The copyright statement in the bottom left corner is true text. The rest is of the text is actually text within a picture.
- Pictures—Web authors can place what are known as **inline images** or **inline pictures** into their documents. Such pictures are, in some cases, links to other documents. Notice the small hand pointer in figure 4.5; this indicates that the image it's pointing to is a link to another document.
- Text links—There aren't any text links in this page. However, Web documents can contain special text that, when clicked on, will cause the browser to display another document. This text is usually underlined and colored blue (though you can change the color used; see chapter 7). We'll see text links later (see fig. 4.6).

What haven't I mentioned yet? The **Address bar** is the large text box near the top of the window. It shows you the URL of the currently displayed Web document. You can also type a URL into this and press Enter to go to a particular URL (we'll learn more about that in chapter 5). The **status bar** is at the bottom of the window. This shows the URL of the link that the mouse pointer is over, and has the **action indicator** on the right side. It also shows information about file transfers.

How do I use the browser?

There are a number of ways to travel around the Web. The most basic method is by clicking on links. As you've just seen, when you point to a link the mouse pointer changes into a small hand. The link may be a picture or colored text. For instance, point at the large *Explore the Internet* image in the middle of the document. The mouse pointer changes to a small hand. Click, and Explorer retrieves the referenced document, which you can see in figure 4.6. (Maybe you *won't* see this; I'm assuming that the home page and the documents linked to it haven't been changed. If they have, you won't see the same things, but the principles are the same, so just explore.)

Explorer's components

Open Start Page
Click on this button to return to the home (or start) page.

Back
Click on this button to see the previous Web document.

Forward
Click on this button to see the next Web document—the one you left by clicking the back button.

Stop
Click on this button to stop the current procedure—to stop transferring the Web document or file.

Open
Click on this button to open an .HTM or .HTML file from your hard disk. It can also be used to specify the URL of a document you want to retrieve from the Web (though you'll usually use the Address text box near the top of the window to do that).

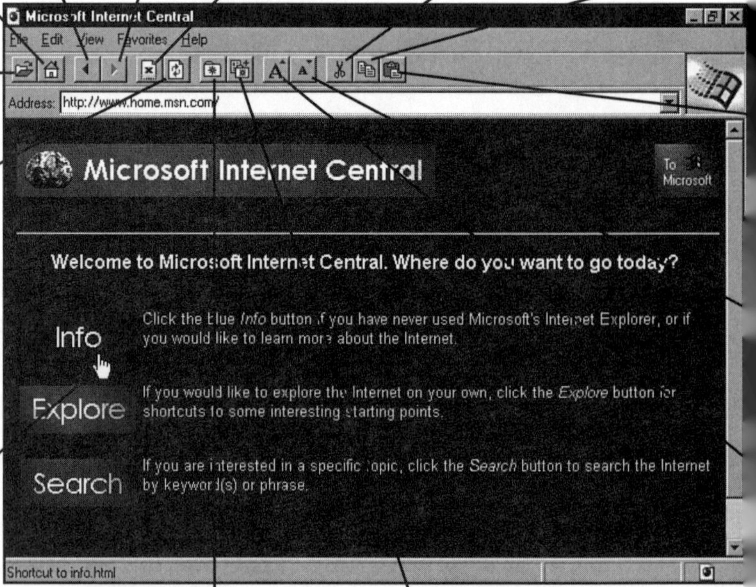

Refresh
Click on this button to reload the current document from the Web again.

Mouse pointer
When the mouse pointer changes to a small pointing hand, it's over a link. When it's a normal arrow pointer it's over an "inactive" part of the document.

Open Favorites
Click on this button to open the Favorites folder so that you can return to a Web document you viewed before.

Add to Favorites
Click on this button to add the current Web document to the list of Favorites.

Cut
Click on this button to cut the selected text from the Address text box, or from a form in a Web document, to the Clipboard. (You'll find out more about forms in chapter 5.)

Copy
Click on this button to copy the selected text from the Web document or the Address text box to the Clipboard.

Paste
Click here if the cursor is in the Address text box or in a form's text field to copy text from the Clipboard to the text box.

Use Smaller Font
Click on this button to use smaller text in the Web document.

User Larger Font
Click on this button to use larger text in the Web document.

Busy Indicator
As long as the clouds are moving across the sky, Explorer is busy doing something; retrieving a document, trying to connect to a Web server, or transferring a file.

Action Indicator
This icon, on the right side of the status bar, indicates what's going on. The icon changes depending on what Explorer is doing.

Internet Explorer is trying to connect to the Web server that holds the document you want to retrieve.

The transfer has finished, and the document is being displayed. Point at this icon and a small box pops up, showing you the address of the displayed Web page.

Explorer has found the document you need, and is transferring it.

Notice that figure 4.6 shows text links. The *Internet Searches*, *Handy Internet services*, and *A sampler of links* text is colored and underlined. You can click on one of these links to go to another document. Just move around in this way, clicking on text and graphic links, exploring "Webspace."

TIP **When you point at a text link, the address is shown in the status** bar. By default the address is shown in a non-standard, simplified manner. You can change it to the normal, Web-standard URL in the Options dialog box. See chapter 7 for more information.

Q&A ***I clicked on a link and got a message saying that the document can't be displayed. Why?***

There are a variety of reasons for documents being unavailable:

The Web server is very busy, and didn't respond to the browser's request.

The Web server is out of action, forever or just for the moment.

The document referenced by the link has gone or been renamed—this is very common.

You are using a Web document pulled from the cache, and the link is outdated (points to a document that has been renamed, moved, or removed). Click on the Refresh button and try the link again. (See chapter 5 for an explanation of how the cache works.)

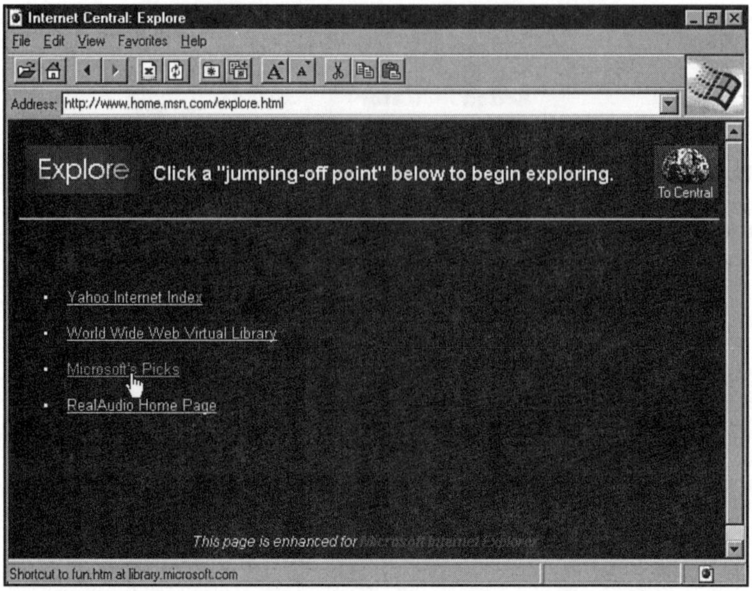

Fig. 4.6
Here's the document you see after clicking on the *Explore the Internet* image in the Internet Explorer home page.

Q&A ***I've got all sorts of different colored text. What's what?***

By default Explorer colors links blue. However, if you have viewed a document referenced by a link, Explorer colors the link purple. (You'll see how to change these default colors in chapter 7.) Also, Web authors can pick their own colors. The document in figure 4.6 (though you can't see it in the illustration, of course) has specially colored text; the links have been colored dark blue. These colors have been added using a special HTML command.

A good way to begin exploring is by clicking on the *A sampler of links* link, which takes you to the *Links to other sites*. From here you'll be able to select a category—*Business & Finance*, *Public Affairs*, *News*, and so on. These take you to various lists of interesting sites (all sorts of weird and wonderful things); like the America's Cup Web page, A Bison's Library of Dreams, Banned Books, Confession Booth, Dilbert's Home Page, Drive-by Shootings, Internet Underground Music Archive, Late Show with David Letterman, Mystery Science Theater 3000, O.J. Central, Planet Earth Home Page, Shakespearean Insult Server, Stark's Museum of Vacuum Cleaners, Surrealist Compliment Generator, The Chihuahua Home Page, The Jihad to Destroy Barney on the WWW, Klingon Language Institute, The Worst Job in the World, and Virtual Pub. This page will be updated often, I'm sure, so take a peek for yourself.

TIP

Started transferring a document and discovered that you really don't want it? Click the Stop button or choose View, Stop to cancel the transfer. Or simply press the Esc key.

Finding your way back

Lost yet? Eventually the question, "How do I get back?" comes to mind. That's easy; use one of these techniques:

To go to the previous page, click the Back button, choose View, Back, or press Backspace.

Having gone back to a previous page, go forward again by clicking the Forward button, or choosing View, Forward.

Go all the way home—to the home or start page—by clicking the Open Start Page button, or by choosing File, Open Start Page.

Open the File menu and choose one of the documents shown at the bottom of the menu (this is the history list, which we'll learn more about in chapter 6).

Look at the bottom or top of the document. You'll often find links provided by the Web author that return you to a particular place. For instance, at the top and bottom of all the pages at the Microsoft site there's a bar, a picture, that has several links inside it. One says To Home. (The others take you to Help, Index, Search Microsoft, and Feedback pages.)

TIP

You can move around inside a Web page by pressing Home and End to move to the top and bottom, the PgUp and PgDn keys to move up and down a page at a time, and the up and down Arrow keys to move a few lines at a time. Make sure you look further down the home page, where you'll find the *Microsoft's Top Ten* link.

You've learned the most basic techniques used for getting around the Web. There are more, of course. We'll look at more advanced skills in the next chapter.

5

Advanced Navigation

In this chapter:

- **Working more quickly—turn off inline images**
- **How can I run multiple Web sessions?**
- **Using URLs to go directly to a Web document**
- **The right-click pop-up menus**
- **The cache and the refresh command**
- **Passwords and forms**

Now that you're on your feet, it's time to start running . . .

You're on the Web, using a few basic techniques to move around. But the Web is a huge place, and if what you learned in the last chapter was all you had, you'd never get very far. Following links is all well and good, but what if the links don't go the way you want to go?

In this chapter you'll find out about more advanced methods for moving around on the Web. These methods will let you go directly to the document you want without having to click on a million links to get there, and will even let you run multiple Web sessions at the same time. Let's start by talking about a way to speed up your work on the Web, by turning off inline graphics.

Work faster—remove the pictures

A Web browser needs a way to turn off inline graphics. As nice as they may be, pictures in Web documents present a problem—they really slow down working on the Web. Much of the time you really *want* the pictures. But if you are "on the way to somewhere on the Web" and really don't need to see the pictures in the documents you are passing through, it's a good idea to remove them so you can move more quickly.

Here's how to turn off the pictures:

1. Choose View, Options. The Options dialog box opens.
2. Clear the Show Pictures check box.
3. Choose OK. Now, when you go to a Web page, you won't see any pictures. Instead, you'll see small icons in place of the pictures. You can see an example in figures 5.1 and 5.2

Now how do I see a picture?

So you're traveling around the Web (inline images turned off), when all of a sudden you decide you've just got to see a particular picture. Or perhaps you *have* to see the image—many Web documents these days simply won't work unless you can see the image, because all the links are inside the image. Or maybe you just decide you want to start seeing all the pictures. Here's what you can do.

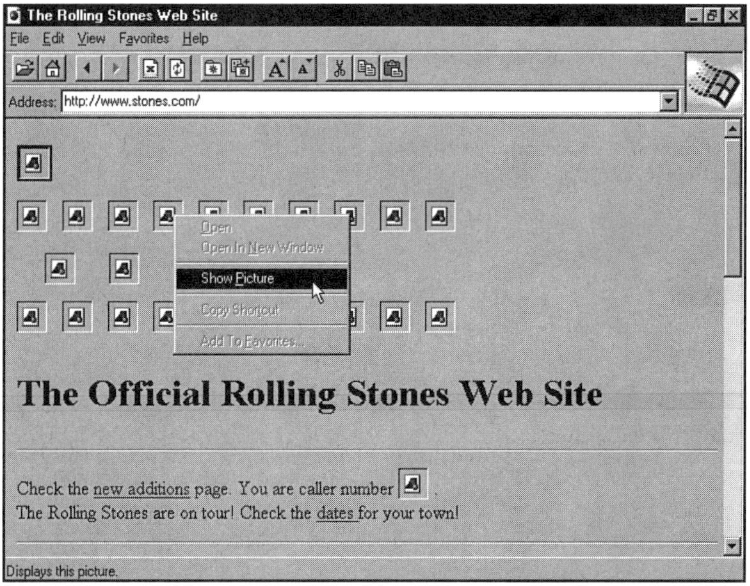

Fig. 5.1
The Rolling Stones site, sans inline images. Notice the pop-up menu that appears when you right-click on one of the icons representing a missing picture.

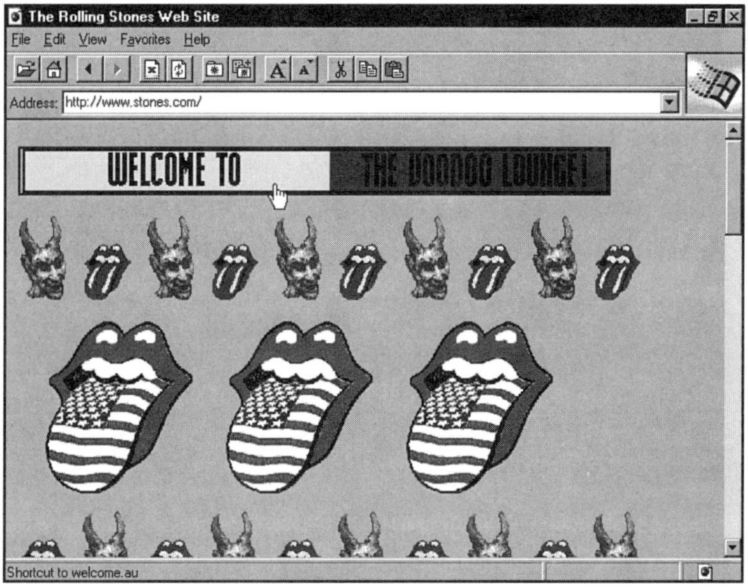

Fig. 5.2
The Rolling Stones page, in all its glory; this time the inline images are turned on.

- If you want to view just one picture, right-click on the icon that represents the missing picture. When the pop-up menu opens choose Show Picture. (You can see this pop-up menu in figure 5.1.)

- To see *all* the pictures in the current document, turn the Show Pictures option back on, then click on the Refresh toolbar button. Then turn the Show Pictures option off again.
- To see pictures in the next Web document you view, and for the rest of the session, turn the Show Pictures option back on.

Q&A ***I turned off inline images; so why did the next page I viewed have pictures?***

It's that cache thing again! Internet Explorer places documents in the cache directory on your hard disk, so it can retrieve them more quickly. If it placed a document into the cache with inline images, the next time you view the document it will be retrieved with inline images. Turning off inline images only affects documents retrieved from Web, not from the cache directory. See "And Now...the Cache," later in this chapter for more information about the cache.

Note that there's a flip side to this, too. If you view a page with the inline graphics turned off, the next time Explorer opens the page from your cache, you won't see the pictures...even if you have turned on inline graphics. Click on the Refresh button to retrieve a new copy of the page—graphics and all—from the Web.

Another way to speed up your sessions

Here's another way you can speed up your work on the Web. You'll notice that when Explorer begins transferring a document from the Web, it displays part of the document before it gets the entire thing. For instance, you may notice that all the text is displayed, but the pictures are not; the clouds in the busy indicator (on the right side of the Address bar) are still floating across the sky, and the little action indicator in the status bar shows that Explorer is still transferring.

You don't have to wait until Explorer has finished. You can start working right away. Scroll down the page to find the information you need. If you discover that everything you want has already been transferred, click on the Stop button or choose View, Stop. Or simply press the Esc key.

If you find a link you want to use, you don't even have to bother stopping the transmission. Just click the link, and Explorer will automatically stop transferring the current document, and begin transferring the one referenced by the link.

Running two (or more) Web sessions

Internet Explorer allows you to run more than one Web session at the same time. You can have one Explorer window open displaying the latest Dilbert cartoon, and another downloading a file from the RealAudio Web site, for instance.

The simplest way to start another Web session is to do so when you use a link. Hold down the Shift key while you click on the link. Or point at it and *right*-click on it. A pop-up menu will open, as you can see in figure 5.3. Choose Open In New Window. Whichever method you use, a new Explorer window will open and the referenced document is opened in *there*. You end up with two windows open, each displaying a different document.

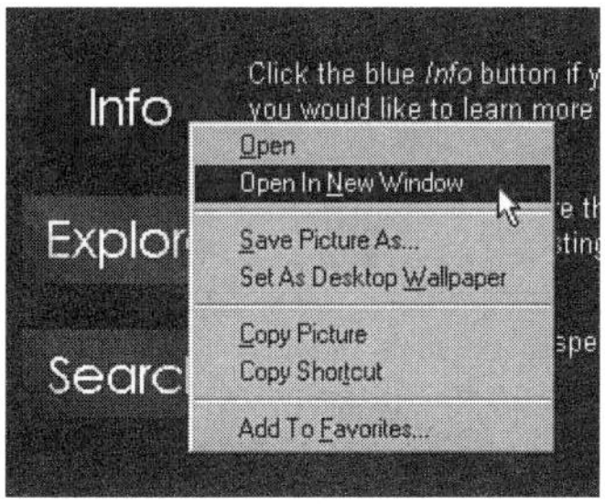

Fig. 5.3
The right-click pop-up menu lets you open another Web session (and do other stuff, too).

There's another way to open a new window, too. You can do so when you enter a URL into the Address text box or the Open Internet Address dialog box, as you'll see next. And in some cases Explorer will ask if you want to open a new window. For instance, if you click on a link while Explorer is transferring a file (see chapter 9), Explorer will ask if you want to cancel the transfer. Answer No, and Explorer will ask if you want to open a new Window. Answer Yes, and you'll end up with two windows, the original one (with the transfer still in progress), and the new one displaying the page referenced by the link you clicked on.

Q&A ***Why doesn't my pop-up menu look like the one in your figure? And what are these other options?***

There are five different pop-up menus, for five different situations. You can right-click on a picture, on a text-link, on a blank area of the background, on a picture icon (which Explorer places into the document, if you've turned off inline graphics), or on text that you have selected. We'll take a quick look at these menus in "The right-click pop-up menus" later in this chapter.

Going directly to a Web page

Now and then you'll find a URL—a Web address—in a newspaper or magazine. Or perhaps you run across one in a newsgroup message, or a friend e-mails you his favorite.

Now you need to know how to go directly from here to there; you don't want to follow links to this document, you want to go directly to it. There are several ways to do this:

- Click inside the Address text box, then type the URL. (When you click in the Address text box the current URL is highlighted, so when you type it's replaced with the new one.) Then press Enter. For instance, type **`http://www.mcp.com/`** and then press Enter to go to the Macmillan Publishing Web site.

TIP **You can omit the http:// bit if you wish, and when you press Enter** Explorer will add it for you. In this example you'd type **www.mcp.com/** and press Enter.

- Copy a URL into the Windows Clipboard from another application, and then paste it into Internet Explorer's Address text box and press Enter. (You can press Ctrl+V, choose Edit, Paste, or click on the Paste toolbar button.)
- Enter a URL into the Address text box (type it or copy it—it doesn't matter), and then press Shift+Enter. This time another Internet Explorer window will open, with the specified Web document inside. The original Internet Explorer window will remain open, so you can run two Web sessions at the same time.

- Choose Open, or choose File, Open; the Open Internet Address dialog box appears (see fig. 5.4.). Type the URL and choose OK.
- Choose Open, or choose File, Open. Click on the Open in New Window check box, then type the URL and choose OK. A new Explorer window will open and display the document.

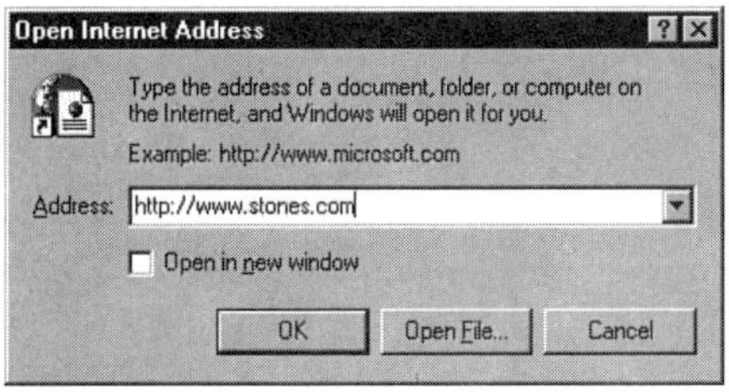

Fig. 5.4
The Open Internet Address enables the Address text box. It also lets you open a file on your hard disk, as we'll see soon.

TIP **Sometimes you'll find that a URL doesn't work, perhaps simply** due to a typo. Try this: remove the rightmost portion and try again. For instance, if you try **http://www.mcp.com/author/pkent** and it doesn't work, try **http://www.mcp.com/author/**. If that still doesn't work, try **http://www.mcp.com/**. (The first URL wouldn't work because there's a typo; it should be **authors**, not **author**. You can actually get to my Web page by using **http://www.mcp.com/authors/pkent**.)

Now, what was that URL?

Let's say you entered a URL a few days ago. Now you want to return to the same document, but you don't remember the URL. You can use the History list, or the Favorites list (if you placed the document there). We'll learn more about those in chapter 6, but there's a quicker way. Notice the small down arrow at the end of the Address text box.

Click on this arrow, or click inside the text box and press the Down Arrow key—the URL list opens up, as you can see in figure 5.5. This shows the URLs you've entered in the past; just click on the one you want, and Explorer will load that document. (You can also use the Down Arrow to move through the list, and press Enter once you've highlighted the one you want.)

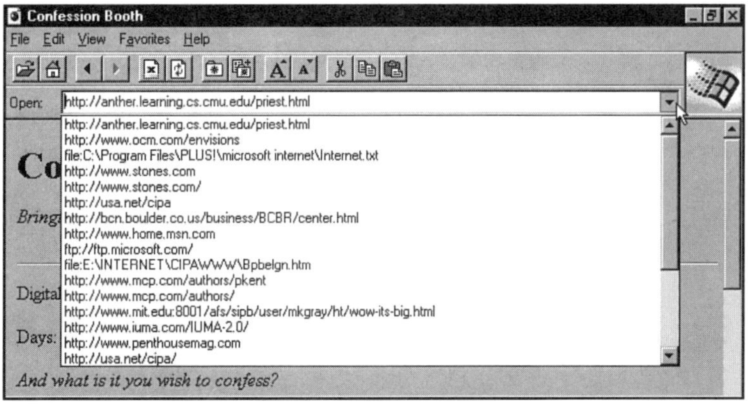

Fig. 5.5
Select a URL that you've used earlier by opening the Address list.

TIP **The problem with selecting from the URL list is that you may not** recognize the URL; they often are not very descriptive. If you can't remember the URL, and you haven't placed the document in the Favorites list, use the History list. The History list uses the document *titles*—which are much more descriptive and easier to remember. See chapter 6.

This URL list appears in the Open Internet Address dialog box, too (the box that opens when you click on the Open toolbar button or choose File, Open).

TIP **Here's a quick way to move to the Address text box. Press Tab,** and the URL is highlighted. Type a new one, or press Down Arrow to open the list box. (This method *won't* work in Web documents that contain forms, because pressing Tab moves to the next field in the form. See "Using forms" later in this chapter.)

How can I share URLs?

You may want to share URLs that you've found. You can copy them from Explorer and paste them into letters, memos, e-mail, and so on. Here's how.

If you want to copy the URL of the page you are currently viewing, click in the Address text box. The entire text will be highlighted. Then press Ctrl+C or click on the Copy toolbar button. This copies the text to the Windows Clipboard. Then you can change to another application, and paste the text.

If you want to copy a URL from a link—in other words, you haven't gone to the Web document, so the URL isn't in the Address text box—point at the link and right-click on it. When the pop-up menu opens, choose Copy Shortcut; the URL referenced by the link is copied to the Clipboard. (Well, maybe it's not. In the first release of Internet Explorer this feature was "broken." Maybe they'll fix it in later releases.) There's that pop-up menu again. We'll get to that in a moment.

TIP **If you are a member of MSN, you can also share shortcuts that** you've placed on your desktop or in the Favorites list, or that Explorer has placed in the History list. Simply copy them to an e-mail or BBS message window. (See chapter 6 for information on creating shortcuts.)

Opening files on your hard disk

Eventually, in your exploration of the Web, you may end up with .HTM or .HTML files on your hard disk. Perhaps you'll even create your own (see chapters 17 and 18). Explorer provides a way to open these files:

1. Click on the Open toolbar button, or choose File, Open. The Open Internet Address dialog box opens.
2. If you want to open the document in a new Explorer window—so the current document remains displayed in the current window—click on the Open in New Window check box.
3. Click on the Open File button. A typical Windows 95 Open File dialog box opens.
4. Use the dialog box to find the .HTM or .HTML file you want to open.

Q&A

What are all these file types in the Files of Type drop-down list?

Oh, you weren't supposed to see those yet. Not only can you load .HTM and .HTML files into Explorer, you can load these formats, too: .TXT (text), .JPG and .JPEG (a compressed graphics format), .GIF (the Graphics Interchange Format), .AU, .AIF, .AIFF (three different sound formats), and .XBM (a UNIX graphics format). You'll learn more about these in chapters 9 and 10.

5. Double-click on the filename or click once and click on the Open button. The document will be loaded into the Internet Explorer window.

TIP

Here's a geek trick for you. If you know the exact path to the file you want to open, and if you can type quickly, click in the Address text box then type **file:** followed by the path. For instance, you might type **file:C:\Program Files\PLUS!\microsoft internet\cache\acro.html** to open a document called acro.html in your cache directory. (Note that you can type the forward or backslash; for instance, if you type **file:C:/Program Files/PLUS!/microsoft internet/cache/acro.html** Explorer will replace the / with \ and grab the correct document.)

The right-click pop-up menus

Now, it's time to look at the right-click pop-up menus. As I mentioned before, there are different menus for different things. To look at what you can get, refer to the following graphics page.

What are all these menu options? Well, most are self-explanatory, and we'll be describing them in more detail in various places throughout the book. Here's a quick run-down.

Pop-up Menu Option	Description
Add to Favorites	Adds current document to the Favorites list.
Copy	Copies the highlighted text to the Clipboard.
Copy Background	Copies the document background to the Clipboard.
Copy Picture	Copies the picture to the Clipboard.
Copy Shortcut	Copies the URL referenced by the link to the Clipboard. (In theory, though this feature currently doesn't work.)
Create Shortcut	Creates a desktop shortcut for this document.
Open	Displays the document referenced by the link.
Open in New Window	Opens a new Explorer window and displays the document referenced by the link.
Save Background As	Saves the background as a graphics file on your hard disk; you specify the name.
Save Picture As	Saves the pictures on your hard disk; you specify the name.
Select All	Selects all the text in the document.
Set As Desktop Wallpaper	Saves the document background (or the inline image you are clicking on) and uses it as your Windows 95 desktop wallpaper.
Show Picture	Displays the missing picture.
View Source	Opens Notepad or Wordpad and displays the .HTM or .HTML document, so you can see all the "codes" or "tags."

Right-click pop-up menus

This menu opens when you right-click on the blank background, or on normal text (text that is neither a link, nor in a picture).

This opens when you right-click on a picture. If the picture has a link on it, then all options are enabled.

This opens when you highlight some text, then right-click on it.

This opens when you right-click on a text link.

This opens when you have inline images turned off, and you right-click on an icon representing a missing image.

And now...the cache

It's time to learn about the cache, and the Refresh command. I've mentioned it a few times already, because it seems to touch on so many areas. So let's learn about it in detail.

When you go back to a Web document that you've previously viewed, you may notice that it's displayed much more quickly. That's because Internet Explorer isn't taking it from the Internet; it's getting it from the **cache**, an area on your hard disk in which it saves pages. This is really handy. Not only does it speed up working on the Web, but because Internet Explorer doesn't throw away the cached pages when you have finished your session, you can view a page later without having to reconnect to the Internet and pay online charges.

By default, these documents are stored in the \PROGRAM FILES\Plus!\microsoft internet\cache directory. This cache can get very big—as big as you allow it. Choose View, Options to see the Options dialog box, and then choose the Advanced tab. You'll see the information shown in figure 5.6. Note that the Folder line, near the bottom of the dialog box, shows which directory is being used as the cache.

Is a link a true shortcut?

The Internet Explorer programmers have changed a few terms. Instead of using *home page*, they use *start page*. Instead of using *URL*, they use *Address*. I can understand the reasoning behind these, and accept them. But I think the next substitution that they've made is simply wrong. Instead of *link* or *URL*, they use the term **shortcut**. For instance, in the previous table you can see the Copy Shortcut menu option. By this, the programmers mean that when you choose the menu option, Internet Explorer will copy the URL from the link to the Clipboard. Why shortcut, then? After all, they're using URL Addresses elsewhere. Also, when you point at a link, the URL is shown in the status bar, preceded by the words *Shortcut to*—the implication being that the link is a shortcut. But the term shortcut already has another meaning in Windows 95, and these links are not true Windows 95 shortcuts. And a link isn't a shortcut in the normal sense, either. It's not a quicker way to get somewhere. Link is a much better and clearer term, so that's the term we'll use throughout this book.

Plain English, please!

In Windows 95, directories on your hard drive are often also known as **folders**. I've been using PCs too long to get used to the idea, though, so I still call them directories. (I know I'm not alone!)

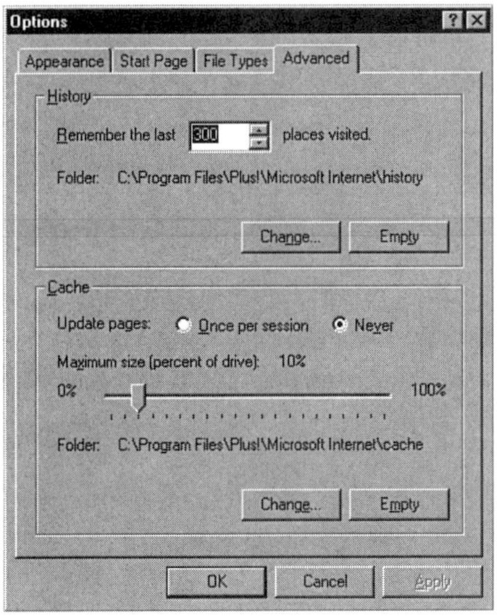

Fig. 5.6
The Options dialog box lets you determine the size of your cache.

At the top, you'll see the History information—we'll come back to this later, in chapter 6. Below that, you'll see the Cache information. Drag the pointer along the Maximum Size bar to tell Internet Explorer just how much of your drive you want to use for the cache. This doesn't stop other programs from using that space, it just means that Internet Explorer can use that much, if available.

But which drive? What if the drive containing the \PROGRAM FILES\Plus!\microsoft internet\cache directory is almost full, but you have another, half-empty drive? First, open Windows Explorer and create a directory for the cache. Then return to Internet Explorer's Options dialog box, choose the Change button, and select the directory you just created.

The cache update options

Now, there are two Update Pages option buttons; Once Per Session and Never. If you choose the Once Per Session option button, each time you start a new session Internet Explorer will only retrieve files from the cache that it placed there in the current session. For instance, let's say you visited the

Rolling Stones Web page (**http://www.stones.com/**) yesterday. Today, you open your browser and go back to the Rolling Stones page; does Internet Explorer take the page out of the cache? No, if Once Per Session is turned on. It does, however, replace the old copy of the Rolling Stones page in the cache.

Q&A *What are all these tmp*.html files in the cache directory?*

Many files on the Web have the name DEFAULT.HTM or DEFAULT.HTML. The Default document is the one that is displayed in a browser if no document is specified. For instance, notice that when Internet Explorer starts and opens the default Microsoft home page, the URL shown is **http://www.home.msn.com/**. This doesn't include a document name, it just shows a Web server name; it doesn't even specify a directory. Because no document is specified, the server sends the default document.

Internet Explorer doesn't save the name of these DEFAULT.HTM and DEFAULT.HTML documents. Rather, it replaces the name with tmp, followed by a number.

If you leave the Stones page and return to it later, Internet Explorer retrieves the document from the cache, because it placed a copy of the page there during the current session.

The other option button, Never, tells Internet Explorer *not* to refresh the page in the cache. In the situation mentioned above, when we access the Stones page for the first time, Internet Explorer takes the document out of the cache—it doesn't grab a new copy from the Web. Actually the term *Never* is not quite accurate. Internet Explorer won't automatically update the pages in the cache, but you can tell it to do so using the Refresh command (which we'll discuss in a moment).

Which of these two options should you use? I prefer Never, because it makes my Web sessions *much* quicker. Whenever I tell Internet Explorer to go to a Web page that's already in the cache, it loads it from the hard disk instead of accessing the Internet. (It's much quicker to load something from your hard disk than over your phone lines!) On the other hand, I have to remember to keep using the Refresh command to make sure I'm viewing the latest version of the Web pages. Some people may prefer to use the Once Per Session option, so that they can be sure of always looking at the latest page.

Clearing the cache

Look at the Empty button in the Options dialog box. Clicking on this button deletes everything in the cache directory (of course, you can also do this from Windows Explorer). Before you do that, read on, because in chapter 9 I'm going to explain how to grab information from the Web—the cache can provide storehouse from which you can extract information, even after you've logged off the Internet.

What's refresh?

Refresh is a "cure" for the cache. What happens if you return to a Web document that's stored in the cache? Internet Explorer gets it from the cache, right? However, that means you are not getting the latest document. Now that won't always matter, but in a few cases, it *does*.

For instance, let's say you want to return to a site you visited several weeks ago. If you have a very large cache, that document may still be there. If you have the Never option button selected in the Options dialog box, you'll be seeing the *old* document, which may have changed in the last few weeks. Or perhaps you are viewing a Web document that changes rapidly, such as a stock quote page. Even if you viewed the page only a few minutes ago, it could already be out of date.

The cure for old stale Web pages is to refresh them. (If you've used other Web browsers, you'll know this as the **Reload** command.) Click the Refresh button, or choose View, Refresh. Internet Explorer overwrites the current document in the cache, replacing it with the latest version.

Searching within documents

Some Web pages are pretty big. In fact some are *very* big—dozens of pages long—with links from the top of the document to "sections" lower down.

So Explorer helps you search long documents. Choose Edit, Find, and the Find dialog box opens (see fig. 5.7). Type the word you are looking for, choose Match Case (if necessary) and Start from Top of Page to make sure you search the entire document. Choose Find Next, and Internet Explorer will move the document so that the first line containing the word is at the top of the window.

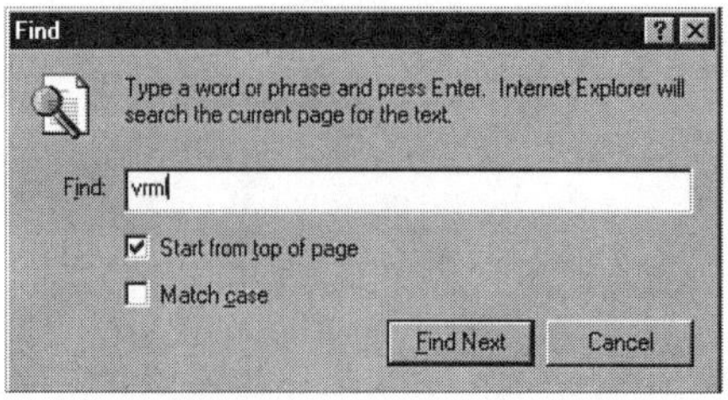

Fig. 5.7
Use the Find dialog box to search large Web documents.

You can't go there!—using passwords

In the not so distant past, the World Wide Web was totally open. If you had a browser connected to the Web, you could view virtually any document available on the Web. That's not the case these days, because there are now a lot of *private* Web sites. More are likely to show up in the near future. (Don't worry though. The Web is huge; you can travel around it for weeks without running into these private sites.)

Which sites are private? Generally sites that have been set up to make money. Of course, a Web author can set up a site as private just to keep "unauthorized" people out. For instance, a company might set up a technical-support Web site for use by registered users of its products, or a club could set up a site for its members. Many sites, though, are being set up as pay-per-view sites. If you want to view the site, you'll have to cough up the bucks.

An example are the "adult" sites. These Web sites show people (mostly women) in various states of undress, often doing things that Pat Robertson would call "abominable." If you want access to such sites you'll have to register, and you'll probably have to pay. A password and account name are normally issued. When you try to enter such a site—or the private parts of such sites (if you'll excuse the pun), as they often have both public and private areas—you'll see the Password dialog box. You can see an example in figure 5.8.

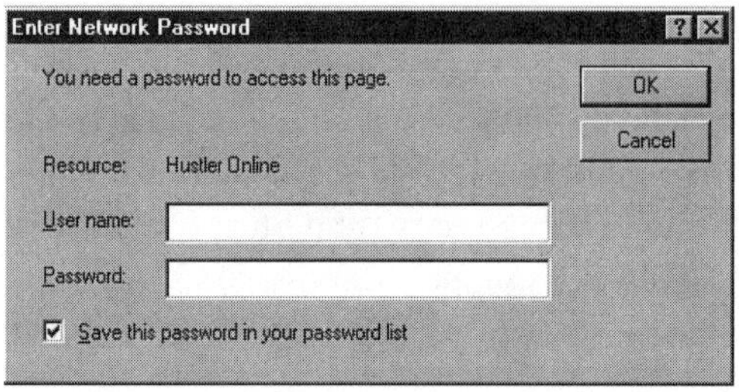

Fig. 5.8
Type your user or account name and password and click on OK to enter a private site. (No, I'm not a subscriber!)

You'll type your account (or User) name and password, then click on OK to gain access to the document. Also, notice the Save This Password in Your Password List check box. Windows 95 stores a list of passwords for each user with a profile on a computer. (Windows 95 lets you set up separate profiles, or accounts, for each user; each person has his own account name and password.)

If you select this check box, Internet Explorer will add the password to the list. The next time you return to this site, you won't have to remember the password—Explorer will enter it for you.

Using forms

Many Web pages contain **forms**. Forms contain text boxes, option buttons, command buttons, list boxes, and other information requested by the host. You can enter the requested information, make certain selections, and carry out procedures.

For example, in figure 5.9 you can see part of a very handy Web document, the *Confession Booth* ("*Bringing the net to its knees since 1994*"). This form lets you enter information about your most worrying sin, and be given a suitable penance. (If you feel the need to repent, go to **http://anther.learning.cs.cmu.edu/priest.html.**)

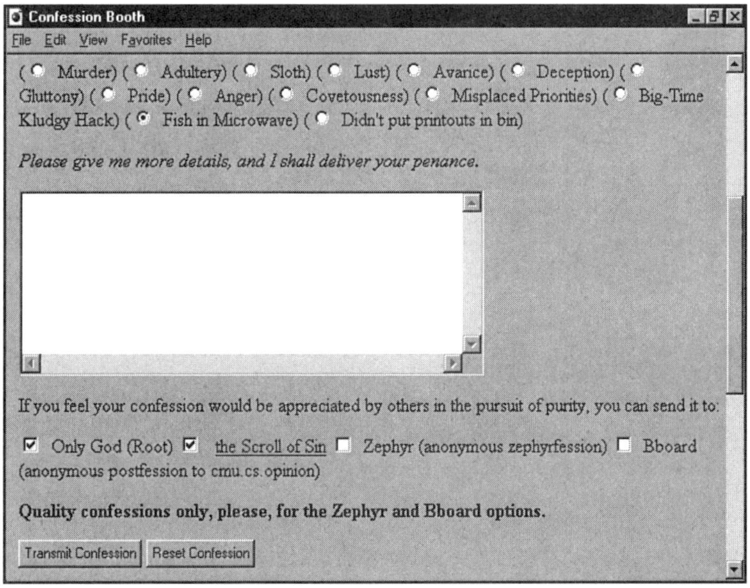

Fig. 5.9
The Confession Booth, an example of a Web form.

This form contains option buttons (select one of the available options: Murder, Adultery, Misplaced Priorities, Didn't put printouts in bin, and so on); a text box into which you can type something; check boxes (select as many as you wish); and command buttons (click on Transmit Confession or Reset Confession).

You can click on components in these forms, or press Tab to move through them one after another (press Shift-Tab to move backward through the list). Note also that you can use the Cut, Copy, and Paste buttons while working in forms.

What's all this about Netscape?

Well, let's be honest—you're going to run into Netscape sooner or later. Netscape is Internet Explorer's major competitor. It's generally regarded as the best browser available, though I think this has been overstated somewhat. It's very good, but as far as "ease of use" goes, so's Internet Explorer. I use Internet Explorer, and am quite comfortable doing so; I don't feel the need to throw it out and use Netscape.

However, there are some things that Netscape has that Explorer (and other browsers) don't. You see, the people who created Netscape decided to short-circuit the HTML development phase, and create their own HTML tags. That is, they came up with special codes that will do things for the Netscape browser, but which are not part of standard HTML. Remarkably they've even been able to convince many Web authors to use these tags. So now and again you'll see sites with messages that say something like "customized for Netscape." That means the Web pages use certain HTML tags that work for Netscape. But many of those tags now work for other browsers, too, as they incorporate the Netscape tags.

You won't find much that Internet Explorer can't display that Netscape can. You may run into Netscape-secure servers now and again, though. These are special https:// servers (s for secure). They are designed to allow the Netscape browser to use special forms that will send encrypted data back to the server. For instance, you could type a credit-card number into a form and click on Send. The browser would encrypt the data, then send it to the server, where it could be decrypted.

This is a neat little system, but also one that isn't used at most Web sites. Yes, you'll quite likely run into such sites, but, for now at least, probably not many. In the meantime, who knows…maybe Internet Explorer will incorporate the security features.

6

The History List, Favorites, and Shortcuts

In this chapter:

- Using the History list
- The GLOBHIST.HTM file—another form of History list
- Working in the History-list window?
- The Favorites list
- How can I add folders to the Favorites window?
- Creating desktop shortcuts, and creating a shortcut to the Favorites window

The Web's so big, you can easily get lost. These three tools will help find your way back to sites you've visited before . . . .

You'll soon find that the Web is an interesting place, but a very big place, too. Now and again you'll discover that it's so big you can't seem to find your way back to that interesting little Web document you were viewing a few days ago. Or maybe you *won't* run into this problem—if you use the tools I'm going to describe in this chapter.

These are the three tools you'll learn about:

- The History list—Internet Explorer keeps a list of all the documents you've viewed, so you can quickly return.
- Favorites—Create your own categorized list of places you know you'll want to return to sometime.
- Shortcuts—Place shortcuts to documents on your Windows 95 desktop.

Using the History list

A **History list** is a list of Web documents that you've visited before. Almost all Web browsers have History lists, but Internet Explorer's list is a little unusual. Most browsers keep a list of sites you've visited during the current session. Internet Explorer, though, saves entries from previous sessions, too.

You can use the History list in a couple of ways. The easiest is to select an entry from the bottom of the File menu—you can see an example in figure 6.1. As you visit sites, Internet Explorer adds the document titles to the File menu. When you select an entry from the list, Internet Explorer displays that document again.

TIP **Remember that when you "return" or "redisplay" a document by** selecting it from the File menu, Internet Explorer may pull that document from the cache on your hard drive. In other words, you are not seeing the latest version. Click on the Refresh button to tell Internet Explorer to refresh the document by getting the latest version from the Web. See chapter 5 for information about the cache.

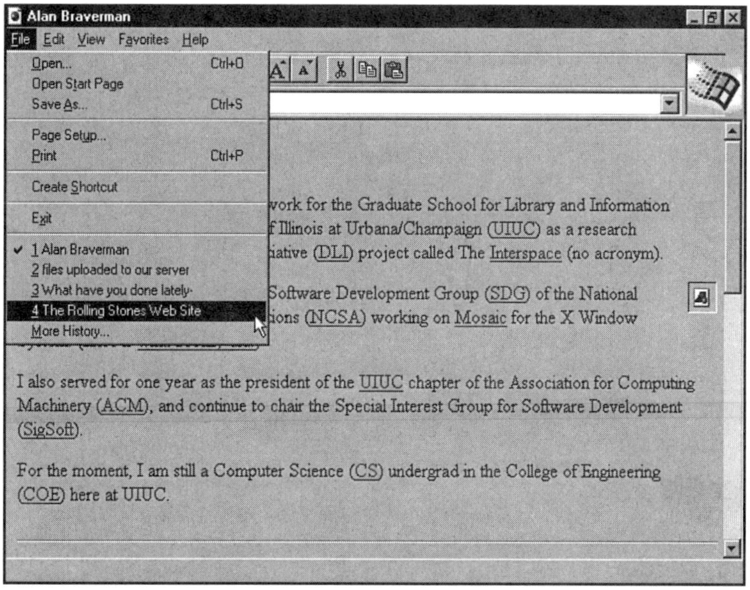

Fig. 6.1
You can quickly return to a document you've seen by selecting it from the bottom of the File menu.

Q&A ***When I double click on an entry in my Favorites or History lists, the Microsoft Network dialog box opens, even though I'm already logged on. What's going on?***

This is just one of those strange little bugs you may run into. Go to the Control Panel, double-click on Add/Remove Programs, click on Microsoft Plus! for Windows 95, and choose Add/Remove. Remove the Internet Jumpstart Kit, and reinstall.

If you want to visit a site from a *previous* session or if you have visited too many documents for them all to be shown in the File menu, choose File, More History. A special History window will appear, as you can see in figure 6.2. (If this History window opens displaying icons, you'll probably want to choose View, List.)

Can you see what this window is? It's actually a Windows Explorer window, showing the contents of the History directory on your hard drive. (The full path to the History directory is *C:/Program Files/Plus!/Microsoft Internet/history*.) Each entry is actually a shortcut file—simply double-click the document you want to return to and Internet Explorer displays that document. (The History window disappears under the Internet Explorer window, but it's still open. You can get back to it by clicking its button in the taskbar.)

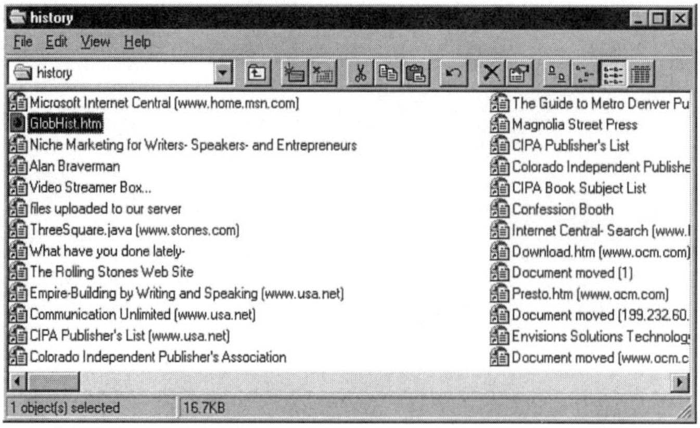

Fig. 6.2
The History list is actually a Windows Explorer window.

Q&A ***My History-list window doesn't look like yours. How can I change it?***

First, if the toolbar isn't displayed, choose View, Toolbar. Then click on the four buttons on the right side until you find the view you prefer. The view in my illustration is the List view. You can also change views by choosing one from the View menu. Also, I've set up my History list so that only the word "history" appears in the title bar. To include the entire path, choose View, Options, then click in the Display the Full MS-DOS Path in the Title Bar check box and click on OK.

Using the GLOBHIST.HTM file

There's also a GLOBHIST.HTM file in your History directory. Each time you close Internet Explorer, it updates the GLOBHIST.HTM file with entries from the History list. Each of these entries in the GLOBHIST.HTM file is a link. So another way to view your History list is to open this file; you can choose File, Open, click on the Open File button, then double-click the file in the History directory. You'll see a Web document inside Internet Explorer (see fig. 6.3), containing a list of all the documents you've viewed. Click on the text to go to a previously viewed document. Remember, though, that the document only shows entries that were in the History list the last time you closed Internet Explorer, so it won't show documents you visited in the current session.

Q&A ***I can't find the GLOBHIST.HTM file—where did it go?***

GLOBHIST.HTM is a hidden file. If you don't see it in the Open File dialog box, try this. Open Windows Explorer, then choose View, Options. Click on the Show All Files option button, then click on OK.

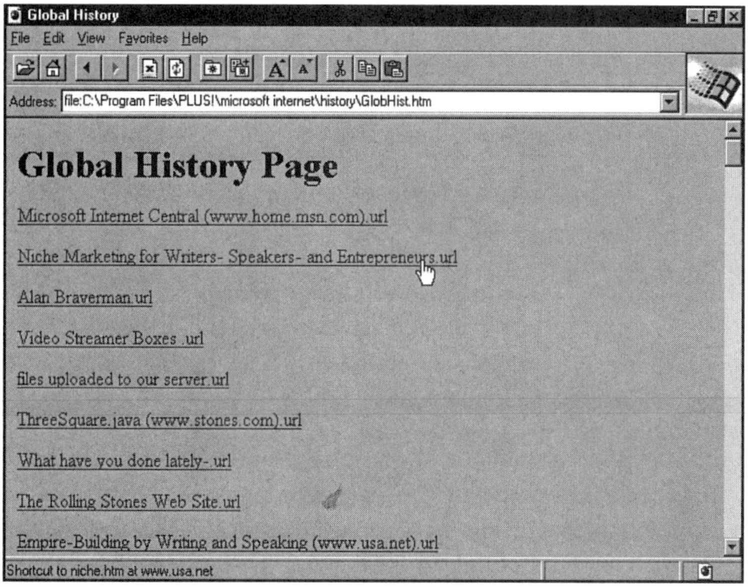

Fig. 6.3
You can also view the History list by opening the GLOBHIST.HTM file.

TIP **If you prefer to use the GLOBHIST.HTM History list, here's a way** to get to it quickly. First, open the file in the way I've just described (choose File, Open, click on the Open File button, then double-click on the file inside the History directory). Now, right-click on a blank area, and choose Add to Favorites. In the Add to Favorites dialog box type **0-History** and click on Add. (That's a zero; it will ensure that the entry will appear near the top of the Favorites menu.) We'll get into the Favorites list in detail in a moment (see "Using the Favorites list").

Opening a document in another window

In chapter 5 you learned how to enter a URL into the Address box or the Open Internet Address dialog box and open the specified document in a new window, leaving the current document displayed in the original window. How can you do that with the History list?

Well, there's no direct way to do that from the File menu or the History-list window. However, if you select a History list entry while Internet Explorer is busy transferring a document into the original window, Explorer will automatically open a new window.

A few things you can do to the History list

Here are a few things you may want to do to your History list:

Delete entries—select them and press Delete, or right-click on them and choose Delete.

Sort the list—Choose View, Arrange Icons. You'll see a cascading menu that enables you to sort the entries by Name or Date. (Date is the default, so the most recent document appears first. You can sort by Size and Type, too, though it's kinda pointless.)

Send an entry to someone else—Right-click on it and choose Send To, Mail Recipient. A Microsoft Exchange e-mail window will open, with a shortcut inside. You can send the message to another MSN user. That user can double-click on it to open Internet Explorer and open the document, or save it to the hard disk.

Copy the URL from the entry—Right-click on it and choose Properties. In the Properties dialog box, click on the Internet Shortcut tab. The URL will be shown in the Target URL text box.

Rename the entry—Click on it, then press F2 and type a new name. Of course if you go to this extent, you may as well add the entry to the Favorites list. (More on the Favorites list later in this chapter.)

Move or copy the entry to the Favorites list—Click on the entry you want to move (hold Shift and click on two entries to select all the entries between, or hold Ctrl while you click on the ones you want). Then right-click and choose Cut or Copy. Open Windows Explorer and find the Favorites directory (it's a sub-menu of the Windows directory). Place the cursor inside the directory, right-click, and choose Paste.

Copy the entry to the Favorites (maybe)—Some Windows 95 system utilities add an entry to the right-click Send To cascading menu. The new option may say Any Folder, for instance. This can be used to copy an entry from the History list to the Favorites.

Create a desktop shortcut—Drag the entry from the History list to your desktop to create a shortcut.

TIP **You can also archive History lists; use the Windows Explorer to** copy the entries to another directory, and then compress them using WinZip or a similar compression utility.

Configuring the History list

In figure 6.4, you can see the History information in the Options dialog box (choose View, Options, then click on the Advanced tab). In this example, the History list is set to 300 entries; in other words, Internet Explorer adds entries until there are 300 in the list, and then removes the oldest ones to make room for the newest. You can increase this number up to 3000, if you want.

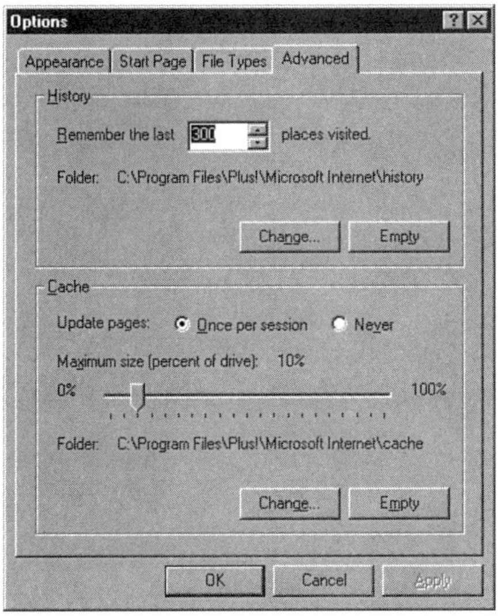

Fig. 6.4
In the options dialog box, you can choose the number of entries in your history list.

You can empty the History list by clicking the Empty button. Each History entry is actually a small text file, stored in the \Program Files\Plus!\Microsoft Internet\history directory. Because each entry is so small—ranging from about 40 to 140 bytes, with about 70 bytes on average—even when the list contains 300 entries, it's still not very large. (If you really feel you need to keep up to 3,000 entries you'll only take up about 200 Kbytes.) If you wish, you can move the list to a different directory by clicking on the Change button. (When you do this Internet Explorer will move all the entries from the History directory to the new one, then delete the History directory.)

Using the Favorites list

History lists can get very cluttered and, even if you clean them periodically, often include lots of files you are not really interested in. So there's another way to get back to where you've been: the Favorites list. This is a collection of shortcuts—again, small text files containing the Web address (URL) that you want to store.

When you reach a document you think you may want to return to, click the Add to Favorites button; or choose Favorites, Add to Favorites; or right-click inside the document and choose Add to Favorites. The Add To Favorites dialog box opens, as you can see in figure 6.5.

The large list box shows the contents of the \Windows\Favorites directory, the default location of your Favorites shortcuts. (It also shows folders, though your list box won't show these yet. I'll explain how to add these under "Add folders to your Favorites window," later in this chapter.) You can modify the entry in the Names text box, if you want. This normally shows the title of the document you are viewing, but you may want to change the text to something you'll find easier to remember and recognize later. Sometimes, you'll also find documents without titles, in which case Internet Explorer has to use the document's file name—GALLERY.HTM, MFR2.HTM, or whatever unmemorable name it happens to be. Change these to something sensible.

Choose Add, and Internet Explorer creates the file, adding the entry to your Favorites list.

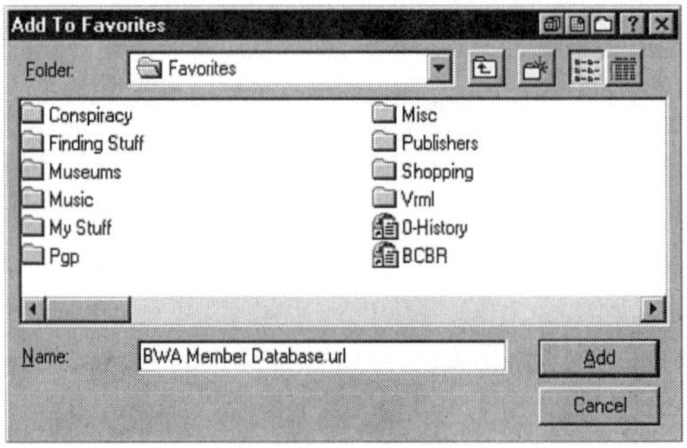

Fig. 6.5
The Add To Favorites dialog box lets you save a route back to your favorite Web sites.

Using the Favorites

There are a couple of ways to use the Favorites list. The quickest is to open the Favorites menu (see fig. 6.6). You'll see the first 19 entries in your

Favorites list. Choose any entry to get Internet Explorer to reload that document (perhaps from the cache, depending on how the cache is set up). Again, you can see folders in my illustration, and your's doesn't have any yet. I'll explain this in a moment (OK, I'm teasing you).

TIP

Sometimes when you try to open the Favorites or History list, it doesn't appear. Take a look in the taskbar—you may find it there. Click on the taskbar button to open the window.

If you have more than 19 entries in your list (and you haven't placed those entries in the folders that I'm going to explain soon), you'll have to open the Favorites window to get to them. Click the Open Favorites button, or choose Favorites, Open Favorites. As with the History list, you'll see a Windows Explorer window displaying the contents of your Favorites directory. Just double-click the one you want to go to.

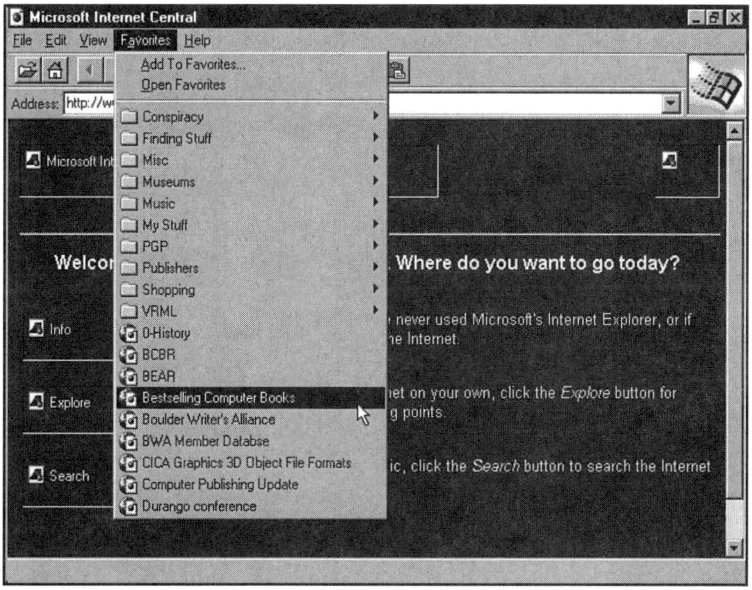

Fig. 6.6
You can quickly select documents from the Favorites list.

TIP

The Favorites window works in the same way as the History window. For an idea of what you can do in this window, see the information about the History window earlier in this chapter.

Here's another little trick you can play; you don't have to add documents to the Favorites immediately, you can wait and add them later—at the end of your session, after you've logged off, or even a week later. Simply open the

Windows Explorer and drag items from the History directory into the Favorites directory. This will move the entries from the History directory to the Favorites directory. (If you want to *copy* an entry from History, press Ctrl while you drag.) Or open Internet Explorer and then use the History list to open the document—retrieving it from the cache. Then add it to the Favorites list using the Add to Favorites toolbar button, and open the next document you want to add.

TIP **There's another way to open the Favorites folder. Create a** desktop shortcut to it, and double-click on the shortcut. See "Managing shortcuts," later in this chapter.

Add folders to your Favorites window

You can customize the way that your shortcuts are stored by creating folders, and categorizing your Favorites. Instead of having a huge jumble of entries, you can have a variety of folders, each for a different subject or purpose.

Open the Favorites window, and then choose File, New, Folder. A new folder icon appears in the window. Type a name for the folder—**Music**, **Multimedia**, **Business**, or whatever else comes to mind—and press Enter. Create as many of these folders as you want, each for a different category. You can create subfolders within those folders, too, if you want. Just double-click on a folder to open it, then create a new folder inside it.

Now, the next time after you add a Web document to your Favorites, you can double-click a folder to place it in the appropriate category. Later, when you want to return to this page, open the Favorites window, double-click the folder icon, and *then* double-click the shortcut to the page.

TIP **You may find that when you double-click on the folder, another** window opens. You can stop this from happening by choosing View, Options, and clicking on the option button labeled Browse Folders By Using a Single Window That Changes As You Open Each Folder.

This method lets you improve the Favorites menu. I told you that you could display only 19 entries in the Favorites menu, but that includes the new folders you've created. Each folder appears near the top of the Favorites menu as another cascading menu. Click on a folder and the menu opens. You can see an example of this in figure 6.7.

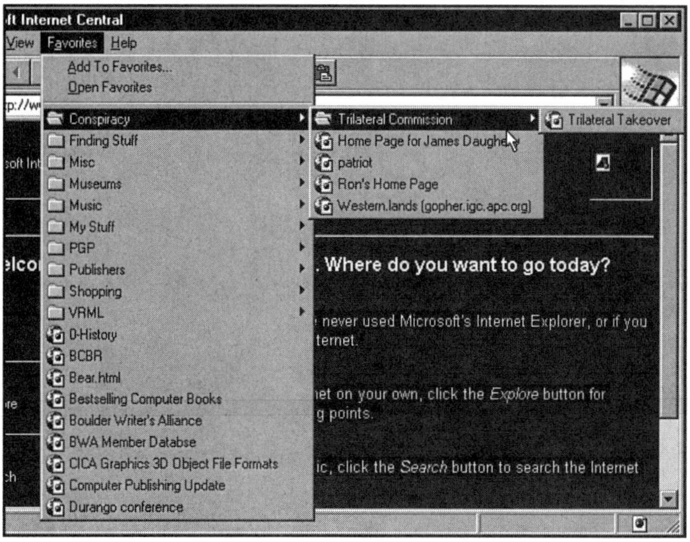

Fig. 6.7
Create a series of cascading menus by adding folders to your Favorites window.

Creating desktop shortcuts

Windows 95 uses desktop icons for two purposes. Many icons directly represent files or folders. Delete one, and you delete the file or folder from your hard disk. But many icons work just as Program Manager icons did in Windows 3.1—they don't directly represent a file or folder, they represent a *link* to something. Double-click on the icon and the file opens, for instance. But delete the icon, and the file or folder still remains on your hard disk.

These icons are known as **shortcuts**. They allow you to get to a file or folder from many different places, but they are not only used for files or folders. You can create a shortcut that "points" at a World Wide Web document. This shortcut can be placed on your desktop. Double-clicking on the shortcut icon will open Internet Explorer, log on to the Internet, and retrieve the document. (As usual, if the document is in the cache, Internet Explorer won't bother logging on—it will grab it from the cache. Click on the Refresh button to make Internet Explorer log on and get a "fresh" copy of the document.)

Creating shortcuts

To create a shortcut to a document you are viewing, choose File, Create Shortcut, or right-click in the document and choose Create Shortcut. You'll see a message box telling you that a shortcut will be placed on your desktop. Click on OK to remove the message box.

Now, minimize all your applications and windows—a quick way to do this is to point at the taskbar, right-click the bar, and then choose Minimize All Applications. What will you see on your desktop? You'll see the new icon, with a small arrow in the bottom-left corner. This arrow shows that the icon is a shortcut.

Managing shortcuts

What can you do with these shortcuts? Well, you can rename them, if you wish. Click on the shortcut and then press F2, type a new name, and press Enter. (Or right-click on the shortcut and choose Rename.)

You can quickly add them to your Start menu, too. Just drag them onto the Start button on your taskbar. You could also create a desktop folder to hold your shortcuts. This would provide you with a way to store a large number of these shortcuts.

However, I think most people will create these shortcuts just now and again, for Web documents they know they'll want to return to once more, though don't wish to place in their Favorites list. The Favorites list provides a more convenient way to save large numbers of shortcuts. So here's a quick way to create a desktop icon that opens the Favorites folder:

1. Right-click on the desktop and choose New, Shortcut.
2. When the Create Shortcut dialog box opens, type **C:\Windows\Favorites**.
3. Click on Next >.
4. Change the name of the shortcut, if you wish. (Internet, or WWW, or whatever you wish.)
5. Click on Finish.

Windows 95 will place a small folder icon with the usual arrow in the bottom left corner showing that it represents a shortcut. Double-click on this icon to open your Favorites folder.

Of course you can do the same thing for your History list, too. This time you'll create a shortcut to C:\Program Files\Plus!\Microsoft Internet\history.

However, there's a small Windows 95 bug here. You can't use the method I just described, because the Create Shortcut dialog box doesn't like seeing directory names with spaces inside them. Instead, open the History window, then click on the Up One Level button in the toolbar. Then right-click on the History directory, and choose Create Shortcut. Windows Explorer will place a shortcut into the Microsoft Internet directory (the directory holding the History directory); you can drag this out of the window onto your desktop.

7

Customizing Internet Explorer

In this chapter:

- **Modifying the Explorer window (slightly)**
- **Changing colors and removing the link underline**
- **What are the address options?**
- **How can I select another home page?**
- **Changing the document font size**
- **Modifying the print margins, headers, and footers**

Here are a few ways to tweak the Explorer interface, to modify the way it looks and runs . . . .

Removing Window components

The quickest and easiest change you can make to Internet Explorer is to increase your viewing area. Choose View, Toolbar to remove the toolbar from the top of the window; View, Address Bar to remove the Address bar from below the toolbar; and View, Status Bar to remove the status bar from the bottom of the window.

Of course all these items are useful, so you may not want to remove them often. Now and again, however, you'll come across a Web document that really requires a larger viewing area than you have available—perhaps there's a picture that doesn't quite fit into the window. Removing these items may provide enough extra space. (You may have noticed that some of the pictures in this book were "snapped" with the toolbar, address bar, and status bar turned off, for this very reason.)

TIP **A few browsers have a useful feature called kiosk mode. It allows** the user to quickly remove the toolbar, menu bar, address bar, and status bar, to maximize the amount of space available to view the Web document. You can't remove the menu bar from Internet Explorer, but if you have a programmable keyboard, programmable mouse, or some kind of macro utility you can set up a particular key, mouse click, or macro to quickly remove or add the toolbar, address bar, and status bar.

Changing program options

Now let's look at the program options that are available. Here's what you can change:

- Turn inline images on and off.
- Select custom colors for text and background.
- Select custom colors for links.
- Turn the URL display off so it doesn't appear in the status bar.
- Change the format of the URL displayed in the status bar.
- Select a different home (or start) page.

- Assign file formats to applications ("viewers")
- Configure the history list and cache.

Begin by opening the Options dialog box—choose View, Options. You'll see the dialog box shown in figure 7.1.

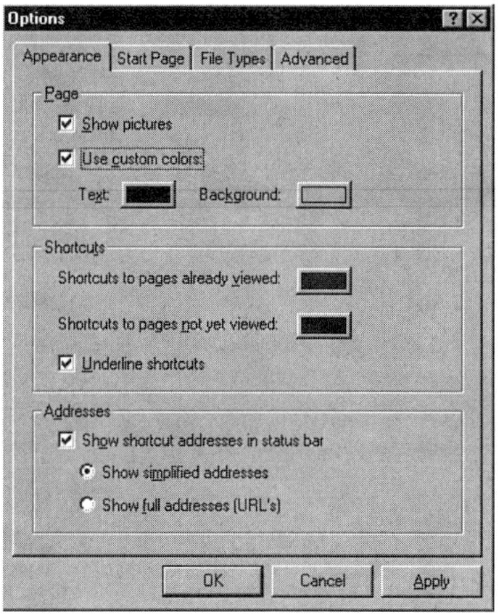

Fig. 7.1
The Options dialog box lets you choose turn off inline images, change colors, and define how URLs are displayed.

Turning inline images off

At the top of the dialog box is the Show Pictures checkbox. Clear this to turn off inline images. As we saw in chapter 5, doing so will cause Internet Explorer to display Web documents without any pictures—a good way to speed things up. (See that chapter for information about quickly viewing pictures that you *do* want to see).

Modifying colors

Now notice the Use Custom Colors checkbox. Use this to modify the text and background colors used in the Internet Explorer window. Click on the checkbox, then on the Text or Background color button. A Color dialog box opens. Choose your color, then click on OK. Back in the Options dialog box you can click on Apply to see what your choice will look like (the Explorer window will change to show you the effect); if you like it, click OK to save your changes. (If you click on Cancel the change will not be saved; the Apply button only applies the change temporarily.)

Q&A

I changed the background color, but the document background didn't change; why didn't anything happen?

Some Web authors use special backgrounds in their documents. If the document you are viewing has a special background, changing the default background color has no effect. Also, remember that authors can define text colors, too; the default text color has no effect on these special text colors, either.

The Shortcuts area lets you define what the hypertext links in Web documents will look like. You can clear the Underline Shortcuts checkbox to remove the link underlining, and you can modify the link colors—click on the colored buttons to open the Color dialog box. Remember that there are two link colors—one for links that will take you to Web pages you've never been to before (Shortcuts To Pages Not Yet Viewed), and one for Web pages that you *have* visited (Shortcuts To Pages Already Viewed). Again, you can use the Apply button to see what the changes look like before you decide to keep them.

Q&A

I've just viewed a Web page that I've never been to before, yet one of the links uses the Shortcuts To Pages Already Viewed color. How come?

Internet Explorer doesn't care if you've used the link before, only if you've been to the referenced document before. The link you are looking at leads to a document that you've viewed before—evidently you got to the document via some other route. Also, if the link takes you to another part of the document you are viewing (perhaps it takes you a few paragraphs down the document, or up to the top of the document), it will be marked as *already viewed.*

How long do the shortcuts to documents you've seen remain colored with the Shortcuts To Pages Already Viewed color? For as long as the referenced document remains listed in the history list. If you delete it from the list, or if it "drops off" the end of the list, in the next session you see a link to that document the link will use the normal, Shortcuts To Pages Not Yet Viewed, color.

The Addresses options

Now we come to the Addresses area of the Options dialog box. When you are working in a Web document and point at a link, the URL for that link will appear in the status bar at the bottom of the window, unless you clear the Show Shortcut Addresses In Status Bar checkbox. You also have two options for how Internet Explorer shows these URLs. The default is Show Simplified Addresses (*Shortcut to "homepage.html" at www.egallery.com* for instance). If you prefer, you can choose to Show Full Addresses (URLs) (*Shortcut to http://www.egallery.com/egallery/homepage.html*, for instance). I think the idea behind this is that the full URL is somehow confusing, but I don't find the "simplified" address to be of any great utility. (I prefer to take my URLs straight!)

By the way, if you use the Simplified Addresses, you'll find that sometimes the status bar only shows the document name, not the host name. It does this whenever the document referenced by the link that you are pointing at is on the same host computer.

I've discussed the term *shortcut*, in chapter 5. These are not shortcuts, they are simply hypertext links to other documents. I think the term shortcut is ambiguous, so I'm sticking with the term link.

Changing the home page

By default, the browser's "home page" (what Internet Explorer calls its **start page**) is the http://www.home.msn.com/ (At least, at the time of writing—it may change, as it has a number of times before. And yes, I know that this URL doesn't actually specify a document. But this is the URL that Internet Explorer uses to call the home page, and the Web server is automatically displaying a default document when this URL is used, so you don't need to know the document name.)

You can make any page you wish your home page. In other words, you can tell Internet Explorer which page to display when it opens. In fact, you can even create your own HTML file on your hard disk, and use that as a home page. (See chapter 17 for more on how to create a simple Web page.)

To set a different Web page, begin by displaying the page you want to use in Internet Explorer; it may be a page on your hard disk, or a page out on the Web somewhere—the Rolling Stones page (**http://www.stones.com/**), the

Internet Underground Music Archive (**http://www.iuma.com/**), or whatever you want.

Now choose View, Options, and when the Options dialog box opens click on the Start Page tab. You'll see the area shown in figure 7.2. Notice that near the top, under the home icon, you'll see the URL (or perhaps a simplified URL, if you selected that option under "The Addresses options" earlier in this chapter) of the page that is currently in use as the start page—in this case www.home.msn.com.

Fig. 7.2
The Start Page area of the Options dialog box is where you define your start (home) page.

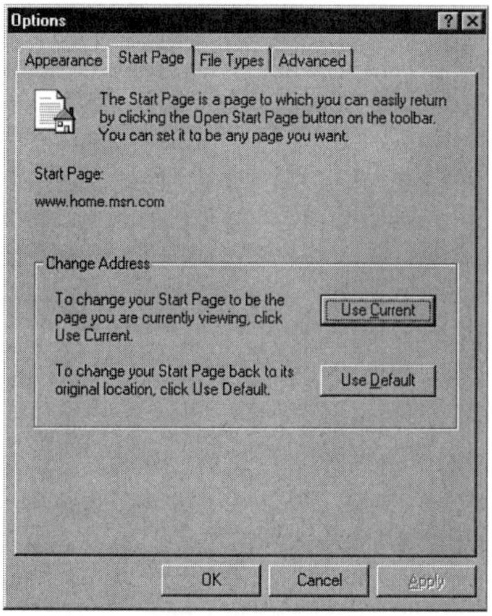

Now click on the Use Current button. You'll notice that the URL changes to show the URL of the displayed document. Click on OK to save your settings. (The Apply button is also active, but it doesn't really do anything here. To make sure your change is saved, you must use the OK button.)

That's it. If you ever want to change back to using the http://www.home.msn.com/ document as the home page, return to the Options dialog box and choose the Use Default button.

The File Types and Advanced settings

The Options dialog box has two more areas. The File Types area, and the Advanced area. The File Types area is used to define how Internet Explorer should handle certain documents it finds. As we'll see in chapters 10 and 11, the Web contains all sorts of neat things—music, video, static images of many kinds, 3-D "fly-through" environments, and so on. When Internet Explorer comes across one of these weird and wonderful formats, it has to figure out what to do with the file, so it looks in the list created in the File Types area.

> **TIP** **With most browsers, using a Web document somewhere out on** the Internet as your home page is a problem. You have to be connected to the Internet to display the home page, and it slows down opening the browser. And what if that document isn't available when you access it? With Internet Explorer, though, the document is in the cache! So, for instance, you could use the Stones Web page as your home page without spending a lot of time waiting for it to load each time. (Make sure you've got the Update Pages Never option button selected under the Options dialog box's Advanced tab, though.)

As for the Advanced area, this is where you set up your history list and cache. We've looked at these elsewhere, so see chapter 6 for information about the history list, and chapter 5 for information about the cache.

Change the document format

If a Web document is a simple ASCII text document, how does a Web browser know how to display the document? How does it know which piece is a heading, which is body text, and how does it know how each element should be displayed?

The HTML tags that I've mentioned before are instructions to the browser. For instance they tell the browser which part of the text is a Heading 1 (the text between the <H1> and </H1> tags), which is bold text (text between <B> and </B>), and so on. But they don't tell the browser how to display the text—just what the author intended it to be. For instance, how should Heading 1 text be displayed? Should it be bold? Should it be 24-point type, or 28-point type? Arial or Times New Roman? The HTML tags don't say. It's up to the browser to decide. That means that the same document looks one way in one browser, and another way in a different browser.

Internet Explorer, unlike some Web browsers, *doesn't* let you select the font for each type of text. It does, however, let you choose an overall text size. Choose View, Fonts, and a cascading menu opens, showing you your choices from Largest to Smallest. Simply select one of these and all the text in the current document will change. If the text is too small or too large, pick another one.

You can also click on the Use Larger Font and Use Smaller Font toolbar buttons to move up and down through the size range.

Preparing for printing

As you'll learn in chapter 9, Internet Explorer helps you retrieve information from the Web in many ways. One of the simplest is by printing the document, so Internet Explorer enables you to set up your page margins, headers, and footers. If you choose File, Page Setup, you'll see the dialog box in figure 7.3.

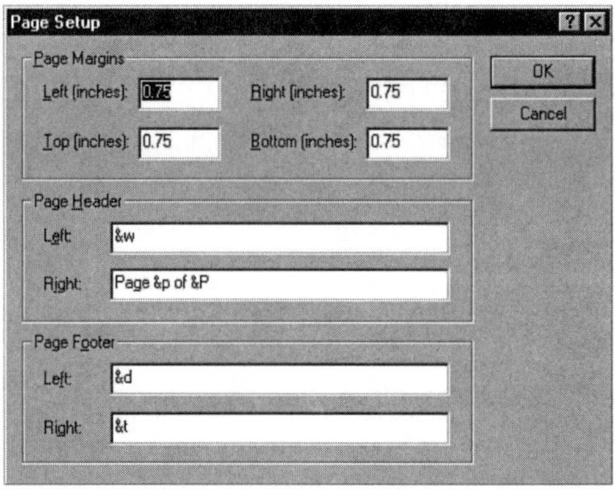

Fig. 7.3
The Page Setup dialog box helps you define the way your printed pages appear; you can even add headers and footers.

At the top of the page you'll find the margin settings. You can enter any margins you wish; in order to make the document fit within the margins Internet Explorer will wrap the text into a narrower area, and, perhaps, cut off parts of the pictures.

You can also create two headers and two footers (one left and one right for each). You can type any text you want into these boxes, and you can include special codes that will tell Internet Explorer to insert information. For instance, you could create this line:

```
&w from &u
```

This means, place the document title, followed by the word "from," followed by the URL of the document. For instance, you'd get this at the Stones Web page:

The Rolling Stones Web Site from http://www.stones.com/

You could include this line, too:

```
Page &p of &P
```

This means, place the word "Page" followed by the sequence number of the printed page, followed by the word "of," followed by the number of pages in the document. For instance,

Page 3 of 7

These are the codes you can insert:

Code	Description
&w	Web page title
&u	Web page address (URL)
&d	Date: mmm dd yyyy (e.g.: Jul 27 1995)
&D	Date: dd mmm yyyy (e.g.: 27 Jul 1995)
&t	Time, 12-hour format (e.g.: 05:25 PM)
&T	Time, 24-hour format (e.g.: 17:25)
&p	Current page number
&P	Total number of pages
&&	A single ampersand (&)

8

Searching for Information on the Web

In this chapter:

- **Searching the Internet with Lycos**
- **Moving through Yahoo's category list**
- **Searching with Yahoo**
- **Finding more search sites**
- **A multitude of searches—from AliWeb to WebCrawler**

Now that you know what to do on the Web, you need to know where to go. . . . .

By now you've learned how to move around on the Web. (You still need to know how to "grab" things from the Web, and how to play the multimedia files you'll find, but we'll get to that in chapters 9 to 11.)

So where you gonna go? You can't just launch out onto the Web and wander around forever. Well, you can I suppose. But what if you want to find something very specific, information about conspiracy theories, Web documents with links to music and video, online shopping…

In this chapter I'll explain how to search for what you need. We'll start by looking at the search tools that Explorer makes quickly accessible, then take a look at a few other places you can go to track down information.

Lycos

We'll start with Lycos, a system developed at Carnegie Mellon University. Why? Because Microsoft recently bought the rights to Lycos. Start Explorer, and click on the *Explore the Internet; Searches, Links and Tools* icon in the middle of the default Internet Explorer home page. Then click on the *Lycos* link that you'll see near the top of the document that appears. You'll now see the document in figure 8.1.

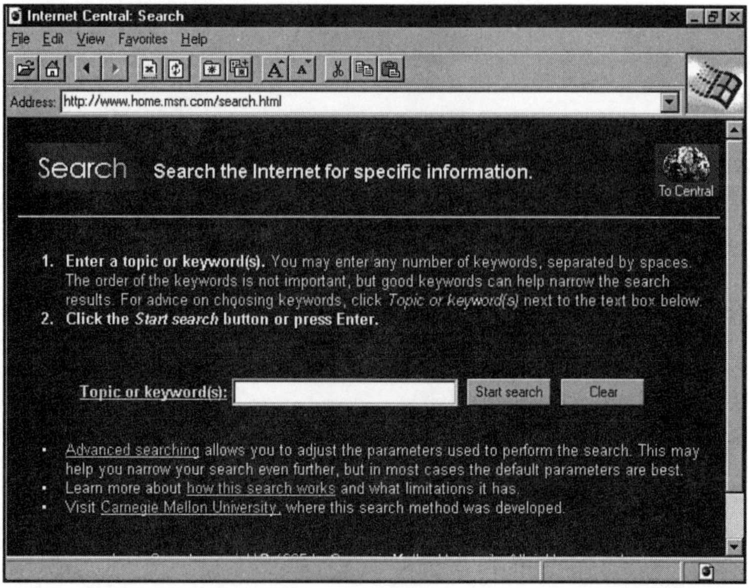

Fig. 8.1
Here's a quick way to search for a subject.

Type a word into the Topic or Keywords text box—**conspiracy**, **music**, **video**, or whatever you happen to be searching for. You must enter at least three characters for each word—letters or numbers—and you must start with a letter (not a number). You mustn't include hyphens and other non-alphanumeric characters within a word. You can enter several terms, if you wish (**music rock**, for instance).

TIP **Place a period after a word if you want Lycos to search for an** exact match. For instance, if you type **fire.** Lycos will only look for the word *fire*, and will ignore words such as *firefly* and *firefight*. Place a hyphen before a word to tell Lycos to score the document lower for that word. For instance, you might search for **conspiracy -kennedy**, if you are interested in conspiracy theories but *not* in theories about the Kennedy assasinations.

Also, note that many common words are not indexed, and thus cannot be found by Lycos.

Then press Enter or click on the Start Search button. Explorer will send the search term off to the computer at Carnegie Mellon, which will search for matching Web documents. In a few moments, with luck, you'll see something like the document shown in figure 8.2.

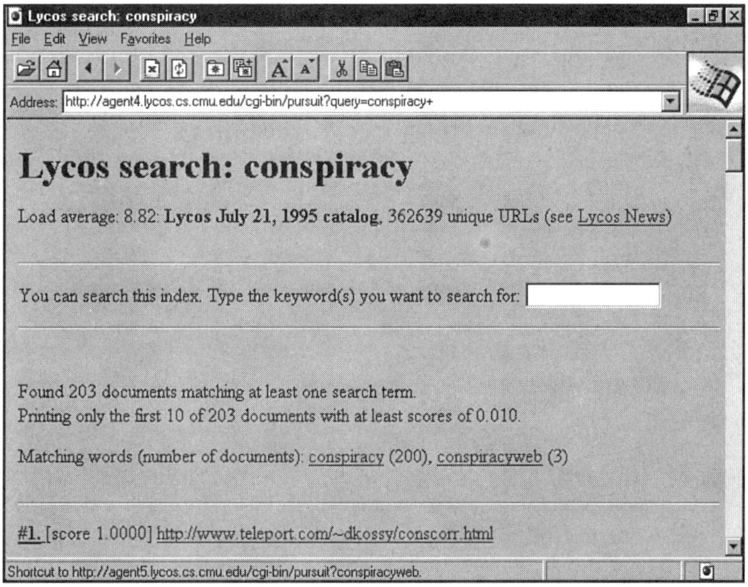
Lycos search: conspiracy
File Edit View Favorites Help
Address: http://agent4.lycos.cs.cmu.edu/cgi-bin/pursuit?query=conspiracy+
Lycos search: conspiracy
Load average: 8.82: Lycos July 21, 1995 catalog, 362639 unique URLs (see Lycos News)
You can search this index. Type the keyword(s) you want to search for:
Found 203 documents matching at least one search term.
Printing only the first 10 of 203 documents with at least scores of 0.010.
Matching words (number of documents): conspiracy (200), conspiracyweb (3)
#1. [score 1.0000] http://www.teleport.com/~dkossy/conscorr.html
Shortcut to http://agent5.lycos.cs.cmu.edu/cgi-bin/pursuit?conspiracyweb.

Fig. 8.2
Here's what Lycos showed me when I searched for **conspiracy**.

TIP **You can retrieve old searches from the History list—for instance, I** found an entry in my History list called *Lycos search-conspiracy*. You can also add searches to your Favorites list (see chapter 7). Create a folder in the Favorites window called Searches, and place all the searches you think you may want to repeat in this folder. Then you can search again quickly by simply selecting that entry from the Favorites list (from the menu or window). There's no need to go to the Lycos search screen first; Explorer will bypass that and simply run the search for you again.

What can we do in this document? Right at the top you'll see a *Start new search* link. If Lycos couldn't find anything, or if it finds something that's no use to you, use this link to search again.

To view what Lycos has found, simply scroll down the page, looking at each entry. What does each entry contain? You'll see a link—click on this link to go directly to the referenced document. Below the link you'll see the URL of the document, which you can copy if you wish. You can copy this URL or simply click on it to go directly to the document.

You may also see an outline; this is the first Heading 1 that Lycos found in the document. And you may also see **excerpts**. These are bits of text grabbed from the document. Sometimes useful, sometimes not. Lycos grabs bits and pieces from within the document, so it sometimes seems a bit garbled. Also, it grabs notes from within the HTML file that are not intended to be displayed when a browser "renders" the file (that is, when it converts the HTML file to something you can see).

At the bottom of the page you'll find a *Show more pages about*. Lycos only puts the first few items it finds in the document it displays. To see the next batch, click on this link.

Yahoo

Here's another very popular Web-search site, Yahoo. You can get to Yahoo at **http://www.yahoo.com/**, or by clicking on the *Yahoo* link you probably saw earlier. (Start Explorer, and click on the *Explore the Internet; Searches, Links and Tools* icon in the middle of the default Internet Explorer home page. Then click on the *Yahoo* link that you'll see near the top of the document that appears.)

You can see in figure 8.3 what you'll see when you go to Yahoo using the **http://www.yahoo.com/** URL. If you use the *Yahoo* link from Microsoft's *Explore the Internet* Web page, you'll see a search form similar to the Lycos one we just looked at. When you search for a word or words, the Microsoft Web site sends the information to Yahoo, which then searches for you. The next document you see will be a Yahoo page. I'm going to take a look at Yahoo proper.

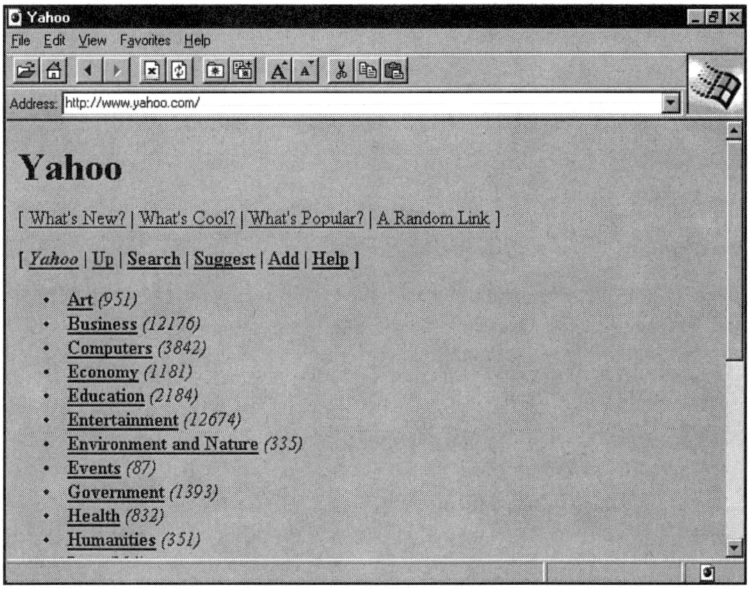

Fig. 8.3
The Yahoo site, one of the most popular places to search the Web.

As you can see, Yahoo is set up a little differently from Lycos. At Yahoo you have a variety of ways to get to the information you need. First, near the top of the page, you'll find these "buttons":

Button	Description
New	Click here to go to a list of documents recently added to the Yahoo list.
Cool	This takes you to a list of particularly "cool" sites—or whatever the people running Lycos think is cool, anyway (it's subjective, after all. Such as Britannica's Lives (who was born on any day), Christ In The Desert (monks invite you to join them in a chant), FBI Top Ten Most Wanted Page, and Idea Futures (betting on disputed science questions with odds available to mass media).

continues

Button	Description
Headlines	Click here to see a list of Web documents containing the latest news stories.
Popular	The 50 most-searched categories in Yahoo. (A note says that these are "asexual." I assume they mean by this that the list does not include searches for sexual subjects—which are quite likely the most used search terms!)
Write Us	Click here if you want to make a suggestion to the Yahoo administrator.
Add URL	This link is for Web authors who want to add their sites to the Yahoo lists.
Random	Don't know where you want to go today? Click here and Yahoo will choose somewhere for you, at random.
Info	Click here for more information about using Yahoo.

You've seen the various "auxiliary" ways to find things in Yahoo—look in the What's Cool or What's New list, for instance—but there are two main ways to find something in Yahoo. You can look in the various lists, or you can search.

Using the Yahoo lists

As you can see in figure 8.5, most of the Yahoo page is comprised of a list of categories: Arts, Business and Economy, Computers and Internet, Education, and so on. (Scroll down to see more categories.)

So, pick a category, and start clicking. You'll see another document, with more subcategories, or perhaps with a mixture of listings and subcategories. For instance, when I clicked on *Education* I saw a page full of subcategories: Adult Education, Alternative, College Entrance, Community Colleges, and so on.

Q&A ***How do you know which is a subcategory and which is a link to another Web site somewhere?***

Generally (though not always), the boldface entries are subcategories. Also, they normally have a number in brackets at the end of the subcategory name, to indicate how many documents are listed within that subcategory. Click on one of these to see *another* list. The normal text links are links that take you out of the Yahoo system, across the Web to someone else's Web site.

I clicked on the *Alternative* link, and found a list of documents and subcategories. For instance, if you click on the *Alpine Valley School* link, you'll go to a Web page set up by the students of that school. If you click on the Alternative Colleges Network, you'll find a document designed for "students interested in exploring alternative institutions of higher learning."

Searching at Yahoo

In the main Yahoo page you'll see a Search text box. You can type a word into that box and click on Enter. To do a more detailed search, though, click on the *Options* link next to the Search text box, or click on the Search button that appears at the top of most Yahoo pages. You'll see a form like that in figure 8.4.

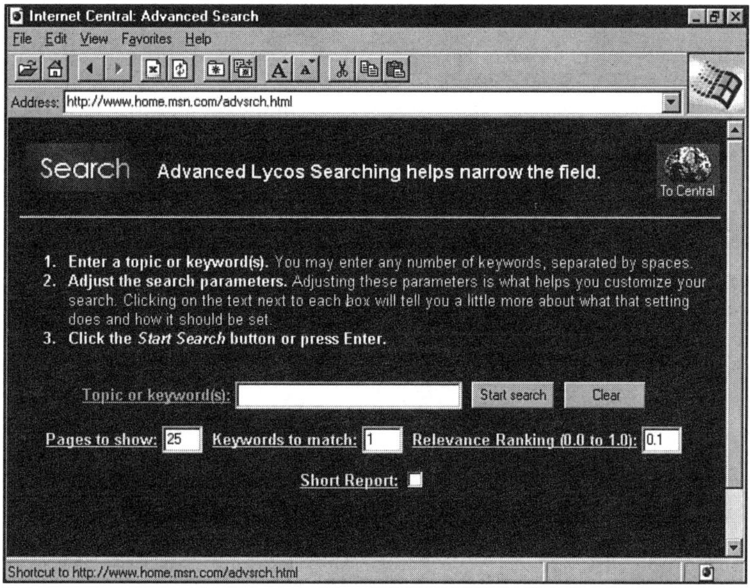

Fig. 8.4
Yahoo allows you to specify various search criteria.

This form allows you to specify exactly what and how you want to search the Yahoo database. You can tell Yahoo to search for the word you enter in the database of Titles, URLs, and Comments. You can also specify Case Sensitive searching; in other words, Yahoo will only show you matches that use the same capitalization that you used.

If you enter more than one word into the Search box, you can also tell Yahoo what to do with those words. Choose At Least One Of The Keys (Boolean Or) to tell Yahoo to search for entries that have any of the words you entered.

Choose All Keys (Boolean And) to tell Yahoo that the entries it finds must contain *all* the words you entered. And choose All Keys As A Single String to tell Yahoo that you want to find entries that contain the words exactly as typed, one word after another.

You can also tell Yahoo that the words are Substrings; that is, the word you typed may be part of a longer word. Or choose Complete Words to tell Yahoo that the word you typed is *not* a fragment of a longer word, but is a complete word.

Other search sites

There are loads of other Web sites set up specifically to help people search for a subject of interest. Try these two sites:

- **http://www.mcp.com/authors/pkent/**—These are two pages I put up on the Web (at the Macmillan Publishing site) when I finished *The Complete Idiot's Guide to the World Wide Web*. The first, Chapter 25, contains links to all the sites I've mentioned later in this chapter, plus a few more. The second, Chapter 26, contains links to a potpourri of interesting sites.
- The Explore the Internet page that we looked at earlier also has a link to InfoSeek, another directory of Web pages.

Let's take a look at a few other directories you may want to visit.

Directories of directories

We'll start with a general category, a list of Web documents that will help you find more specific directories.

TIP **Remember that URLs sometimes end with .html, and sometimes** with **.htm**. Make sure you use the correct one. And if it doesn't work, try the other.

The World Wide Web Initiative

"Everything there is to know about the World Wide Web is linked directly or indirectly to this document." From the W3 Organization, the people planning the future of the Web.

http://www.w3.org/hypertext/WWW/TheProject

The Mosaic Communications Internet Directory

This is a "directory of Servers," leading you to other useful listings (most of which are mentioned in this chapter).

http://home.mcom.com/home/internet-directory.html

Mosaic Communications also have a document that points you to other Web search tools:

http://home.mcom.com/home/internet-search.html

ANANSE—Internet Resource Locators and Search Engines

Links to lots of other directories.

http://ananse.irv.uit.no/law/nav/find.html

List of Robots

This is a directory of programs that dig around on the Web, creating indexes and measuring its size.

http://web.nexor.co.uk/mak/doc/robots/active.html

General directories

The following lists are directories of Web documents. You can search or browse for just about any subject.

The World Wide Web Worm (WWWW)

The World Wide Web Worm is a system that digs around on the Web looking for documents. It follows links through the Web, and builds an index of Titles and URLs. You can enter keywords to search for any subject—you'll find detailed instructions on how to search.

http://www.cs.colorado.edu/home/mcbryan/WWWW.html

Web Crawler

This system crawls around on the Web, creating an index. You can search that index.

http://www.webcrawler.com/

The Web Crawler Top 25

The Web Crawler also publishes a document that lists the 25 most-referenced documents on the Web. That is, the documents that are referenced by other document links more than any others.

http://www.webcrawler.com/WebCrawler/Top25.html

The JumpStation

Another simple index that you can search.

http://www.stir.ac.uk/jsbin/js

Wandex

Wandex—the World Wide Web Wanderer Index—lets you search an index of thousands of documents.

http://www.netgen.com/cgi/wandex

The Spider's Web

Over 1000 links to "cool places."

http://gagme.wwa.com/~boba/spider1.html

Nikos (Formerly Nomad)

This is an index created by Rockwell Network Systems and Cal Poly, San Luis Obispo. Type the keyword you are looking for.

http://www.rns.com/cgi-bin/nomad

RBSE's URL Database

The RBSE (Respository Based Software Engineering) spider "walks the web" grabbing URLs. You can search the resulting database.

http://rbse.jsc.nasa.gov/eichmann/urlsearch.html

Best of the Web '94

A list of the "best" Web documents, chosen in an online contest and announced at the International W3 Conference in Geneva. From the NCSA (Best Overall Site) to the Sports Information Service (Best Entertainment Service) to Travels With Samantha (Best Document Design) to the Xerox Map Server (Best Use of Interaction).

http://wings.buffalo.edu/contest/

ALIWEB

ALIWEB stands for *Archie-Like Indexing for the Web.* It lets you search for Web sites in the same way you can use Archie to search for FTP files (we'll get to that in chapter 13). There are several different interfaces—a form-based search, a multiple-keyword form-based search, and a simple index search.

http://web.nexor.co.uk/aliweb/doc/search.html

The Mother-of-all BBS

Search this giant database of Web sites, or select a category first; from Agriculture to Writing on the Net, and subjects as diverse as Underwear and the Sheffield Ski Village.

http://www.cs.colorado.edu/homes/mcbryan/public_html/bb/summary.html

NCSA's What's New on the Web

A list of new Web pages. You can view the current month's crop of new stuff, or go back and view previous months. This is a great way to get a feel for just how much new information is being added to the Web.

http://www.ncsa.uiuc.edu/SDG/Software/Mosaic/Docs/whats-new.html

The same lists are also available from Mosaic Communications.

http://home.mcom.com/home/whats-new.html

NCSA's Starting Points

This site is handy for newcomers wanting to get an overview of what's on the Web. You'll find links to useful services and other directories.

http://www.ncsa.uiuc.edu/SDG/Software/Mosaic/StartingPoints/NetworkStartingPoints.html

The WWW Virtual Library

This is at CERN, the home of the Web. Select a category and you'll be shown a list of related Web sites.

http://www.w3.org/hypertext/DataSources/bySubject/Overview.html

The CUI W3 Catalog

This directory (the Centre Universitaire d'Informatique W3 Catalog in Geneva) lists thousands of Web pages. You type the word you are looking for, and the catalog looks for matches. It's actually an index of the WWW Virtual Library.

http://cuiwww.unige.ch/w3catalog

Virtual Libraries

This site points you to Web reference documents, such as Scott Yanoff's Internet Services List and Big Dummy's Guide to the Internet. You'll find pointers to useful directories as well as individual documents.

http://www.w3.org/hypertext/DataSources/bySubject/Virtual_library

ElNet Galaxy

This site is another directory that can be searched by entering a keyword, or by browsing through links to different subjects. There's also a What's New page.

http://galaxy.einet.net/

The Harvest WWW Home Pages Broker

Another searchable index of Web sites. This system also displays information about a Web document that it finds, even showing part of the document's text.

http://www.town.hall.org/brokers/www-home-pages/

W3 Servers

This is a *very* big list. It's an almost complete list of Web servers, broken down by geographical location. If you are going to view this document, go take a break—it'll take a while to load this. Or skip this, and go to the next one ("W3 Servers—By Area").

http://www.w3.org/hypertext/DataSources/WWW/Geographical.html

W3 Servers—By Area

This provides an easier way to work with the W3 Servers list. Select the continent, country, and state to see a list or "clickable" map showing servers in that area.

http://www.w3.org/hypertext/DataSources/WWW/Servers.html

GNN NetNews

This one isn't really a directory, but it's worth mentioning because it's a great way to discover lots of interesting things. It's an online magazine about the Internet. A great place to find out about new programs and services, Internet news stories and controversies, and neat stuff on the net.

http://nearnet.gnn.com/news/index.html

Internet Services List

Scott Yanoff's Internet Services List has been around in text files for about three years, but it's now available on the Web, in interactive form, of course. When you find something of interest—whether a Web site, an FTP site, a chat service, or whatever—you can go right there.

http://slacvx.slac.stanford.edu:80/misc/internet-services.html

Commercial and business lists

These are lists of Web documents maintained by businesses.

Open Market's Commercial Sites Index

A large alphabetical listing of commercial Web documents. You can also search for a keyword, or look at the What's New section.

http://www.directory.net/

Interesting Business Sites on the Web

A small list of interesting business Web pages. There's no searching, just select a category—Pick of the Month, Financial Services, Virtual Malls, and so on.

http://www.rpi.edu/~okeefe/business.html

Sell-it On the WWW

This is a Directory of Advertisers' Web sites. You'll find links to companies selling CD recordings, business supplies, computer equipment, books, and general services and stuff.

http://www.xmission.com/~wwwads/index.html

CommerceNet

A Silicon Valley–based directory. You can find out about products and services, associations, news, information and events related to the participants in CommerceNet. Companies like American Express, Amdahl, Apple, FedEx, and many more. (Cool graphics in this directory.)

http://www.commerce.net/

MecklerWeb

Select the category you are interested in—Business and Finance, Travel, Seniors, Arts & Entertainment, Computing, Education, and so on—and you'll see information about companies related to that subject. Or view a list of companies with information at this site. Mecklermedia, the owner of MecklerWeb, publishes *Internet World* magazine.

http://www.mecklerweb.com/

More specific stuff

The following are directories that are designed to help you find more specific information.

Web Newspaper List

This lists magazines and newspapers on the Web. It also contains links to other lists of publications.

http://www.jou.ufl.edu/commres/webjou.htm

Campus Newsletters on the Net

This list has links to dozens of college newspapers.

http://ednews2.asa.utk.edu/papers.html

Journalism and Communications Schools

Links to Journalism and Communications colleges.

http://www.jou.ufl.edu/commres/jouwww.htm

The Journalism List

In theory this provides information about Internet and Web resources that might be of use to journalists. But it's a great list for *anyone* who wants to find their way around. Not only does it have Web resources, but newsgroups, finger, FTP, gopher, WAIS, and more.

http://www.jou.ufl.edu/commres/jlist.htm

Internet Law Sites

These are good places on the Web to find information about the law. The General Lists of Various Law Sites (**http://ananse.irv.uit.no/law/nav/law_ref.html**) and Law related sites on the Internet (**http://www2.waikato.ac.nz/law/law-related.html**).

Multimedia Information Sources

This is an index to Web sites related to multimedia. You'll find links to documents with information about current events in multimedia, various company sites, software archives, and more.

http://cuiwww.unige.ch/OSG/MultimediaInfo/index.html

Web Exhibits

This list links to dozens on Web exhibits, from art to the Dead Sea Scrolls.

http://155.187.10.12/fun/exhibits.html

U.S. Government Web

This is a Web site that lets you search for U.S. Government Web documents. White House press releases, the National Trade Data Bank, the President's speeches (audio files), and more.

http://sunsite.unc.edu/govdocs.html

Irena, Australia's Beauty

Irena is, apparently, named after "one of the most attractive women in Australia" (perhaps it's an inside joke understandable only to Australians). It lets you search the Web server at the Australian National University for information on the social sciences, humanities, and Asian Studies.

http://coombs.anu.edu.au/bin/irena.cgi/WWWVL-Aboriginal

9

Saving Stuff From the Web

In this chapter:

- **Saving documents—as text and HTML files**
- **How can I grab images out of Web documents?**
- **How can I save the document background?**
- **Printing documents**
- **Saving URLs**
- **Transferring files across the Web**

Now that you've found it, how are you going to save it from the Web to your computer?. . . . .

Internet Explorer provides a number of ways for you to get information from a Web document into your other Windows applications, or saved on the hard disk. Here are the things you can save:

- Save the document text.
- Save the HTML "source" document.
- Save inline images in graphics files, as desktop wallpaper, or to the Clipboard.
- Save document backgrounds as graphics files, as desktop wallpaper, or to the Clipboard.
- Save URLs to the Clipboard, so you can copy them into another program.
- Grab files directly from the cache.
- Save computer files referenced by links.

TIP **Remember, much of what you come across on the Web is copyright material.** In fact, unless you are sure that what you are viewing is not copyright, you should assume it *is*. You can take this material for private use, but not for publication. For information about what you can and can't do with copyright material, refer to a book on copyright law. (Many writer's references contain copyright law information.)

Saving document text

Let's begin by looking at how to get text out of a Web document. Use any of these methods:

- Choose File, Save As. In the Save As dialog box, select *Plain Text (*.txt)* from the Save As Type dropdown, select the directory you want to place it in, enter a Filename, and click on Save. Explorer will save all the text in the document (not the underlying HTML "codes," though).
- Position Explorer and another program such that you can view both at the same time. Use the mouse to highlight the text you want to save,

then drag the text from Explorer onto the other program (see fig. 9.1). (You may need to hold the mouse button down for a moment or two before you begin to drag the text out of Explorer.) Release the mouse button and the text is dropped into the other program. (This doesn't work with all programs; it works with Word for Windows, but not with WordPad or Notepad, for instance. And you can't save pictures this way, only text.)

TIP **To highlight text, choose Edit, Select All; or right-click inside the** document and choose Select All; or point at the beginning of the text you want to highlight and click the mouse button, hold the button down, and drag the pointer across the text. (Make sure you are not clicking inside a link, of course, or you won't highlight the text, you'll see another document.)

- Highlight the text and choose Edit, Copy; or right-click and choose Copy; or click on the Copy toolbar button; or press Ctrl+C. The text is copied to the Clipboard, so you can now go to another application and paste it.

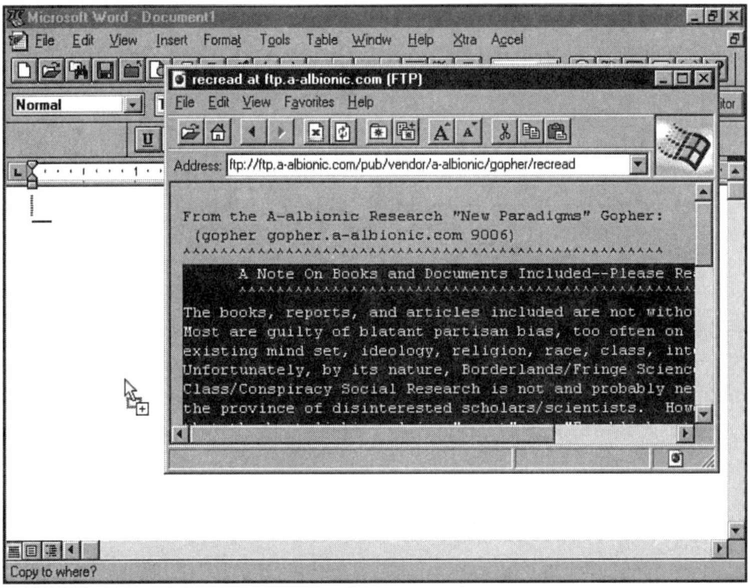

Fig. 9.1
You can drag text from Explorer onto some other programs.

Save the HTML "source" document

Why would you care about the "source" document? Most people won't want the source document, but if you are interested in creating your own Web pages you *will*. If you view a source document, you can learn the techniques other Web authors have used to create documents.

The source document is the ASCII text document that is the basis of the Web page you are viewing. As we saw back in chapter 2, each Web document is an ASCII text document with special codes, or tags, which tell Web browsers what to do. When you transfer a document to the browser, the browser "renders" the document; that is, it takes a look at all the codes, then figures out what it has to do to turn the document into something you can read.

To save the source document, choose File, Save As. Enter a Filename, choose a directory, and make sure that *HTML (*.htm, *.html)* is displayed in the Save As Type dropdown. Then click on Save. (If you don't include an extension with the filename, Explorer automatically saves the document with the .HTM extension, not .HTML.)

TIP **You may want to use the following method to see the HTML codes** first, before you decide whether to save the file. Right-click anywhere on the document except on a link or on a picture—you can click on blank background, or normal text. Then select View Source from the pop-up menu. A Notepad window will open (or, if the document is very big, a WordPad window). Take a look at the document, then choose File, Save As to save the file on your hard disk.

Saving Inline Images

You can save pictures that you find inside Web documents. Use one of these methods:

- Right-click on the picture, then choose Save Picture As. You'll see a Save As dialog box, which lets you save the file onto your hard disk as a .GIF, .JPG, or .BMP file. (.BMPs can be opened in Paintbrush, .GIFs and .JPGs cannot.)
- Right-click on the picture, then choose Save As Desktop Wallpaper. Wait a few moments, then minimize all your programs and you'll find that the picture is in the middle of your desktop.

- Right-click on the picture, then choose Copy Picture. The picture is copied to the Clipboard. You can now go to another application and paste it.

TIP **When you create desktop wallpaper, from an inline image or from** the document background, Explorer creates a file called *Internet Explorer Wallpaper.bmp*. Your Windows desktop will be replaced with this file. (Each time you use this command, Explorer creates a file with this name, replacing the current one—if you want to save the file, rename it first.)

To remove this picture, right-click on your desktop and choose Properties, then select another wallpaper from the list in the Background area of the Display Properties dialog box (the wallpaper you were using previously will still be there). You can also click on the Tile option button to cover the desktop with a small inline image (the image is repeated to fill in all the blank space).

Save document backgrounds

A new feature that's becoming popular on Web pages these days is the background pattern. A Web author can add a special background to his documents; the background may be a plain color, or perhaps some sort of pattern. Many Web sites use a sort of watermark in the background, with the company name or logo. Others are some kind of marble or rock background. (Some authors aren't doing a good job here; a lot of Web pages are almost illegible these days, thanks to a poorly chosen background color.)

If you find a nice background, you can copy it to your system. In fact you have three choices:

- Right-click on the background and choose Save Background As; you'll see the Save As dialog box, so you can save the background on your hard disk (as a .GIF, JPG, or .BMP file).
- Right-click on the background and choose Set As Desktop Wallpaper. Explorer will use the background as wallpaper, in the same way it does when you set an inline image as wallpaper.
- Right-click on the background and choose Copy Background (see fig. 9.2). It's copied to the Clipboard, so you can paste it into another application.

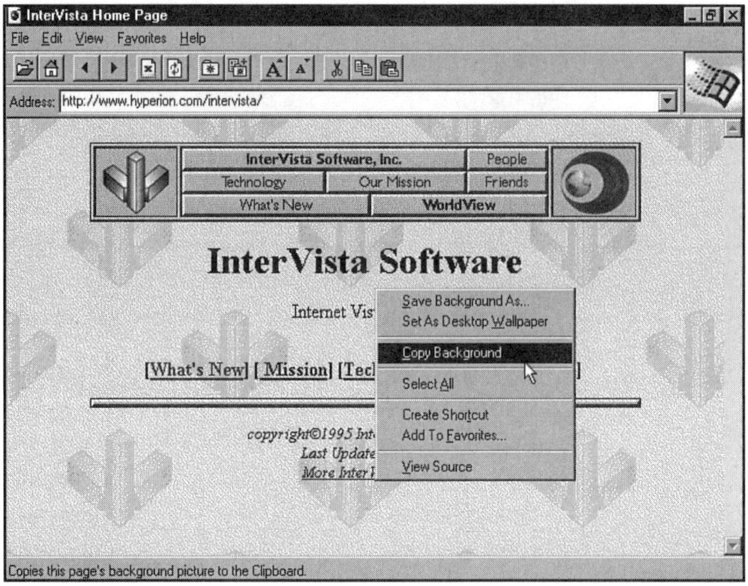

Fig. 9.2
You can save a document's background—this one has a sort of "watermark"—as desktop wallpaper or a graphics file or to the Clipboard.

Printing the document

If you want a paper copy of something you've found in a Web document, you can print the document directly from Explorer. (See chapter 7 for information about setting up the default document margins, headers, and footers.)

Choose File, Print to see a typical Windows Print dialog box. You can pick the printer you want to use, select which pages you want to print (you'll have to guess here a little, because a Web document is a single, perhaps very long, page while it's on the screen), and how many copies you want to print.

Saving URLs to the clipboard

Once you're a regular Web user, you'll find that you want to save URLs, the Web "addresses." Perhaps you want to share them with a friend or colleague. Maybe you want to include a URL in a memo or article you are writing, or want to save the URL in a database with other research materials. Explorer provides a few ways to save URLs:

- Click in the Address text box and the URL of the current document will be highlighted. Then click on the Copy toolbar button, or press Ctrl+C; the text is copied to the Clipboard.

- Right-click on a link (a text or graphic link), and choose Copy Shortcut from the pop-up menu. This is a very handy method for copying a URL without even going to the referenced document. It would be handier still if it actually worked. Unfortunately in the first release of Explorer this feature *doesn't* work. Presumably it will be fixed in later versions.
- To copy the URL of a document listed in the History list or Favorites list, open the History or Favorites window, right-click on the entry, choose Properties, and click on the Internet Shortcut tab. You'll see the URL in the Target URL text box, already highlighted. Press Ctrl+C to copy it to the Clipboard. (See fig. 9.3.)

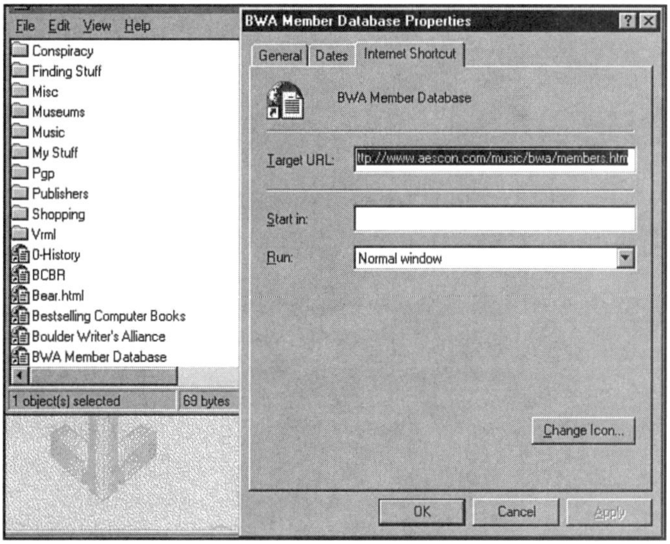

Fig. 9.3
You can copy URLs from entries in the History and Favorites lists.

Stealing directly from the Cache

Long after you've been to a Web document you can grab information from that document by reloading the document using the History list. As you've learned by now, the document is pulled from the cache (assuming that the Update Pages Never option is selected—see chapter 7).

You may at times find it convenient to pull things directly from the cache. You may, for instance, want to grab a special file format from the cache—a sound or video file, for instance. You could open the document you think you originally reached the file from, or you could just go to the cache directory and find the files with the appropriate file extensions.

Open Windows Explorer and display the cache directory (by default, it's the \Program Files\Plus!\microsoft internet\cache directory). You'll find all the inline images—.GIF, .XBM, and .JPG files—from your cached documents, along with the .HTML documents themselves, and a variety of other file formats you may have loaded (see chapters 10 and 11). You can simply open them in another application, or copy them to another directory.

TIP **If you right-click on these files you can choose Open. In most** cases Explorer will open and display the file. In some cases, depending on the format of the file that you chose, this command will open another application (Notepad, for instance, if it was a .TXT file). You may also be able to choose Quick View to view the contents of the document in a small view window that opens more quickly than most applications.

Downloading files from the Web

Many links on the Web point not to other Web documents, but to computer files of various kinds. We can group these files into two types:

- Files that you want to transfer to your hard disk. For instance, a link may point to a program that is in an .EXE or .ZIP file. You want to transfer this program to your computer and then install it.
- Files that you want to play or view; sound files (music and speech), video, graphics of many kinds, word processing documents, Adobe Acrobat documents, PostScript files, and so on.

Of course in order to play or view a file it has to be transferred to your hard disk, and you may choose to save it. So in one sense there's no difference between these two types of files—in each case a file is transferred to your computer. But if you want to play or view a file, that's part of the "hypermedia" or "multimedia" experience of the Web, and so the purpose of the transfer is different.

But it's also different in another way; you may have to configure a special **viewer** so that when Explorer transfers the file it knows how to play or display it. (For the first of these file types, though, Explorer doesn't care what happens to the file; it's simply going to save it to your hard disk and let you figure out what to do with it later.) We're going to look at viewers in chapters 10 and 11. For now, we're only interested in the first type of file, one that you want to transfer and save on your hard disk.

File transfers

Why transfer files back to your computer? In chapter 13 you'll learn how to use Explorer to run FTP—File Transfer Protocol— sessions. FTP is an Internet-wide system that allows you to copy files to your computer from software archives all over the world. You can get shareware programs, clip art, various documents, sound clips, and more. There are literally millions of files waiting for you at these archives.

But Web authors can also distribute computer files directly from their Web documents. They create special links from their documents to the files that they believe their readers may want to transfer. Clicking on the link begins the transfer to your computer. Here are a few reasons for grabbing files across the Web:

- Many sites are run by companies that want to distribute their shareware, freeware, or demo programs. (We'll look at one of these in a moment.)
- Some authors want to distribute non-Web documents. They may create links to PostScript, Word for Windows, Adobe Acrobat, and Windows Help documents, for instance.
- Some authors have placed clip art archives on the Web. You can transfer the files and then use them in your own Web documents.

As you can see, we have some overlap here between the two types of files mentioned before. The bulleted list above points out that a Web author may want to distribute an Adobe Acrobat file (Acrobat is a hypertext document format). But Acrobat files fall into the second category of files, ones that are part of the multimedia experience, that Internet Explorer wants to "play."

Well, they may be files that can be played, depending on two factors:

1. How is the document formatted? If the file has its original extension, and is in its original format, the Web author has set it up so it can be played. For instance, the Acrobat extension is .PDF, and when the file is transferred Explorer can automatically send this file to an Adobe Acrobat viewer, so you can view the document immediately. But the Web author may have saved the file in a compressed, or archive, format. The extension may be .ZIP, for instance (a PKZIP compressed file) or .EXE (a self-extracting archive file). This means that the Web author

expects people to transfer the file, extract the software, and then load the file into another program.

2 Have you set up Explorer to play the file? If you haven't set up Explorer to play a particular file, then the only thing Explorer can do is transfer it to your hard disk. So even if the file extension is .PDF, for instance, if you haven't configured Explorer to "call" an Adobe Acrobat viewer, it can't do so and will want to simply transfer the file and drop it onto your hard disk.

Here's how it works

Let's take a quick look at how all this works. As an example, I'm using the WorldView Web site. WorldView displays (and allows you to interact) with 3-D images (you'll learn more about this in chapter 11). I wanted to download the program so I could then run the 3-D images that are beginning to blossom on the Web.

I went to the WorldView page (**http://www.webmaster.com/vrml/wvwin/**) and found a link that said *Download WorldView*. I followed that link and arrived at another part of the document (remember, links can take you to other documents, or to a different part of the document you are viewing), and found a heading that said *Download WorldView*. Below that was another link that said *WorldView for Windows*. I clicked on this link, and Explorer opened the Confirm File Open dialog box, which you can see in figure 9.4.

Why did Explorer display this dialog box? Because it recognized that the file is a program file, and knows that it's possible to "run" the file. (The file extension is .EXE, which denotes some kind of program file—the file is WRLDVW32.EXE. This file is actually a self-extracting archive, a program file that, when run, will extract compressed files from within itself.). Now, if you click on a link that leads to a file type that Internet Explorer recognizes and knows how to handle, it will automatically do what it's supposed to; display or view it or send it to the appropriate program. If the file is an .EXE file, or one that it doesn't recognize, though, it has to be told what to do.

As you can see in figure 9.4, you have three options:

- **Save As**—Click here if you want to save the file on your hard disk. You'll see a normal Windows Save As dialog box, so you can tell Explorer where to place the file.

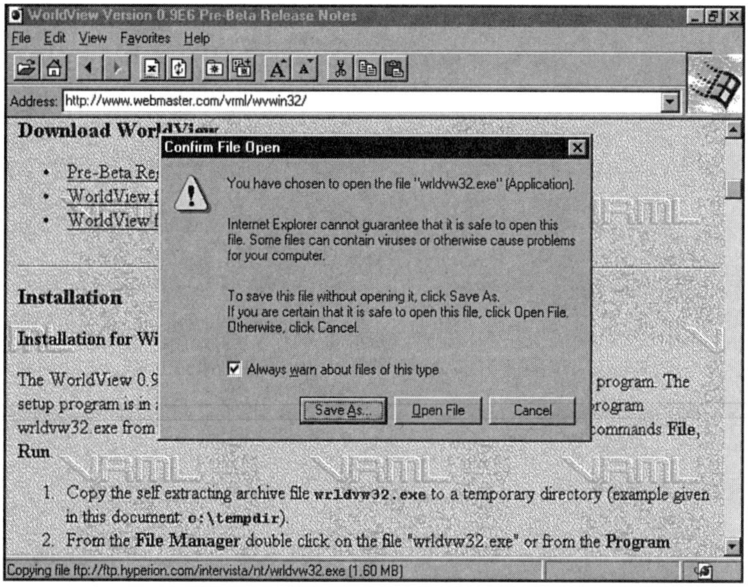

Fig. 9.4
The Confirm File Open dialog box appears whenever you begin transferring a file that Explorer doesn't recognize.

- **Open File**—Click here if you want to save the file to a disk (in the `\Program Files\Plus!\Microsoft Internet\cache` directory), and then *run* the program. After the file has been transferred, Explorer will "open" it—it will run the program. This is usually a bad idea!
- **Cancel**—Click here if you want to cancel the transfer. You may sometimes click on a link without realizing that it will begin a file transfer. (For instance, in our example, the link *WorldView for Windows* is ambiguous—it might have led to a document *describing* the program.)

Notice also the Always Warn About Files Of This Type check box. I suggest you leave this checked. If you *clear* this check box, you won't see this dialog box anymore. Rather, Explorer will automatically transfer and run the file.

If you choose the Save As or Open File options, Explorer will begin transferring the file. You'll see a progress bar in the bottom right corner of the Explorer window—when the blue blocks reach the right side of the bar, the transfer has finished.

You can cancel a transfer before it's finished by clicking on the Stop button, or by choosing View, Stop.

TIP **You don't have to sit and twiddle your thumbs while the file is** being transferred. You can enter another URL into the Address text box, or click on a link, or choose an entry from the History or Favorites lists. When Explorer notices that you are trying to do something else, you'll be asked if you want to cancel the transfer. Click on No. Then you'll be asked if you want to open another Explorer window. Click on Yes, and the document you requested will be loaded into another window.

This means you can transfer multiple files, too. When you click on a link to another file, follow the same procedure and Explorer will open a blank window, and begin transferring the file.

Why shouldn't I automatically open files?

Why not just automatically run the file each time? There are a couple of good reasons *not* to automatically run .EXE files. Many, if not most of these files, are **self-extracting archives**. The WRLD08D1.EXE file, for instance, is not a true program file. Rather, it's an archive file (a single file containing a file called SETUP.EXE inside it). When you run it, it automatically extracts the compressed file from within.

When Explorer runs self-extracting files, the files that are extracted will be automatically placed into the cache directory, where you probably don't want them! You'll have to dig through the cache directory to figure out which file is which; it'll be difficult to know which files are from the archive file, or even how *many* are from the archive.

Also, you should really check .EXE files with a computer-virus program before using them; many sites on the Internet don't check for viruses, so you don't always know for sure what you are getting. (Windows 95 does not have a virus-checking program, but there are a number of commercial and shareware programs available.)

Downloading other types of files

What if the file you are getting is not an .EXE file, but some kind of file that Explorer can't recognize? For instance, if you go to the **http://www.stones.com/audio/index.html** Web page, you'll find links to various types of sound files. Click on one of the RealAudio links, and Explorer will begin transferring a .RAM file, a new kind of sound file (which you'll learn about in chapter 10). In this case you'll see the dialog box in figure 9.5.

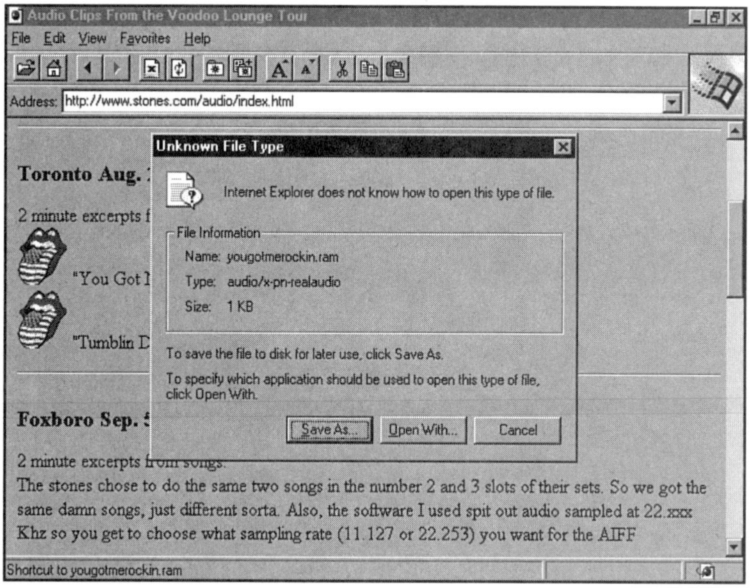

Fig. 9.5
I found this RealAudio file at the Rolling Stones site. Explorer doesn't recognize it, so I have to tell it what to do.

You can now choose the Save As button, then tell Internet Explorer where to place the file it's going to download and what to call it. Of course you could click on the Open With button, instead…but that's the subject of the next chapter.

10 Music, Video, and Other Neat Things—Installing Viewers

In this chapter:

- **How Explorer handles sound, video, 3-D, and other file formats**
- **What file formats will I run into?**
- **Three ways that Explorer handles sound**
- **The RealAudio sound format**
- **How do I install a new viewer?**

The really neat stuff is yet to come—working with a multitude of file types . . . .

What happens when you click on a link in a Web document? Well, it might take you to another Web document. That's pretty much what this book has been about so far. It might also be an .EXE file, a program or self-extracting archive file that you want to transfer to your hard disk. We covered that in chapter 9. But it might be something different. Here's how Internet Explorer works with a variety of file formats:

File Format	Description
Explorer can handle all of the following file formats, displaying or playing them itself.	
.AU, .AIF, .AIFF, .AIFC	Sound files—Explorer can open a special sound utility and play these.
.EXE	A program file, or a self-extracting archive file. We saw these in chapter 9. Explorer will let you save the file to your disk, or will save it for you and run the file.
.GIF, .JPG (or .JPEG),.XBM	These are graphics files. They share one thing in common; they are the formats that are used for inline graphics images. But a Web author may also place one of these files at a Web site with a link pointing to it. The file will be transferred, but it won't be "inline." That is, it won't be part of a Web document. They will appear in the Explorer window.
.HTM, .HTML	You know all about these; the basic Web document format.
.TXT	A text file. These are displayed in the Explorer window.
Explorer needs a "viewer" for the following files—Windows 95 has built-in programs that can handle these:	
.AVI	Video for Windows. This will play in Media Player.
.BMP, .PCX,	Common bitmap graphics formats. These can be displayed in Paintbrush.
.DOC	If you have Word for Windows, .DOC files will open in that program. However, Windows 95 comes with a word processor called WordPad, which can also open Word for Windows .DOC files.

File Format	Description
.FLC, .FLI, .AAS	Autodesk Animator files. These can play in Media Player.
.HLP	Windows Help files. The Windows WINHLP32.EXE program opens them.
.MID, .RMI	MIDI (Musical Instrument Digital Interface) sounds. These will play in Media Player.
.MMM	Microsoft Multimedia Movie Player files. Again, these run in Media Player.
.RTF	Rich Text Format, word-processing files that work in a variety of Windows word processors. If you haven't installed a program such as Word for Windows, the .RTF files are opened in WordPad.
.WAV	The standard Windows "wave file" sound format. These can play in Sound Recorder.
.WRI	Windows Write word processing files. These can be opened in WordPad.
The following file types don't have built-in Windows 95 viewers, so you'll have to find something else:	
.EPS	A PostScript image.
.MOV	The QuickTime video format.
.MPEG, .MPG, .MPE	The MPEG (Motion Pictures Expert Group) video formats.
.MP2	An MPEG audio format.
.PDF	The Portable Document Format, an Adobe Acrobat hypertext file. This format is becoming a very popular way to distribute electronic documents.
.PS	A PostScript document.
.RAM, .RA	RealAudio files. This is a sound format that plays while it's being transmitted. Click on a link to a RealAudio file and it begins playing within a few seconds, rather than waiting for the entire file to be transferred before starting.

continues

File Format	Description
.SGML	A document format.
.TIF	A common graphics format.
.WRL	A VRML (Virtual Reality Modeling Language) 3-D object.
.ZIP	A PKZIP archive file. These files contain other, compressed, files within them.

TIP **You'll find compressed files in a variety of formats. If you find a** .ZIP, .LZH, or .ARC file, it's probably for a DOS or Windows computer. (The .ZIP format is currently by far the most-used archive format; you'll rarely find the other formats these days.) The .EXE self-extracting archive is very common in the DOS and Windows world, too, as we saw in chapter 9. If the file is an .HQX, .SEA, or .SIT file it's for the Macintosh. The .Z, .TAR, and .GZ files are generally for UNIX computers (although the .GZ format can work on all three of these computer types, you'll rarely find a .GZ file for the PC or Mac).

Have I missed some? Sure, there are as many possible file formats on the Web as there are file formats in existence. But the ones I've mentioned here are the ones you'll most likely find (I think I've covered the ground pretty well with this list).

Let's take a look at how Explorer figures out what it's supposed to do when it transfers a file.

What happens when Explorer transfers a file?

When you click on a link, Explorer looks at the file extension at the end of the link to see what type of file it is. Here's the procedure it follows:

1. If the extension is .HTM or .HTML, it knows just what to do—display the file in the Explorer window, because it's a Web document.
2. If the extension is .TXT, it's not a true Web document, but it can be displayed easily (it's a text document), so Explorer displays it in the

window. (You'll often find .TXT files when working in Gopher sites—see chapter 12.)

3 If the extension is .GIF, .JPG, .JPEG, or .XBM, Explorer displays the file in the Explorer window; all of these are graphics files.

4 If the extension is .AU, .AIF, .AIFF, or .AIFC, Explorer opens its sound program and plays the sound—all of these are sound formats. (*Sound program*, what sound program? We'll get to that! See "Example 1: .AU and .AIF" later in this chapter.)

5 If the extension is .EXE, Explorer knows that it's a program or self-extracting archive file. It displays a dialog box asking if you want to save the file to a particular directory, or save it to the cache directory and run it (see chapter 9).

6 If the file is "none of the above," Explorer goes to the Windows 95 file-association list and takes a look. For instance, let's say it finds a .WAV file. It looks in the file-association list and finds that the .WAV format is associated with Sound Recorder. So it "sends" the file to Sound Recorder.

Plain English, please

The **file-association** list is a list that all Windows programs can refer to. It shows which file types are associated with which applications, so one program can run another when needed. For instance, when you double-click on a file in Windows Explorer, that program looks at the list to see which program it should run. You can look at the file-association list by choosing View, Options and clicking on the File Types tab.

7 If the file is not in the file-association list, Explorer is stuck; there's nothing more it can do, so it has to ask you. It displays the dialog box shown in figure 10.1. You have two choices; you can choose Save As to save the file to your hard disk—absolving Explorer from any further responsibility. Or you can choose Open With, to tell Explorer which application it should use to open this file type. See "Adding viewers—the RealAudio player," later in this chapter, for more information.

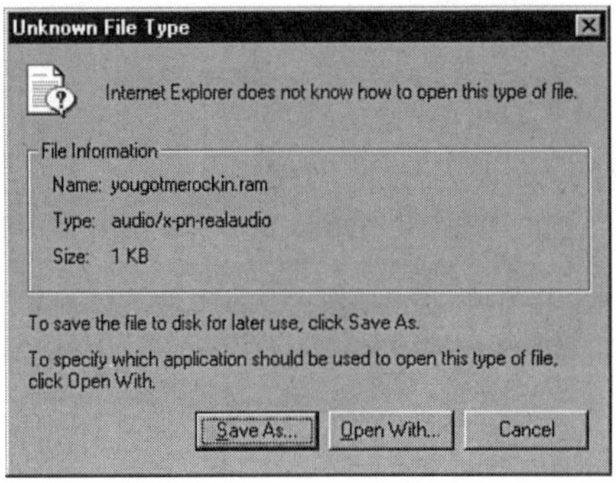

Fig. 10.1
If Explorer doesn't know what the file is, it will have to ask for your help.

Three examples—working with sound

Let's look at three examples; file formats that Explorer can handle, a format that it can't handle but knows what to do with, and a format that you've probably not come across yet (unless you've been working on the Web for a while) and which Internet Explorer won't recognize.

For instance, you are visiting the Rolling Stones Web site (I'm sure many of you *will*—the Stones' Live Audio Clips page had logged over half a million visits last time I looked). As you've seen earlier, you can get there by typing **http://www.stones.com/** into the Address box and pressing Enter, then select the RealAudio link; or go directly to the Live Audio Clips page using the **http://www.stones.com/audio/index.html** URL.

In the Live Audio Clips page at the Stones site you'll find links to music. You click on one of these links, and the file is transferred. Unfortunately, sound files tend to be big, so this will take a while!

Example 1: .AU and .AIF

If you click on a link to an .AU or .AIF file (or .AIFF or .AIFC, same thing—different extension), Internet Explorer can deal with it directly. Explorer has a built-in sound application—you can see it running in figure 10.2. As soon as Internet Explorer has finished transferring the sound file, it opens the sound player and begins playing. After it's finished you can choose File, Save As and save the sound file on your hard disk. Or you can use the buttons and scroll bar to replay the music. (Of course none of this will work if you don't have a sound board properly installed.)

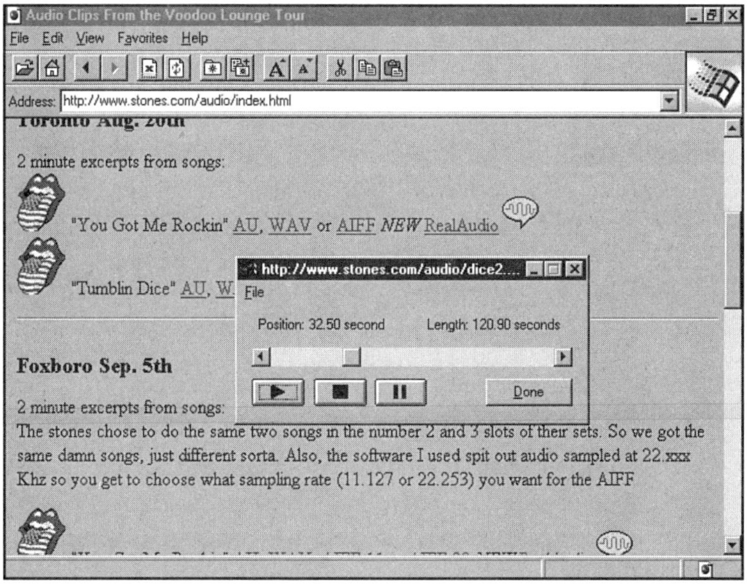

Fig. 10.2
Internet Explorer's built-in sound program plays .AU, .AIF, .AIFF, and .AIFC files.

Example 2: .WAV files

What about .WAV files, another common sound format? The .WAV format is a Windows sound format, and until recently has not been common on the Web (you'll find plenty of .WAV files now, though, including at the Stones site). The Internet Explorer sound program doesn't play .WAV files, though. So Internet Explorer looks at the Windows 95 file associations, and finds that .WAV is associated with Sound Recorder. Once Explorer has finished transferring the file, it opens Sound Recorder and gives it the .WAV file; the sound will begin playing right away.

TIP **Sound Recorder is optional. If you didn't load it when you installed** Windows, you can do so now. Double-click on the Add/Remove Programs icon in the Control Panel; click on the Windows Setup tab; click on the Multimedia item in the list; click on Details; click on Sound Recorder in the list; click on OK a couple of times. You may also want to install Volume Control and Media Player, if you haven't done so already.

Example 3: RealAudio (.RAM & .RA)

The **RealAudio** links at the Rolling Stones site are to .RAM files, a new format that greatly improves the way that sound is played over the Web (you'll also find RealAudio files with an .RA extension). With the other sound formats we've looked at, you click on a link and then wait. Twiddle your thumbs for a while, or go for coffee, because it can take a long time to transfer a sound file. Once the transfer has finished, Explorer plays the file or sends it to Sound Recorder.

But RealAudio begins playing almost immediately. Explorer begins the transfer, then starts the RealAudio player within a few seconds. (You don't have the RealAudio player yet—I'll explain how to find it in a moment.) The music (or radio broadcast; National Public Radio uses RealAudio files for their broadcasts—go to **http://www.npr.org/**) begins playing right away, and continues playing while the file is being transferred. In fact this is the way that a radio works, isn't it? The radio receives signals over the airwaves and plays the signal immediately (it doesn't wait until it's received the entire song to play it).

The first time Explorer looks for a .RAM or .RA (RealAudio) format, it won't recognize it. If you click on a RealAudio link you'll see the dialog box shown in figure 10.1. So let's look at how to install the RealAudio **viewer** or **player**, the program that will be used to play these sounds.

> **Plain English, please!**
>
> Programs that Web browsers "call" to display or play file types that they can't handle are generally known as **viewers** or **helpers**.

Adding viewers—the RealAudio player

The first thing you must do is transfer the RealAudio player. Follow this procedure:

1. Go to the RealAudio Web site, **http://www.realaudio.com/**. You'll find lots of background information, and links to sites that use RealAudio sounds.

2 Download the RealAudio Player. Last time I looked one had to choose the *Download* link and then the *Download the RealAudio Player for Windows Version 1.00* link, though this may change.

3 Explorer displays the Confirm File Open dialog box. Click on the Save As button, and find a directory to save the file into. (Remember, you can use the second toolbar button in these Windows Save As dialog boxes to create a new directory—a new "folder" in Windows 95-speak.) Click on Save to begin the download.

4 When the download has finished, open Windows Explorer, find the file you've just downloaded and double-click on it. The RealAudio Setup program begins. Follow the instructions to install the program. I suggest you select the Custom installation, which lets you choose the directory into which you want to place the program.

5 The Setup program will modify the file-association list, then inform you that it has "registered" the player as an external viewer for Internet Explorer.

6 Next the Setup program looks for various other Web browsers on your hard disk, and asks if you want to install the RealAudio player for those browsers, too. If you don't have these browsers, you can simply click on the Cancel button.

7 Finally, the RealAudio player opens and informs you—vocally—that the setup is complete.

You've installed the RealAudio player, but you got through it a little too easy. The Setup program modified the file-association list for you, so RealAudio is ready to play. You won't be so lucky with most viewers—later in this chapter we'll look at how to configure a viewer "manually."

For now, though, let's go back to the Rolling Stones site (**http://www.stones.com/audio/index.html**) and find a RealAudio file. Or go to NPR (**http://www.npr.org/**), or back to the RealAudio page (**http://www.realaudio.com/othersites.html**) where you'll find links to RealAudio sites all over the world.

Playing RealAudio

Find a RealAudio link and click on it. You'll see the Confirm File Open dialog box (see fig. 10.4).

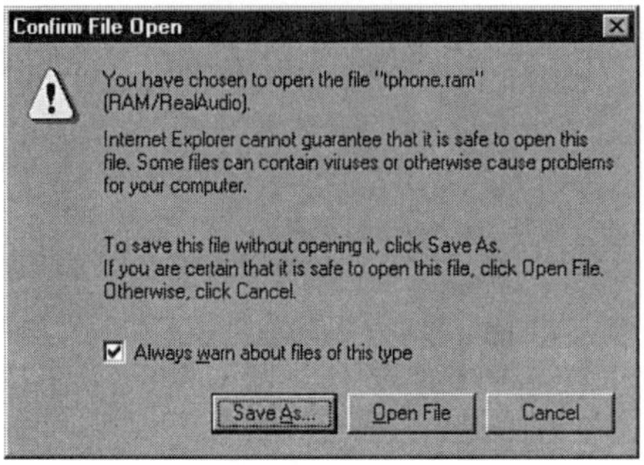

Fig. 10.4
Now that Explorer knows that it *can* play the file, it wants to know if you want to do so.

You may remember from chapter 9 that this dialog box lets you save the file to disk without playing it (click on Save As), or saves it to disk—in the cache directory—and then plays it (Open File). If you want to make sure that Explorer always plays this sort of file, without asking you what to do first, clear the Always Warn About Files of This Type check box.

Click on Open File. The RealAudio program opens, Explorer starts transferring the file, and the music begins!

Now, whenever you click on one of these links, up will pop your RealAudio program (see fig. 10.5), and the music plays. (If you *didn't* clear the Always Warn About Files of This Type check box, though, you'll always see the Confirm File Open dialog box, so you'll be able to save to disk rather than listen to the music.)

You can click on the Stop button in the RealAudio player (the big black square) to cancel a file transfer. You can use the other controls to determine which parts of the sound file you play:

Button	Description
	Click on this button to pause the transmission, and to restart.
	Click here to stop the transmission and move to the beginning.
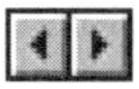	Click on these buttons to move back or forward through the sound.
	Drag this slider up and down to adjust the volume.

You can also drag the vertical bar along the horizontal scroll bar—immediately below the toolbar buttons—to move to a different part of the sound.

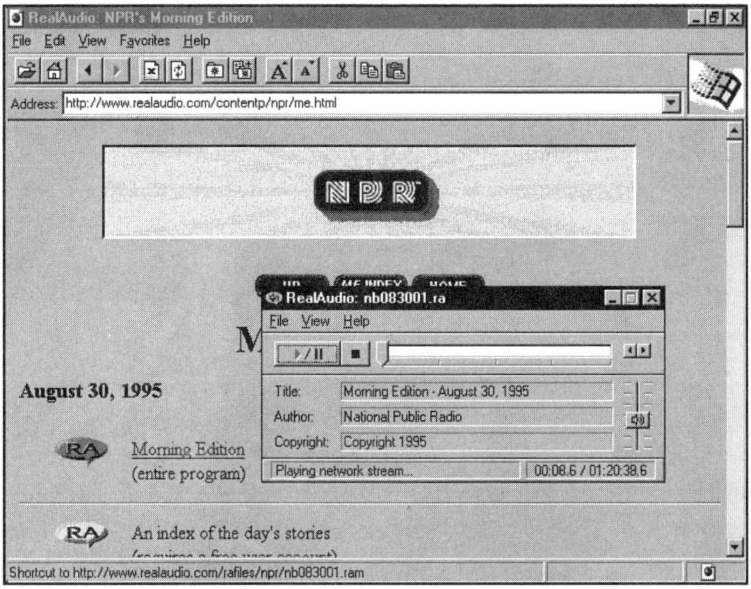

Fig. 10.5
Listening to the radio over the Internet. RealAudio and National Public Radio's *Morning Edition*.

Q&A ***Why's the sound so bad?***

Well, for a start, RealAudio doesn't sound as good as the .WAV, .AU, and .AIF formats. I guess it's a compromise between instant gratification and sound quality. Also, if you have a low-quality sound card, and cheap speakers, you'll get low-quality sound. Finally, sound files can vary in quality, depending on how they were recorded.

Associating programs "manually"

Many of the viewers that you want to use *won't* automatically associate themselves with the appropriate file extension. They leave it up to you to do so. Let's take a quick look at how.

As an example I'm going to use the WorldView VRML viewer (see chapter 11 for information on where to find this program).

We'll assume that I've already downloaded the program from the WorldView Web site and have installed it. Now I'm at a site that has 3-D VRML images—the IUMA site (**http://www.iuma.com/IUMA-2.0/vrml/**

Click on one of the links to a VRML file. Up pops the dialog box you saw in figure 10.1. Internet Explorer doesn't know what the file is and wants you to tell it what to do. Follow this procedure:

1 Click on Open With. The Open With dialog box appears (see fig. 10.6).

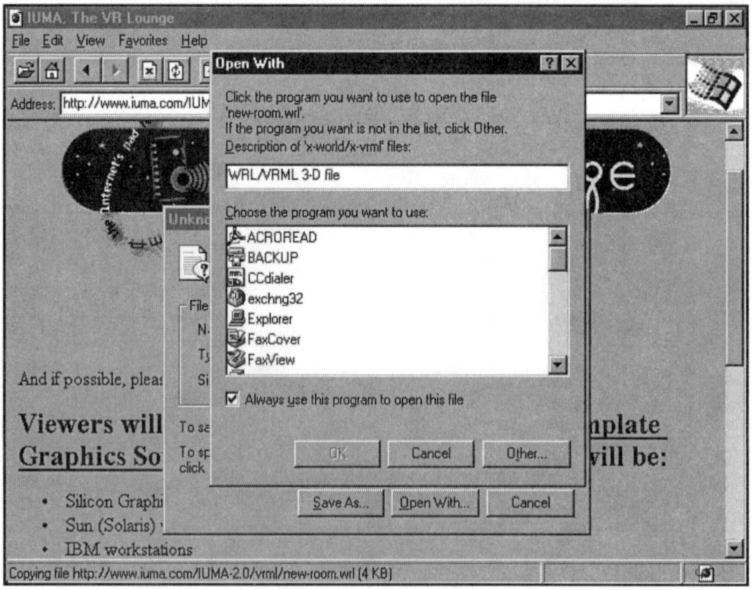

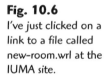

Fig. 10.6
I've just clicked on a link to a file called new-room.wrl at the IUMA site.

2 Near the top of this dialog box you can see the filename, and the file extension; in this case, new-room.wrl. Type **WRL/VRML 3-D file** or something similar into the Description Of text box. (I like to begin this description with the file extension, as it makes it easier to find this association in the list later.)

3 Click on the Other button. This displays a typical Open dialog box. Use this to find the directory holding the WorldView program that you've just installed.

4 Double-click on the WorldView program (it's called WRLDVIeW.EXE), placing the filename into the Open With dialog box.

5 Click on OK. Both the Open With and Unknown File Type dialog boxes close.

6 Now the Confirm File Open dialog box appears (see fig. 10.7).

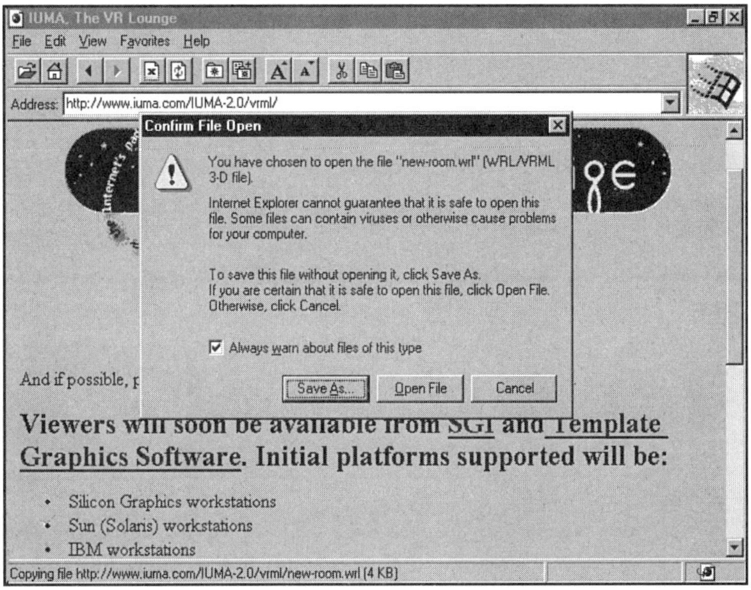

Fig. 10.7
Now that Explorer knows that it *can* play the file, it wants to know if you want to do so.

7 If you want to make sure that Explorer always plays this sort of file, without asking you what to do first, clear the Always Warn About Files of This Type check box.

8 Click on Open File. The WorldView program opens and displays the 3-D image.

Next time you click on a link to a VRML file you won't have to dig your way through this procedure. Now, whenever you click on one of these links, up will pop your WorldView program, and the music plays. (If you *didn't* clear the Always Warn About Files of This Type check box, though, you'll always see the Confirm File Open dialog box, so you'll be able to save to disk rather than view the file.)

TIP **Some file types come with different extensions. If you associate** one of the type's extensions with the appropriate program, you'll still have to do the same when you run into the same file type using a different extension.

There are two more ways to associate files with programs. You can double-click on a file in Windows Explorer; it there's no association for the file type, you'll be given the chance to associate it with a program. Or you can choose View, Options, click on the File Types tab, then click on the New Type button. See your Windows documentation for more details.

Part III: Traveling the Internet

11

More on Viewers

In this chapter:

- **Saving the multimedia files you play**
- **Where can I find more viewers?**
- **Why's Adobe Acrobat (.PDF) so important?**
- **How can I view a .ZIP file?**
- **Playing videos**
- **Viewing (and moving through) 3-D Images**

Playing what you find, and saving what you play, on the multimedia World Wide Web. . . . .

In chapter 10 you learned the basics of adding viewers to Explorer. In this chapter we'll cover a bit more information that you will find useful—how to save the multimedia files that you find on the Web, where you can find more viewers (mostly freeware or shareware), and some details about specific viewers that you'll find useful.

Saving what you've played

Once you've played a file, you can save it for future use if you wish. There are two ways to do so:

- Save the file using a command in the viewer.
- Copy or move the file from the cache.

Most viewers have some kind of command to help you save the file. For instance, if you play a .WAV file, Sound Recorder opens. This program has a File, Save command which lets you save the sound to whatever directory you wish.

But when Explorer transfers a file, it places it in the cache directory (\Program Files\plus!\microsoft internet\cache\—see chapter 5 for more information about the cache). So if you save it from the viewer, you actually end up with two copies on your hard disk, though the one in the cache will eventually be removed by Explorer (when it runs out of cache space and wants to save a more recent file).

If you are short of disk space, you may want to open Windows Explorer and simply move the file to another directory, so it won't be removed from the cache. There's another reason to grab files from the cache—some programs *don't* have a Save command.The RealAudio player doesn't have a Save command, for instance. Grabbing files from the cache, though—moving or copying it to another directory—provides a way to save the file for later use.

What viewers do I have?

You have plenty of "viewers." As you've already seen, Explorer can deal with .TXT, .GIF, .JPG, .JPEG, .XBM. .AU, .AIF, .AIFF, and .AIFC files itself, and it can send .WAV files to Sound Recorder. But how about other types of files? Well, you saw in the table near the beginning of chapter 10 that Windows 95 already has a variety of built-in viewers—Sound Recorder, Media Player, and WordPad. You may have installed more, without knowing it, too. For instance, I installed Hijaak Pro, a graphics program. The Setup program automatically modified the file-extensions list, so that Hijaak is now association with *loads* of file formats, including .TIF and .EPS, two common graphics formats.

You can quickly see what file associations have already been made. Choose View, Options, then click on the File Types tab. You'll see the dialog box in figure 11.1.

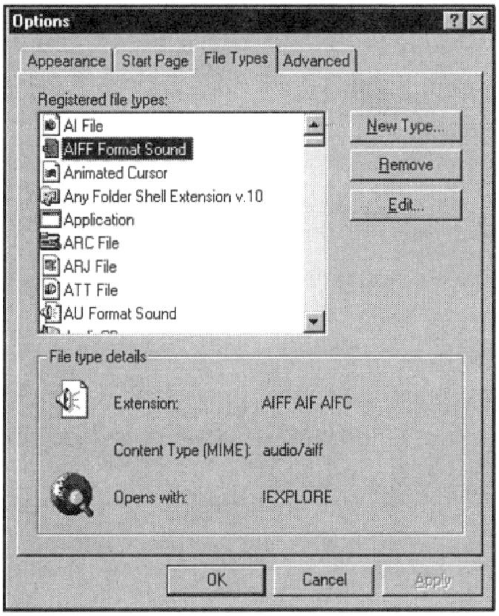

Fig. 11.1
The File Types list shows you which files are associated with which applications.

Look through this to find out what you have installed—you may be surprised. Most of the file types you'll never see on the Web. But you may discover that some program you have installed has associated itself with a few file types you will run into, though.

Q&A ***How can I remove file associations?***

To remove file associations—perhaps so that you can associate a different program with a particular association, or perhaps a program has been incorrectly associated with a file type—find the file type in the Registered File Types list. Then click on the Remove button. You can now associate another application in the manner I described in chapter 10. It's also possible to associate files directly in this dialog box, using the New Type button. See your Windows 95 documentation for more information.

Finding more viewers

You can find more general purpose viewers on the Internet. These are often freeware or shareware. I've already shown you how to find a RealAudio player, but you may want to take a look at the following Web sites to see what else you can pick up:

http://www.ncsa.uiuc.edu/SDG/Software/WinMosaic/viewers.htm

http://vsl.cnet.com/

http://www-dsed.llnl.gov/documents/WWWtest.html

http://www.iuma.com/IUMA-2.0/help/help-windows.html

http://www.law.cornell.edu/cello/cellocfg.html

TIP **Be careful when entering URLs; note that the first one, above,** ends in **.htm**, while the rest end in **.html**. Add an *l* when it's not needed, or miss it when it is, and you won't get to the document.

You can also try these FTP sites. (See chapter 13 for instructions on getting into FTP sites.)

ftp://ftp.law.cornell.edu in the **/pub/LII/Cello/** directory

ftp://ftp.cica.indiana.edu (you'll have to dig around a bit to find anything, but there's a *lot* of software in here.)

TIP **See the rest of this chapter for information about finding viewers** for archive files (.ZIP, .ARC, .ARJ, & .LZH), Adobe Acrobat (.PDF), Video (.MPEG, .MPG, .MPE, & .MOV), MPEG Audio (.MP2), and VRML 3-D images (.WRL).

If you can't find what you need through these sites, try searching the Web (see chapter 8) or use Archie (see chapter 13).

Adobe Acrobat (.PDF) files

We're going to see a lot of .PDF files on the Web very soon, for several reasons. You might think of .PDF as a sort of extension of the Web's "hypertext" or "hypermedia." Adobe Acrobat files are self-contained hypertext documents, with links between pages. Unlike HTML, though, Acrobat files allow the author to determine exactly what the document will look like.

When a browser "renders" an HTML file into the document you see on your screen, the browser decides how to display the different document components—the headers, body text, pull quotes, and so on. But with Acrobat this control is left in the hands of the author; the Acrobat viewer displays the document just as the author intended. Also, Acrobat files are independent of the Web. You can take an Acrobat file and send it to anyone with an Acrobat reader—they don't need a Web browser. In fact Acrobat began its life far from the Web; it was intended to help companies distribute online documentation to a variety of different computer systems. The same document can be read by viewers on Windows, DOS, Macintosh, SunOS, and Solaris computers, with more viewers to be added soon. It also allows companies to produce online documents that look the same as their paper documents.

Another reason we're going to see lots of .PDF documents is that two of the most important companies on the Web—Netscape Communications and Spyglass—have decided that it will be so. ("Let there be .PDF".) Both companies plan to make their browsers work with .PDF, though in different ways. Your browser, Internet Explorer, is licensed from Spyglass, which has a product called *Enhanced NCSA Mosaic* (in turn licensed from NCSA, the National Center for Supercomputing Applications, the originators of the first graphical Web browser, Mosaic). I don't know how .PDF will be handled by Internet Explorer, but I'd bet that eventually the browser will have some kind of built-in support. Also, Adobe is working on a system called Weblink (go to **http://www.adobe.com/Acrobat/Weblink.html** for information) that will allow Acrobat authors to add links from their Acrobat files to Web sites. Users will be able to click on a link in Acrobat, causing their Web browser to retrieve the specified Web document. In the meantime, you'll have to add a .PDF browser if you want to view Acrobat files.

You'll find the Adobe Acrobat reader in a variety of places, but you might want to try the source first, Adobe itself, at **http://www.adobe.com/Software.html** (the viewer is free; Adobe wants to sell the authoring tool, so they've made the viewer easy to get). Once you've installed the program (just run the file you download and follow the instructions), you can try it out at a variety of sites:

Web Sites with Cool PDF—**http://www.adobe.com/Acrobat/PDFsites.html**

US Patent Office—**http://www.uspto.gov/hearings.html**

Centers for Disease Control Morbidity and Mortality Weekly Report—**http://www.crawford.com/cdc/mmwr/mmwr.html**

Time-Life Virtual Garden—**http://www.timeinc.com/vg/TimeLife/Project/**

TimesFax—**http://nytimesfax.com/**

Axcess Magazine—**http://www.internex.net/axcess**

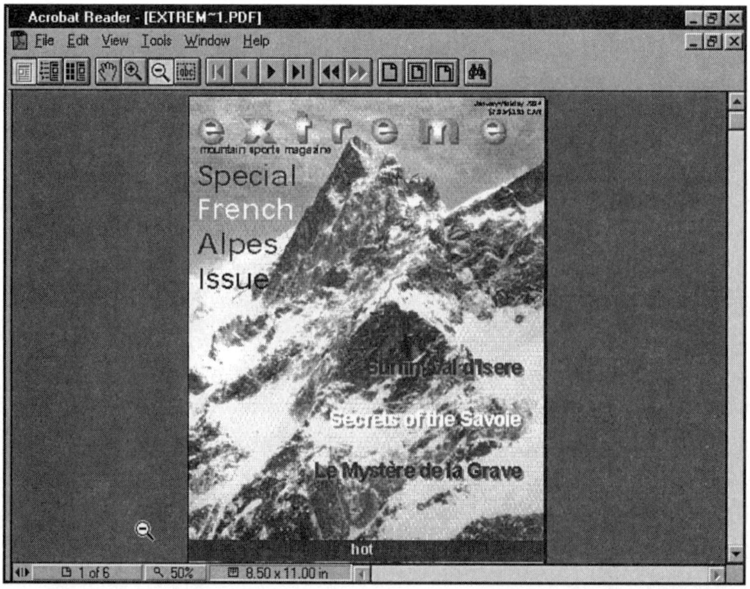

Fig. 11.2
Extreme Mountain Sports magazine, in the Adobe Acrobat Reader. (I found this at **http://mole.uvm.edu/skivt-l/skishop.html**.)

.ZIP, .ARC, .ARJ, & .LZH files

You may want to associate these file types with an application. These are all archive, or compressed, file formats. If a Web author wants you to be able to transfer a very large file, or a collection of files, he can compress it in one of these formats, so it is transferred more quickly. You'll often find .ZIP files (PKZIP files); more rarely you *may* run across .ARC, .ARJ, and .LZH files.

If you have a Windows Explorer utility that lets you view these files as if they were directories, you probably won't want to associate these files with anything. For instance, I have Norton Navigator, which has a Windows Explorer replacement. This program treats .ZIP files as if they were directories—click on one and you can see the contents, drag files to other directories, and so on.

If you don't have a utility like this, you can associate these files with an archive-specific program, such as WinZip. (You can find WinZip from the **http://www.winzip.com/winzip** Web page.) Once associated, Explorer will automatically place the archive file in the cache directory, then open WinZip. WinZip will display the contents of the file (as you can see in figure 11.3), and let you extract the compressed files to another directory.

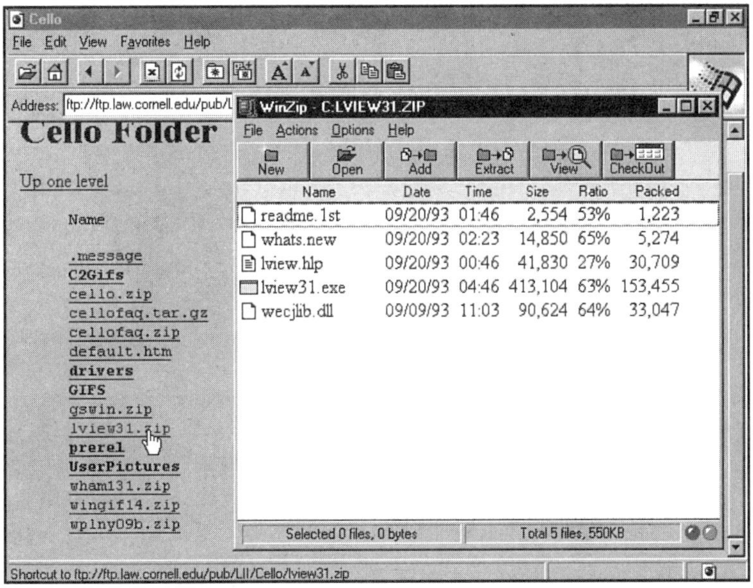

Fig. 11.3
I've just transferred a file called LVIEW31.ZIP, and Explorer sent it to WinZip, which is displaying the contents.

Video viewers

You'll find a variety of video images on the Web. Perhaps the most popular are the MPEG (.MPEG, .MPG, .MPE) and Quicktime (.MOV) formats, neither of which can be played by Widows 95's Media Player.

I've installed MPEGPLAY program. (I found it at the **http://www-dsed.llnl.gov/documents/WWWtest.html** Web page.) It plays MPEGs well, but it has a size limit—I'm not exactly sure what the limit is, but it won't play 5MB movies, for instance. (When you register the program you'll get a version that has no limit.) You can also try VMPEG, which you can find at the Virtual Software Library (http://vsl.cnet.com/) among other places.

TIP **As "neat" as video on the Web may be, it can get old fast. The** problem is that transferring video across the Internet is very slow, even if you are using a 28,800 bps modem. If you have an ISDN—Integrated Services Digital Network—connection, you're okay, but most people are still working with 14,400 or 28,800 bps modems, which take a *long* time to transfer the 5 or 6 MB that many videos on the Web take up. The diving video in figure 11.4 can take an hour to transmit with a 14,400 bps modem!

You can see an example of a movie running in MPEGPLAY for Windows in figure 11.4. This is from the South Florida Dive Journal, at **http://www.florida.net/scuba/videos/movie.html**.

Incidentally, Microsoft plans to add MPEG support to Windows 95 at some point, probably by late 1995 or early 1996. It's not entirely clear how the program will be distributed, but it might be part of the "Tune-Up" packs that Microsoft says will be available. Also, there *may* be another way to play MPEG movies—using Apple's QuickTime for Windows. (Most of you *won't* be able to use this method, though, as I'll explain in a moment.)

Fig. 11.4
An MPEG movie playing in MPEGPLAY—from the South Florida Dive Journal.

QuickTime is another very popular movie format (.MOV). I ended up using QuickTime for Windows, which, in theory, plays both MPEG and QuickTime movies. I couldn't find a shareware QuickTime program for Windows 95. There's *QuickTime extensions for Windows mplayer*, a system that runs in Windows 3.1 (by somehow making the Windows Media Player program compatible with QuickTime), but it doesn't seem to work in Windows 95. Apple sells QuickTime for Windows for only $9.95, so I downloaded that program.

Unfortunately, while QuickTime for Windows plays .MOV files well, it only plays MPEG movies if you have a special MPEG video board installed in your computer, which, of course, few people have.

See **http://quicktime.apple.com/ordering-qt.html** to download the file from the Web (or call 800-637-0029). There are a couple of things you should know about downloading this program. First, you can only download from the Web if you have a First Virtual account. This is a special account that allows you to use your credit card online, without using your actual credit-card number (you'll use a special account number that you choose when you open an account). It costs $2 to open an account, and you can learn more about this in chapter 19 (or go to First Virtual and follow instructions: **http://www.fv.com/newacct/**).

Also, the instructions in the QuickTime Web document say that "*Your browser must be properly configured to accept a mime type of application/ octet-stream BEFORE you purchase and download this file!*" Don't worry about this, Internet Explorer will download the file just fine without any changes.

Once you've downloaded and installed the program, you can go in search of QuickTime movies. The best places to start are **http://quicktime.apple.com/ content.html** and **http://www.iac.net/~flypba/qt.html**, where you'll find lists of QuickTime sites. You can see an example in figure 11.5.

Fig. 11.5
I found this Simpsons video at **http:// www.springfield.com/ episode.html**.

MPEG audio

There's another MPEG format, MPEG *audio* (MPEG stands for the Motion Picture Experts Group, after the people who came up with the file format.) These files have the .MP2 extension. They are a great way to play sound; the files are compressed, so really high quality sounds can be squeezed down into quite a small space. You won't find a lot of these on the Web, though— most sounds are in the .AU, .AIF, .WAV, or .RAM formats.

I installed XingSound, which I found at the **http://www.iuma.com/IUMA-2.0/help/help-windows.html** Web document (this is at IUMA, the Internet Underground Music Archive). It was very easy to install, and works well.

Viewers for VRML 3-D images

The new fad on the Web is 3-D images. Click on a link in a Web page, and up pops your 3-D viewer, with a 3-D image inside. Move around in this image, or "walk around" the image (some images are of landscapes and buildings you can "move through," others of objects that you can rotate).

Check these sites for viewers:

WorldView	**http://www.webmaster.com/vrml/wvwin/**
WebSpace	**http://www.sgi.com/Products/WebFORCE/WebSpace/**
AmberGL	**http://www.divelabs.com/vrml.htm**
NAVFlyer	**ftp://yoda.fdt.net/pub/users/m/micgreen**
Pueblo	**http://www.chaco.com/pueblo/**
VRWeb	**http://hgiicm.tu-graz.ac.at/B7B43623/Cvrweb**
WebFX	**http://www.paperinc.com/webfx.html**

Note that not all of these were available for Windows 95 at the time of writing, though all had some kind of Windows version. WebSpace, for instance, wasn't available for Windows 95 at the time of writing, and I couldn't get the Windows NT version to run in Windows 95 (though others have told me it does run, sometimes). Keep checking, though; a Windows 95 version should be out soon.

You can also check this page to see an up-to-date list of VRML viewers: **http://www.sdsc.edu/SDSC/Partners/vrml/software/browsers.html**

> ***Plain English, please!***
>
> Just to confuse you a little...programs that display VRML images are often known as VRML **browsers**, rather than **viewers**.

Note also that at the time of writing the Windows VRML viewers were a little buggy, and didn't work too well. That may change quickly, though. Also, working in 3-D often requires relatively powerful computers. To run WorldView, for instance, you'll need a 486/50 or better, 8 MB of RAM, and must be running in 256-color video mode.Download a viewer and install it—read the installation instructions carefully. Then, go to one of these Web pages, where you can find links to VRML objects you can test.

- **http://nemo.ncsl.nist.gov/~sressler/projects/vrml/vrmlfiles.html** (VRML Samples from the Open Virtual Reality Testbed)
- **http://vrml.arc.org/gallery95/index2.html** (The Arc Gallery - a la VRML)
- **http://www.well.com/user/spidaman/vrml.html** (look under the *Actual VRML sites* heading for links to VRML sites)
- **http://nemo.ncsl.nist.gov/~sressler/hotvr.html** (Hot Virtual Reality Sites)
- **http://www.lightside.com/3dsite/cgi/VRML-index.html** (loads of links, some of which are to actual VRML sites, though most to sites with information *about* VRML)

You can also search for *VRML* to find more VRML sites (see chapter 8).

Now, when you've found a link to a VRML object (it will have the .WRL extension; look in the status bar), click on it and run through the procedure we looked at earlier for associating file types (see chapter 10). When you've finished, Explorer will transfer the file and load your viewer. You'll then be able to move around in (or about) the 3-D picture. See figure 11.6 for an example.

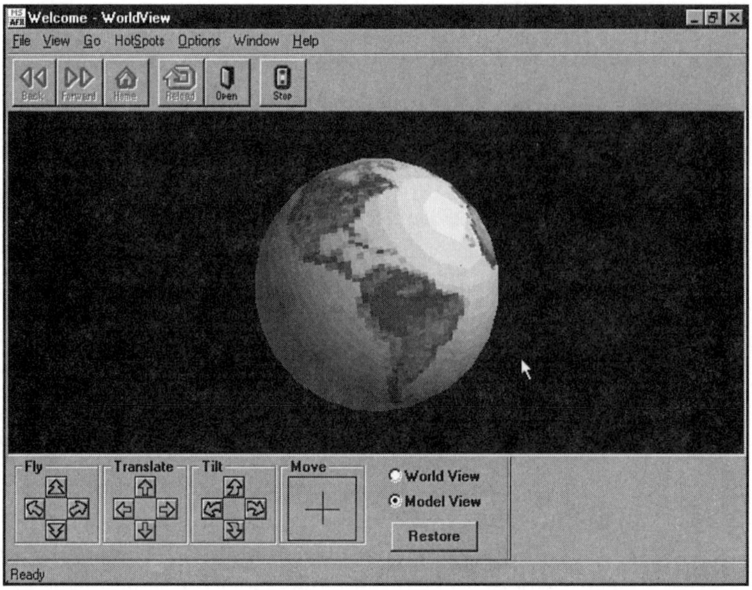

Fig. 11.6
A 3-D image in WorldView—you can revolve the globe to look at it from any angle.

TIP **This Web page is a good place to try out all sorts of viewers** (including VRML viewers): **http://www-dsed.llnl.gov/documents/WWWtest.html**. You can also find unusual viewers here; viewers for .PDB "chemical objects," .MA Mathematica files, .V5D dataset objects, and so on.

Note, by the way, that VRML is very new, and there will probably be many changes over the next year. Right now the viewers are likely to be rather "buggy." You'll soon find lots of new and improved viewers, and perhaps new file formats (there are lots of different 3-D file formats, though most of the files you'll find on the Web are currently .WRL files). You'll also find that some images have Web links inside them. For instance, you'll be able to walk through a museum, click on a door, and go into another room. For information about VRML, go to the **http://vrml.wired.com/** and **http://www.lightside.com/3dsite/cgi/VRML-index.html** Web pages.

TIP **There's another Virtual Reality/3D system on the horizon,** QuickTime VR. This system, from Apple Computers, is already available for the Mac, but not for Windows. They promise it will be out soon, so check the **http://quicktime.apple.com/** Web page now and again.

Voyager CDLinks

Here's a brand new format that's an interesting link of CD-Rom and Web site. Voyager CD-Link provides a way for Web authors to link their Web sites to a music CD in your computer's CD-Rom drive. These CDs don't have to be created to work with a Web site. A Web site can be created to work with an existing CD. For instance, two of the first CDLink sites were designed to work with Frank Zappa's *Hot Rats* CD (**http://northshore.shore.net/rykodisc/fzcdlink.html**) and Elvis Costello's *Imperial Bedroom* CD (**http://northshore.shore.net/rykodisc/eccdlink.html**). You can read reviews of these CDs, and click on links in the reviews to play specific portions of the music. (See figure 11.7.) You can download Voyager CDLink from **http://www.voyagerco.com/cdlink/cdlink.html**

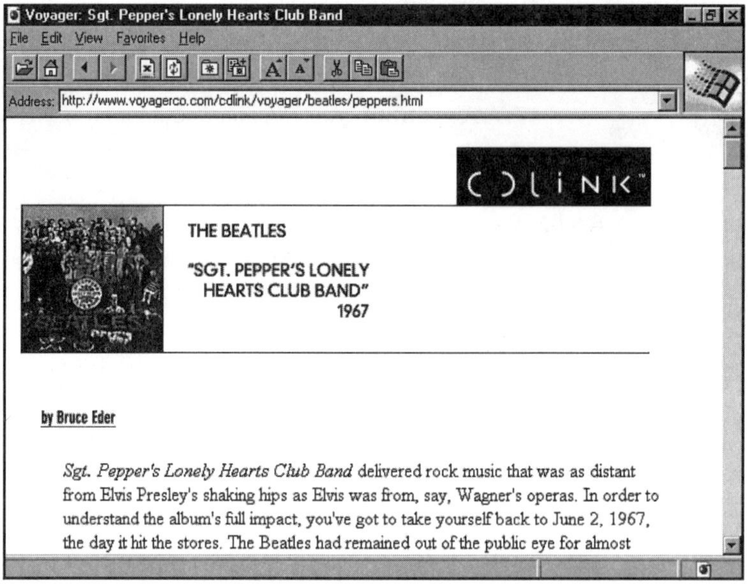

Fig. 11.7
This Web page (**http://www.voyagerco.com/cdlink/voyager/beatles/peppers.html**) contains links to CDLink. When I click on a link, CDLink (which is hidden in the background) plays music from the CD in my CD-Rom drive.

TIP **To find a registry of Web sites that use the CDLink program—and** the music CDs they work with, go to **http://www.voyagerco.com/cdlink/registry/registry.html**. You'll find sites working with CDs from Selena, Amy Grant, Bob Dylan, The Traveling Wilburys, The Beatles, Bon Jovi, and plenty more.

12 Not By Web Alone—WebGopher and More

In this chapter:

- **Using non-World Wide Web resources through Internet Explorer**
- **What is a Gopher system?**
- **Searching Gopher servers with Jughead**
- **Searching the whole of Gopherspace with Veronica**
- **Using special Jughead and Veronica commands, and Boolean searching**

Not by Web alone...there's plenty of other things to be found on the Internet, and Explorer can help you find them . . .

So far in this book we've looked at the standard http:// URLs (http stands for *HyperText Transfer Protocol*, the basic "language" of the Web). When your Web browser sees a **URL** that begins with **http://** it knows that the destination is a Web document. But some URLs begin with other things, such as these:

- **gopher://**—Takes you to a gopher-menu system.
- **ftp://**—Takes you to a File Transfer Protocol site, a site set up so that you can transfer files back to your computer. See chapter 13.
- **mailto:**—Used to send e-mail. See chapter 16.
- **news:**—A special newsgroup protocol, allowing you to read newsgroups from Web browsers. See chapter 15.
- **telnet://**—Starts a Telnet session in which you can log on to another computer on the Internet. See chapter 14.
- **tn3270://**—Starts a 3270-mode session, which is very similar to Telnet (you're connecting to a different type of computer, an IBM 3270). See chapter 14.
- **wais://**—A relatively little-used URL. This one is for Wide Area Information Servers, systems that are used to search databases. While Internet Explorer can't use the **wais://** URL, you can still use WAIS through special "gateways." See chapter 16.

In other words, you can access systems that are not true Web systems. You can use Gopher, FTP, and Telnet, you can send e-mail from Web links, and you can read newsgroup messages. There are even special "gateways" through the Web to systems for which your Web browser isn't prepared. For instance, your Web browser cannot communicate directly with Archie, a system used to search FTP sites for computer files (you type a filename, and Archie tells you where to find it). But there are Web documents that do the work for you, using forms. You type the name of the file into a form, and a special program at the Web server communicates with Archive for you (see chapter 13 for information about Archie).

Finding Internet resources

If you'd like to find the sort of non-Web things that you can get to through the Web, take a look at some of these documents:

Inter-Links

Select a category to see lists of related documents and tools.

http://www.nova.edu/Inter-Links/

Directory of Service Types

If you want to see where you can use WAIS, newsgroups, Gopher, Telnet, FTP, Whois, and other Internet services through your Web browsers, take a look at this Web document.

http://www.w3.org/hypertext/DataSources/ByAccess.html

ArchiePlex

This is a directory of ArchiePlex servers throughout the world—servers that let you search Archie directly from the Web. You'll find sites for browsers both with and without forms support.

http://web.nexor.co.uk/archie.html

Internet Resources—Meta-Index

This is a list of directories containing references to various Internet resources—the Web, Gopher, Telnet, FTP, and more.

http://www.ncsa.uiuc.edu/SDG/Software/Mosaic/MetaIndex.html

What's Gopher?

The World Wide Web has grown tremendously in the last couple of years. At the end of 1993, even well into 1994, the World Wide Web was a sideshow on the Internet. Few people knew how to use it, and fewer still bothered. It wasn't hard to use, but there wasn't much incentive—for the vast majority of Internet users there was no way to display pictures, listen to sounds, play video, or do any of the neat things you've learned to do with Internet Explorer. It wasn't just that the Web was primarily text, with little else. It was because the software simply wasn't available.

TIP **Interested in a little history? Want to see just how people less** fortunate than you have to use the Web? Go to http://www.w3.org/hypertext/WWW/FAQ/Bootstrap.html to find a list of Telnet sites that let you use the old Line Mode and Lynx Web browsers. Then see chapter 14 for information on using Telnet, and go try them out.

So, back in the distant past (okay, a couple of years or so), what was the hot "navigation" system on the Internet, in the days Before Web? **Gopher**.

If you never used the Internet in the old command-line days, if Internet Explorer and the other graphical user interface systems that abound are your only taste of the Internet, you don't know just how difficult the Internet could be. (Actually millions of people are *still* using the Internet through a command-line interface—that is, typing complicated commands to get anything done.) Many people who tried to use the Internet just a year or two ago, when the cyberhype all began, were so turned off by the experience that they went away and never came back. FTP (which you'll learn about in chapter 13) was extremely difficult. Telnet (chapter 14) was pretty clunky—still is. E-mail was just about bearable. All in all, the Internet was *not* a user-friendly place.

Gopher—a brave new world

Then along came Gopher. This tool was a revolution in simplicity, providing a nice menu system from which users could select options. Instead of remembering a variety of rather obscure and arcane commands to find what they needed, users could use the arrow keys to select options from the menu. Those options could take the user to other menus, or to documents of some kind. In fact the Gopher system was, in some ways, similar to the World Wide Web. It was a world-wide network of menu systems. Options in the menus linked to menus or other documents all over the world. These Gopher menus made the Internet much easier to use, and much more accessible to people other than long-term cybergeeks.

For a while Gopher looked like the future of the Internet, at least to a number of people who invested time and money in Internet software. A variety of "graphical point-and-click" Gopher programs were published, some shareware, some freeware. You may have heard of WinGopher, for instance, an excellent Windows program for navigating through the Gopher system.

Then along came the Web. Or rather, along came the graphical Web browsers, which all of a sudden made the Web not only easy to use, but exciting, too. Interest in Gopher subsided rapidly, and everyone rushed off to learn how to create Web documents. So where's that leave Gopher? Still alive and well, actually, for a couple of good reasons. First, there were already many Gopher systems set up. And secondly, there are still millions of Internet users who don't have access to graphical Web browsers, for whom Gophers are the easiest tools available. There's a lot of interesting information on Gopher servers around the world. And, fortunately, you can get to it with Internet Explorer. That's right; Internet Explorer may be primarily a Web browser, but you can use the Web to access Gopher.

" ***Plain English, please!***

Gopher was developed at the University of Minnesota. Why call it Gopher? Three reasons. The mascot of the U of M is a gopher. A gopher "digs around in the dirt"; Gophers dig around on the Internet. And a gopher, as an American colloquialism, refers to someone who's a "dogsbody," someone at the beck and call of others; he "goes fer this and goes fer that." **"**

Digging around with Gopher

Gopher servers are systems that provide a menu interface. Users can select options from a list. Each option can lead to another list of options or directly to some kind of data, such as a text file or a picture (mostly text files). In one sense, Gophers are like Web sites; they have connections across the world to Gopher servers elsewhere. So selecting one menu option might take you to a Gopher server in Australia, while selecting another might land you in Zimbabwe.

You can get to a Gopher server in two ways: by clicking a link that some author has provided, or by typing the **gopher://** URL into the Address text box and pressing Enter. For instance, **gopher://earth.usa.net** will take you to Internet Express' Gopher server, which you can see in figure 12.1.

In some cases you can ignore the **gopher://** bit. You've already learned that you can type a URL into the Address text box without including the **http://** bit. Well, if the gopher address starts with the word **gopher** you can type the address and forget the **gopher://** part. For instance, you could type **gopher.usa.net** instead of **gopher://gopher.usa.net**.

TIP **For a list of links to Gopher servers, go to gopher:// gopher.micro.umn.edu/11/ Other%20Gopher%20and%20Information%20Servers**. Or, if you don't want to type all that, go to **http://www.w3.org/hypertext/ DataSources/ByAccess.html** and click on the *Gopher* link.

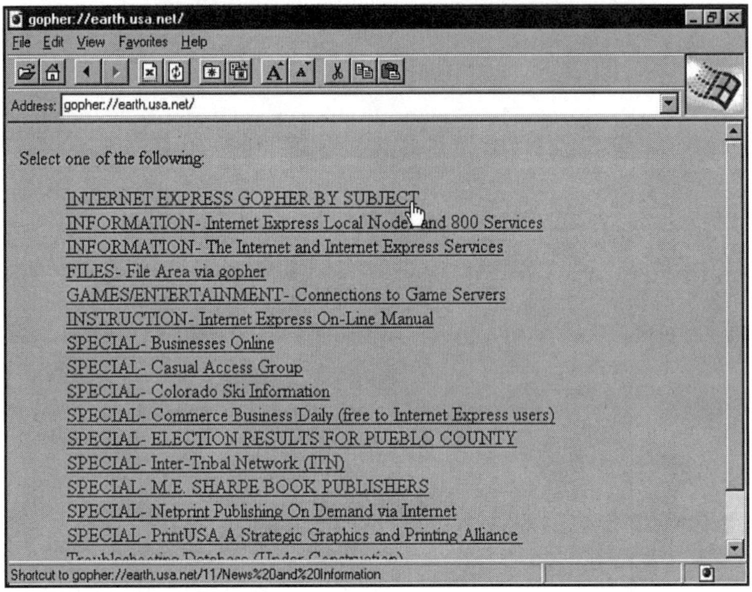

Fig. 12.1
A Gopher is an Internet menu system—and you can use these menus through Internet Explorer.

You can also include "directories" in the URL. For instance, if you type **gopher://earth.usa.net/00/News%20and%20Information/ Ski%20Information/ A%20List%20of%20Today%27s%20SKI%20CONDITIONS** into the Address box and press Enter, you'll go to the Internet Express Gopher server, and then automatically select the Colorado Ski Information and Ski Conditions menu options. (Too much for you to type? If you visit a Gopher site and find a useful Gopher menu, add it to your Favorites list; see chapter 6.)

How, then, do you use a Gopher server with Explorer? The Gopher menu options are represented by links—click the link to select that option. If the option leads to another menu, that's what you'll see in the window. If it leads to a file of some kind, the file is transferred in the normal way, and, if Explorer can display or play it, it does so. If it can't…well, you'd better go back and see chapters 10 and 11.

You'll find that most of the documents at Gopher sites are text documents. But as you'll remember from chapter 10, Internet Explorer can display these text documents within its own window. Of course, you won't find any links to other documents within these text documents—they're not true Web documents, after all—so once you've finished you'll have to use the Back toolbar button to return to the Gopher menu you were just viewing. In figure 12.2 you can see a text document that I ran across at the Internet Express Gopher site. I found a menu option entitled *A List of Today's SKI CONDITIONS*; when I clicked on the option I got the text document.

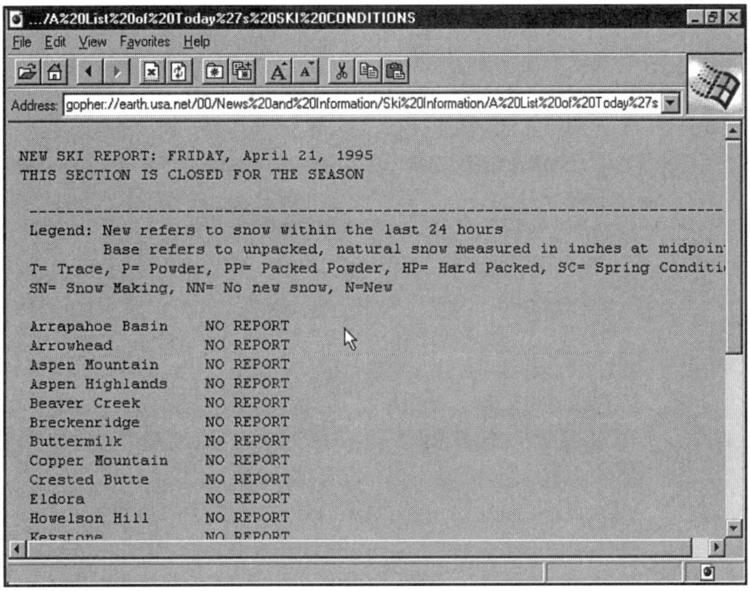

Fig. 12.2
A text document at a Gopher site. (Ski season hasn't started yet—but it won't be long!)

Back to the cartoon world: Veronica and Jughead

Gopher servers have two types of search tools: **Veronica** (Very Easy Rodent-Oriented Net-wide Index to Computerized Archives) and **Jughead** (Jonzy's Universal Gopher Hierarchy Excavation And Display). Do these acronyms mean much? No, but you try to create an acronym from a cartoon character's name!

> **Plain English, please!**
>
> Why **Veronica** and **Jughead**? They are characters in the famous Archie cartoon strip. **Archie** arrived on the Internet first. Archie is a system that enables you to search the Internet for particular computer files—you can type a filename, and Archie will tell you where the file is (you'll learn about this in chapter 13). Why Archie? The legend is that Archie is derived from the word *archive*. Remove the V, and what have you got? *Archie*. Some say this is *not* how the name was derived, so who knows. Personally it makes sense to me. Anyway, the people who created the Gopher search systems figured Archie needed company, and named their systems Veronica and Jughead.

Veronica lets you search Gopher servers all over the world. Jughead lets you search the Gopher server you are currently working with (though many Gopher servers don't yet have Jugheads).

If you want to search **Gopherspace**—this giant system of gopher menus that spread across the Internet—find an appropriate menu option somewhere. For instance, at the **gopher://gopher.cc.utah.edu/** Gopher site, you'll find menu options that say *Search titles in Gopherspace using Veronica* and *Search menu titles using Jughead.* At the Internet Express site we were just looking at, you have to go down a couple of levels. First you'd select *INTERNET EXPRESS GOPHER BY SUBJECT*, then *Search Gophers through the Internet for Keyword (Veronica)*. (You might have to dig around to find menus on some sites; sometimes they are several levels down the menu system.) Many sites don't have Jughead, but virtually all have a link to Veronica.

Jughead

When you select the Jughead option, you'll see a few more links; you'll often find links to other Jughead servers at other sites, and probably a link to information telling you how to work with Jughead.

Of course, there's also a link to the actual search itself (for instance, at the **gopher://gopher.cc.utah.edu** site I would choose *Search menu titles using Jughead* and then click on *Search University of Utah Menus Using Jughead*). When you click this link, you'll go to an index-server form (see fig. 12.3). Type a word into the form, and press Enter. For instance, you might type the word **book.** The Gopher system will search for all menu options containing that word.

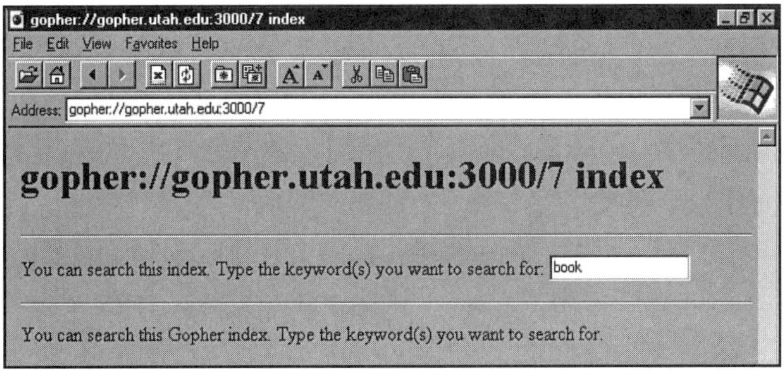

Fig. 12.3
Type the word you want to search for, then press Enter.

TIP **Case Doesn't Matter. You can enter the search statement in** upper- or lowercase, Jughead doesn't care. It regards **BOOK** as being the same as **book**.

Soon you'll see another Gopher menu, one created specially for your search, containing a list of all the items that Jughead has found for you. Click one to see what it is. (When you are working with Jughead, the response will probably be fairly quick. Veronica's much slower.)

If you don't find what you are looking for, you can click on the Back toolbar button to return to the form, and try again. This time, you might enter **book or publication**, for instance. This is what is called a *Boolean* search, a search in which you can enter more than one thing to search for. I can then press Enter to search again.

The Boolean operators

You can use these Boolean operators when you type your search term: **or**, **and**, **not**. For instance:

a and b Search for a menu item containing word a *and* word b.

a or b Search for a menu item containing word a *or* word b.

a not b Search for a menu item containing the word a, but don't include it if it also has the word b.

When I search for **book or publication**, I get a few more menu options. When I search for **book or publications or publications** I get even more.

Wildcards wild

You can also use "wildcards" to search. That means that you can use a character to take the place of another character. For instance, if you search for **pub***, you're telling Jughead to search for any word beginning with **pub**. The asterisk simply means "some other stuff here."

The term **book or pub*** actually means "search for the word book or any words beginning with pub." Words such as publication, publications, publicity, public, and publican.

> **TIP** **Follow These Rules** **Jughead only has one wildcard—you can only** use the * character, not the ? character, a common wildcard in many other systems. Also, remember these basic rules: you can't *start* a word with the asterisk, and you can't put an asterisk within a word. (It's ignored if you do.)

So you could search for **book or pub*** instead of typing out **book or publication or publications**. Searching like this will increase your "hit" rate dramatically; you may end up with hundreds of items. Do you want all this extra stuff? Well, the *publishers* and *publishing* entries that are found may be useful, but *public* and *pubs* gives us lots of extra stuff we really didn't want, like *Title 53A - State System of Public Education, Chapter 11 - Students in Public Schools, Part 3 - Immunization of Students*.

More Boolean searching

Let's take a quick look at the Boolean stuff again. If you enter several words on a line, without one of the Boolean operators between the words (the *and*, *or*, or *not*), Jughead assumes you mean *and*. So, for example, both **book and pub*** and **book pub*** mean exactly the same thing: "find entries that contain both the word book and a word beginning with pub."

There are a few other things to be aware of, though. If Jughead sees any special characters **(!"#$%&'()+,-./:;<=>?@[\]^_'{|}~)** in the search statement, it treats them as if they were spaces, replacing them with the Boolean operator *and*. For instance, if you are searching for **This.file**, Jughead searches for **this and file**. That's not necessarily a problem, though. If I search for **Pubs_by SCERP_Researchers**, I will still find the correct menu item, because Jughead will still search for the words *Pubs*, *by*, *SCERP*, and *Researchers*. (Remember, each Jughead is different, so what you find at one Jughead is not the same as what you'll find at another.)

Also, because you are using the words *and*, *or*, and *not* as Boolean operators, you can't actually search for these words. But there again, you'll probably never need to do so, anyway.

Special commands

Jughead currently has four special commands you can normally include in a search string. (At the time of writing these commands will not work with Internet Explorer; they may by the time you read this). You can use these commands:

?all *what* This tells Jughead to include *all* of the hits it finds. Usually it limits the hits to 1024, so if it finds 2,000 matching entries, you won't see 976 of them. Mind you, 1024 is an awful lot, more than you are likely to need. For instance, if you search for **?all book or pub***, Jughead will search for the words *book* and *pub**, and, if it finds more than 1024 matches (it probably won't) will display them all.

?help [*what*] The ?help command tells Jughead to create a menu option that lets you get to the Jughead help file. You can use the ?help command by itself, if you want, or do a search at the same time. For instance, **?help book or pub***.

?limit=*n* *what* This tells Jughead to limit the number of menu items it gives you. For instance, **?limit=10 book or pub*** will cause Jughead to only display the first 10 items it finds.

?version [*what*] This gives you the Jughead version number. You'll see this menu option: 1. **This version of Jughead is 1.0.4** (or whatever the actual version number is). You can then use the menu option to read the Jughead help file. You can use the ?version command by itself, if you want, or do a search at the same time. For instance, **?version book or pub***.

You cannot combine these commands, by the way—only one may be used for each search. And, as I mentioned before, you may not be able to use them at all right now for Internet Explorer. If you do, you may just get a blank page back. This is a bug, so later versions of Explorer may work with these commands.

Veronica

Working with Veronica is very similar to working with Jughead, with a couple of important differences. First, when you select a Veronica menu option, you'll get the choice of servers. Veronica searches *all* of Gopherspace—Gopher servers all over the world. Something called a **Veronica server** stores an index of menu options at all of these Gopher servers, so you are actually searching one of these indexes; you get to pick which one.

But at the same time, you have to decide whether you want to limit your search. You can search all menu options, or only menu options that lead to other menus. Let's assume, for instance, that you went to **gopher://gopher.cc.utah.edu**, then chose the *Search titles in Gopherspace using Veronica* option. If you now select *Find GOPHER DIRECTORIES by Title Word(s) (via U of Manitoba)*, you will be looking for menu options that lead to other menus (often called **directories** in Gopherspeak) using the University of Manitoba Veronica server. If you select the *Search GopherSpace by Title Word(s) (via University of Pisa)*, you will be searching all menu options, both "directories" and options leading to files and documents, at the University of Pisa Veronica server.

When you make your selection, you'll see the same Index Search dialog box that you see when doing a Jughead search. Type the word and press Enter. What happens then? Well, there's a good chance you'll get a message saying **** Too many connections - Try again soon. ****, or something similar. Try another server. Or perhaps Explorer just seems to wait and wait; the clouds keep moving across the busy icon's background, but nothing seems to happen. These servers are very busy, so it often takes a long time to get a result. When you finally *do* get a result, though, you'll get a much bigger list than you did from the Jughead search. After all, you are searching the world's Gopher servers, not just one.

Veronica details

Veronica searches are very similar to Jughead searches, with a few differences. You can use Boolean searching, and you can use the * wildcard; as with Jughead it must appear at the end of the word, not the beginning nor within the word. (With Veronica, putting the * inside the word will cause the search to abort. Jughead just ignores the asterisk if it's within the word.)

TIP **For detailed information about Jughead and Veronica searches,** read the help files that you'll find in the Gopher menus near the Jughead and Veronica menu options.

Veronica has a special **-t** command. This is placed within the search string (at the beginning, middle, or end, doesn't matter), and is used to define the *type* of item you are looking for. For instance, **book -t0** means "search for the word book, but only find text documents." Or **book -t01** means "search for the word book, but only find text documents and Gopher menu items."

These are the numbers you can use with the **-t** command:

Number or letter	Description
0	Text file
1	Directory (Gopher menu)
2	CSO name server (a searchable database used to track down other Internet users)
4	Macintosh HQX file
5	PC binary file
7	A searchable index
8	Telnet session (see chapter 14)
9	Binary file
s	Sound file
e	Event file
I	Image file (other than GIF)
M	MIME multipart/mixed message (MIME is a system used by Internet e-mail systems to transfer binary files)
T	TN3270 Session (a similar system to Telnet)
c	Calendar
g	GIF image
h	HTML Web document

You can also use the **-m** command to specify the maximum number of items to find. For instance, **-m300 book** tells the Veronica server to show up to 300 items that it finds.

TIP **If you don't use the -m command, the Veronica server will only** search until it's found the default limit, 200 items. Use **-m** to tell the server to find more than the default number.

13

Software Libraries—Using FTP

In this chapter:

- **Using FTP to grab files from the Internet**
- **Finding the files you need at the FTP site**
- **How can I search for computer files on the Internet?**
- **Finding an Archie site**
- **Searching with Archie**
- **Advanced Archie**

The Internet contains millions of computer files just waiting for you to grab. Explorer will help you do so . . . .

We've already seen how to transfer files from the Web back to your computer (see chapters 9 to 11). The Web contains many files that you might find useful—shareware and demo programs, clip art, press releases, music, video, and plenty more.

But before the Web was born, there was already a system for grabbing files from the Internet—**FTP**, File Transfer Protocol. Using this system you can log into a computer somewhere on the Internet, then transfer files back to your computer.

There are many publicly accessible software archives on the Internet. These are known as **anonymous FTP** sites. This refers to a procedure by which anyone can log in to a public FTP site. When you log in, you use the account name *anonymous*, and then type your e-mail address as the password. (Those unfortunate souls still using the Internet through a UNIX command line actually type these entries when they log in to an FTP site; you have Internet Explorer to do it automatically for you, though—you won't even see Explorer log in for you.)

TIP **Explorer currently only works with anonymous FTP. Some FTP sites** are set up with *real* account names and passwords—rather than *anonymous* as the account name and an e-mail address as the password. If you have been given access to one of these private FTP sites, you won't be able to get to it using Explorer.

Explorer may have trouble connecting to some other forms of FTP sites, too. If you want an FTP program that can do just about anything, try WS_FTP. You can find this program at **ftp://ftp.usma.edu/pub/msdos/winsock.files**; retrieve the file called WS_FTP32.ZIP, which contains the 32-bit version of the program.

For instance, here are a couple of FTP sites that contain a lot of Windows shareware utilities: **ftp.cica.indiana.edu/pub/pc/win95/** and **ftp.wustl.edu/systems/ibmpc/win3**. Or go to **http://hoohoo.ncsa.uiuc.edu/ftp/**, to the Monster FTP Sites list, to find thousands of FTP sites.

What does all this information mean? First, there's the FTP site name (or host name): **ftp.cica.indiana.edu**, for instance. This identifies the computer that contains the files you are after. Then there's the directory name: **/pub/pc/win95/**. This tells you which directory you must change to in order to find the files.

There are two ways to use the Web browser for an FTP session. You'll either click a link to an FTP site that some kind Web author has provided, or enter an FTP URL into the Address box and press Enter. The FTP URL begins with **ftp://**. Let's say, for instance, that you want to go the **ftp.cica.indiana.edu/pub/pc/win95/** ftp site to see what shareware is available. You would type **ftp:// ftp.cica.indiana.edu/pub/pc/win95/** into the Address text box at the top of Internet Explorer, and press Enter. Watch the status bar and you'll see the progress messages (*Opening*, *Finding*, *Connecting*, *Logging on*, *Sending commands*, *Receiving Information*, and so on.) When you connect, you'll see something like figure 13.1.

TIP **As with the http:// and gopher:// URLs, you don't always need to** include **ftp://**. If the ftp site name begins with ftp, you can forget the **ftp://**. For instance, you can type **ftp.cica.indiana.edu/pub/pc/win95/** instead of **ftp://ftp.cica.indiana.edu/pub/pc/win95/**.

Each file and directory is shown as a link. In the right-most column, you'll see a description of each item—*file* or *folder* (meaning directory). In the Size column, you can see the file size, so you'll know how big a file is before you transfer it. The Modified date can come in handy, too, providing an indication of how old the file is. (Unfortunately Internet Explorer drops the year from the date.)

Click a directory link to see the contents of that directory. Explorer will display another Web document, showing the contents of that directory. There's also a link back to the previous directory—the *Up one level* link, at

Forward slash or backslash?

If you're used to working in DOS and Windows, FTP-site directory names may appear pretty strange, for two reasons. First, I've used a forward slash (/) rather than a backslash (\) to separate each directory in the path. In the DOS world, we use a backslash (\), but in the UNIX world—and most of the Internet still runs on UNIX computers—the forward slash character (/) is used instead. The directory names are often long, too. In DOS, you can't have directories with more than 12 characters in the name (if you include a period and an extension). Of course in Windows 95 you *can,* as this new operating system allows long file and directory names. And UNIX computers allow long names, too.

the top of the page. (This is not the same as the browser's Back command, of course. It takes you to the parent directory, the one of which the current directory is a subdirectory.)

Fig. 13.1
Using Your Web browser as an FTP program.

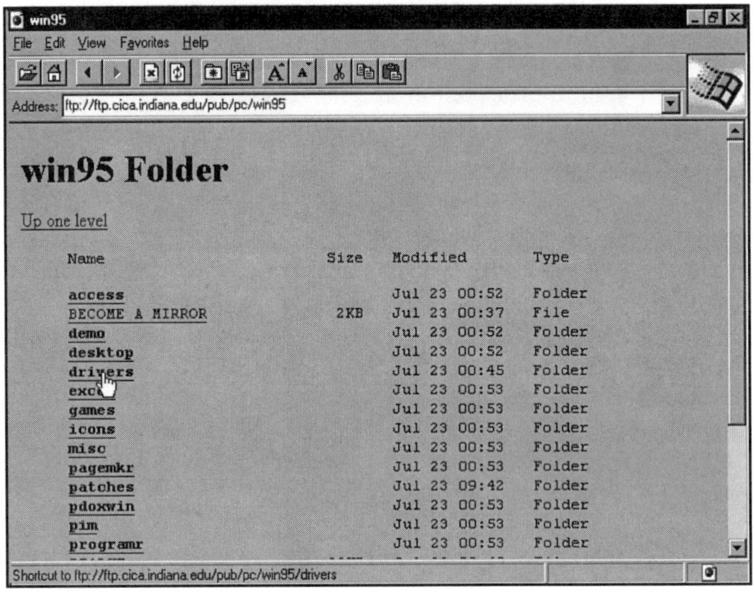

TIP **Don't forget Archie! Archie is a system that lets you search an** index of FTP sites throughout the world for just the file you need. See "How Can I Find Files," later in this chapter, for more information.

What happens when you click a link to a file? The same thing that would happen if you did so from a true Web document. If Explorer can display or play the file type, it will; if it can't, it will try to send it to the associated application; if there is no associated application, it will ask you what to do with it, allowing you to save it on the hard disk. This all works in the same way as it does when you are at a Web site—Explorer looks at the file type and acts accordingly. (See chapters 9 to 11 for more information.)

How can I find anything?

Finding files at an FTP site is often a little difficult. There are no conventions for how such sites should be set up, so you often have to dig through directories that look as if they might contain what you want, until you actually find what you want.

Remember, though, that Explorer can display text files. When you first get to an FTP site, look for files that say INDEX, README, DIRECTORY, and so on. These often contain information that will help you find what you need. The more organized sites even contain text files with full indexes of their contents, or at least lists of the directories and the types of files you'll find.

TIP **Many FTP sites are now accessible directly through Web** documents. For instance, instead of going to **ftp:// ftp.cica.indiana.edu/ pub/pc/win95/**, you could go to **http://www.cica.indiana.edu/**.

How can I find files?—working with Archie

With millions of files to choose from, and thousands of FTP sites spread around the Internet, it's difficult to know where to go to find the file you need. That's why Archie was developed.

Designed by a few guys at McGill University in Canada, *Archie* is a system that indexes FTP sites, listing the files that are available at each site. Archie lists several million files at thousands of FTP sites, and provides a surprisingly quick way to find out where to go to grab a file in which you are interested. Well, sometimes. As you'll find out, Archie is extremely busy, sometimes too busy to help you!

More client/server stuff

As with many other Internet systems, Archie is set up using a "client/server" system. An Archie *server* is a computer that periodically takes a look at all the Internet FTP sites around the world, and builds a list of all their available files. Each server builds a database of those files. An Archie *client* program can then come along and search the server's database, using it as an index. Your Web browser is *not* an Archie client. That is, there is no **archie://** URL! Rather, you'll have to use an Archie interface on the Web. There are dozens of these. Go to **http://web.nexor.co.uk/archie.html** to find a list. Just in case that's busy, here are several Archie sites you can try:

http://www.lerc.nasa.gov/Doc/archieplex.html
http://hoohoo.ncsa.uiuc.edu/archie.html
http://src.doc.ic.ac.uk/archieplexform.html

When you arrive at an Archie site, what sort of search are you going to do? Most of these sites offer both forms and non-forms versions. Internet Explorer is a forms-capable browser, though. That is, it can display the forms components we've seen earlier—text boxes, command buttons, option buttons, and so on. So select the forms search.

TIP **It's generally believed in Internet-land that it doesn't matter** much which Archie server you use because they all do much the same thing; some are simply a few days more recent than others. This isn't always true. Sometimes you may get very different results from two different servers. If, for example, one server finds two "hits," another might find seven.

How do I search?

In figure 13.2 you can see an example of an Archie form, this one at Imperial College in London located at **http://src.doc.ic.ac.uk/archieplexform.html**. The simplest way to search is to type a filename, or part of a filename, into the What Would You Like To Search For? text box and press Enter (or click on the Start Search button). For instance, if you are trying to find the WS_FTP program I told you about earlier in this chapter, you could type **WS_FTP** and press Enter.

Archie searches are often very slow. In fact they often simply don't work, because the Archie server you are working with is busy (I'll show you how to choose another server in a moment). You will see a listing of links to the WS_FTP files. These are links to the host (the computer that contains the file you are looking for), the directory on the host that contains the file you want, or directly to the file you want. For instance, if you clicked on one of the *ws_ftp.zip* links, Explorer would begin transferring the file.

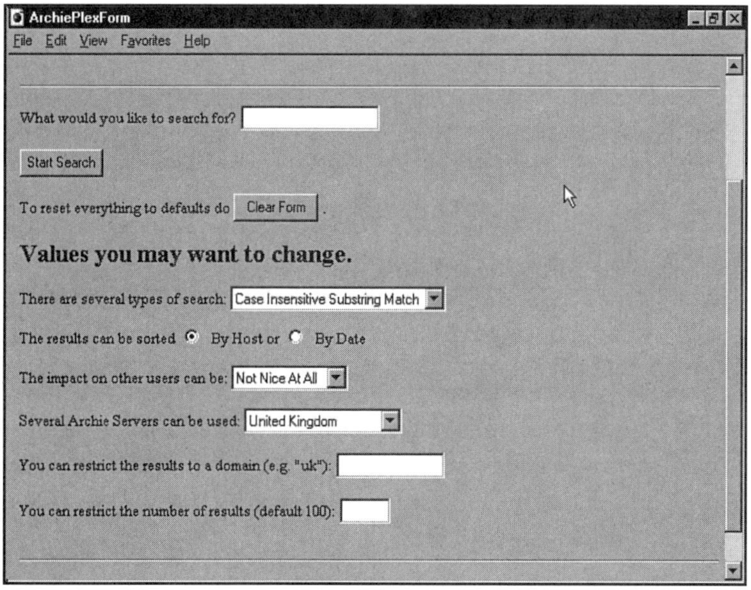

Fig. 13.2
The dozens of Archie Web sites provide a way for you to search Archie from your browser.

TIP **Remember, you can choose Edit, Find, to search the list of files.** For instance, if you are searching for WS_FTP, you don't really want the WS_FTP.ZIP files; those are probably the 16-bit versions, for Windows 3.1. Rather, search for `WS_FTP32` to find the 32-bit versions, for Windows 95.

Archie's options

Below the text box are some more components, which provide more options for your search. Here's what you'll find:

Search Type—There are four types of searches, which I'll explain in a moment.

Sort By—The list of files that is returned to you may be sorted by file date, or according to the host containing the file. The file-date search is a good idea, as it will help you pick the latest version of the file.

Impact On Other Users—You can tell Archie that you are not in a hurry (so other users can go first), or that you want the results right away.

Archie Servers—There are Archie servers all over the world, and you can select the one you want to use from a list. If you find that the Archie server you tried is busy, or it can't find what you want, try another one. You might want to try servers in countries that are currently "asleep," and, therefore, less busy than during the day.

Restrict The Results To A Domain—You can tell the Archie server that you only want to see files in a particular domain (a particular host-computer type): UK (FTP sites in the United Kingdom), COM (commercial FTP sites), EDU (educational FTP sites) and so on.

Number Of Results—You can tell the Archie server how many results you want to see, though this setting is not always accurate. At the example site you saw in figure 13.2, for instance, the default is supposedly 100 entries. Yet the actual default setting seemed to be much less—more like 100 *lines* rather than *finds*.

What are the Search Types?

Before you begin searching for a file name, you should figure out the *type* of search that you want to use. You have the following choices:

Exact or **Exact Match**—You must type the exact name of the file for which you are looking.

Regex or **Regular Expression Match**—You will type a UNIX regular expression. That means that Archie will regard some of the characters in the word you type as wild cards. (If you don't understand regular expressions, you're better off avoiding this type of search.)

Sub or **Case Insensitive Substring Match**—This tells Archie to search within file names for whatever you type. That is, it will look for all names that match what you type, as well as all names that include the characters you typed. If you are searching for *ws_ftp*, for example, archie will find *ws_ftp* and *ws_ftp32*. Also, when you use a sub search, you don't need to worry about the case of the characters; Archie will find *ws_ftp* and *WS_FTP*.

Subcase or **Case Sensitive Substring Match**—This is like the sub search, except you need to enter the case of the word correctly: if you enter *ws_ftp*, Archie will find *ws_ftp* but not *WS_FTP*.

TIP **The Substring Matches *won't* always find filenames that contain** what you typed. That is, if you type **ws_ftp**, it may not find *ws_ftp32*, or it may only find one or two when there are many files named *ws_ftp32* at many FTP sites. Why? Because it will show you the *ws_ftp* matches before it shows you the *ws_ftp32* matches, so if there are a lot of *ws_ftp* matches it may exceed the find limit (see Number Of Results in the table under "Archie's options"). You can increase the number of results and search again, though, to see if there are any *ws_ftp32* files. Or search for *ws_ftp32*.

More often than not, you'll want to use the sub search (Case Insensitive Substring Match), and you'll probably find that sub has been set up as the default. It takes a little longer than the other types, but it's more likely to find what you are looking for.

You should know, however, that file names are not always set in stone. With thousands of different people posting millions of different files on thousands of different computers, sometimes file names get changed a little. If you have trouble finding something, try a variety of different possible combinations.

TIP **If you are looking for shareware, go to— http://vsl.cnet.com/. This** site lets you search for programs by description rather than filename.

14 Launching Telnet Sessions

In this chapter:

- **What is Telnet?**
- **Starting a Telnet session**
- **Using HYTELNET**
- **Logging on and choosing a terminal emulation type**
- **Changing Windows Telnet preferences, and keeping a record of the session**
- **IBM Mainframe (3270) sessions**

Explorer can't run Telnet sessions, but it can get you started. Here's how to run programs on computers all over the world . . . .

Telnet is a system that lets you log on to other computers that are connected to the Internet. You can play games, search library catalogs, dig through databases, and so on. Explorer can't do this for you directly; rather, it will start the Microsoft Telnet program that Windows 95 loaded onto your hard disk.

Many Internet users have private Telnet accounts. A researcher, for example, may have several computers he works on regularly, and may have been given a special login name and password by the administrators of those computers. But many computers also allow "strangers" into their systems. This is done on a purely voluntary basis, depending on the good will of the people who own or operate a particular computer. If a Telnet server is open to the public, anyone can get on the system and see what's available.

Starting Telnet

There are several ways to start Telnet sessions. You'll occasionally find links from Web documents to Telnet sites (using the **telnet://** URL). Clicking on one of these links will launch Microsoft Telnet. A good place to find loads of telnet:// links is at HYTELNET, which we'll look at next.

You can also start a Telnet session by typing **telnet://** followed by a Telnet host address into Explorer's Address text box and press Enter. For instance, if you type **telnet://pac.carl.org** and press Enter, Windows Telnet launches and connects to the Denver Public Library's site. (Type PAC and press Enter to log on.)

When Telnet opens, choose Connect, Remote System, type the Telnet address into the Host Name text box, and press Enter.

You can also open Telnet directly. It's TELNET.EXE in the Windows directory. (You may want to place a shortcut on your desktop or Start menu, so you can open it directly, without having to open Internet Explorer first.) Whichever method you use, Windows Telnet opens, and begins the Telnet session.

Using HYTELNET

Here's a good place to start if you want to find some interesting Telnet sites: **http://www.cc.ukans.edu/hytelnet_html/START.TXT.html**. This will take you to the Web-document version of HYTELNET, a Telnet directory, from where you can launch Telnet sessions on computers all over the place. (Also see the directories mentioned in chapter 12, which have links to Telnet and other resources on the Internet.) In figure 14.1 you can see the first page of HYTELNET. The two most important links in this page are the *Library Catalogs* and *Other Resources* links. They take you to directories of Telnet sites (the other links take you to information about working with Telnet).

Fig. 14.1
The HYTELNET Web page is probably the best place to go to find interesting Telnet sites.

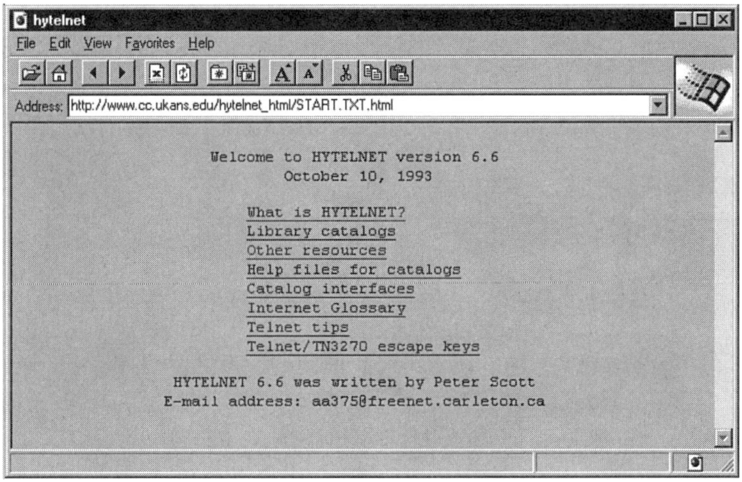

Click on the *Other Resources* link, for instance, and you'll be taken to another page with links to *Databases and bibliographies*, *Electronic books*, *Fee-Based Services*, *NASA databases* and more. Travel further down the hierarchy of documents, and you'll come to information about individual Telnet services, such as the one in figure 14.2. This shows information about the National Radio Astronomy Observatory Telnet site; it shows the Telnet address (ZIA.AOC.NRAO.EDU or 146.88.1.4), and the name you must use to log in once connected. It also shows a list of commands you can use once connected. Note that it also has a link; the word *telnet* is a link that, when clicked on, launches Windows Telnet and begins the Telnet session.

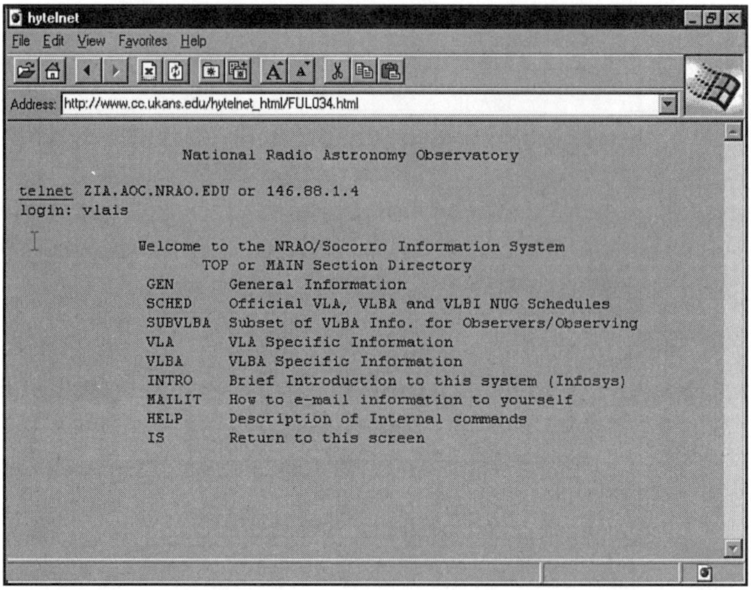

hytelnet
File Edit View Favorites Help
Address: http://www.cc.ukans.edu/hytelnet_html/FUL034.html
National Radio Astronomy Observatory
telnet ZIA.AOC.NRAO.EDU or 146.88.1.4
login: vlais
Welcome to the NRAO/Socorro Information System
TOP or MAIN Section Directory
GEN General Information
SCHED Official VLA, VLBA and VLBI NUG Schedules
SUBVLBA Subset of VLBA Info. for Observers/Observing
VLA VLA Specific Information
VLBA VLBA Specific Information
INTRO Brief Introduction to this system (Infosys)
MAILIT How to e-mail information to yourself
HELP Description of Internal commands
IS Return to this screen

Fig. 14.2
HYTELNET provides information about the Telnet site, so you'll know what login name to use to work with the system, for instance.

I'm connected—what next?

After Windows Telnet has connected to the Telnet site, you'll have to log in. To do so you'll need to know the account name you should use. HYTELNET describes Telnet sites, including the required account names. And when you find a Telnet site described in a book or magazine the account name is often included. In some cases you *won't* have to log in—the computer will let you right in, without asking for further information. And in other cases, the introductory screen you see when you first connect may tell you what to use.

When you connect to a Telnet session, you often have to identify the type of computer terminal you are using. Of course, you are using a PC, but your Microsoft Telnet program can **emulate** (pretend to be) a standard terminal program. By default, it's set to emulate a VT-100 terminal, which is good because the VT-100 setting works in most cases you'll run into. If you run into a site that doesn't like the VT-100 setting—perhaps the text on your screen isn't displayed properly during the session—you can try changing the emulation, although you don't have many choices. (Okay, you have only *one* other option, actually.)

Choose Terminal, Preferences to see the dialog box shown in figure 14.3. This box lets you change the emulation to VT-52. You can modify a few other settings, although you probably won't need to:

- **Local Echo** Select this if you can't see the text you type in the session.
- **Blinking Cursor** Select this if you want to make the text cursor flash on and off.
- **Block Cursor** Select this to make the text cursor a block (rather than an underline).
- **VT100 Arrows** Select this to make the arrow keys work in the session; pressing an arrow key would move a selection up and down a text menu, for instance.
- **Buffer Size** You can increase this setting to specify how many lines the session should save. A scroll bar will be added to the window, so you can scroll back up to see what happened earlier.

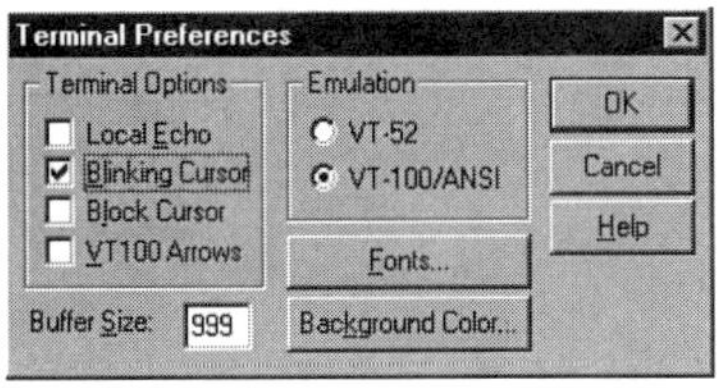

Fig. 14.3
The Terminal Preferences dialog box lets you set up your Telnet session.

You can also click on the Fonts and Background Color buttons to change the appearance of the window.

Working in a Telnet session

Every Telnet system is different. Windows Telnet is simply a way for you to transfer what you type to the computer you have connected to, and for the computer to send text back to you. In effect you've turned your computer into a dumb terminal connected to another computer, so you have to follow the rules of that system. You'll have to read any menu and command options carefully, to see what you can do. In figure 14.4 you can see an example of a Telnet session once you've logged on; this is CARL, the Colorado Alliance of Research Libraries. (You can reach this from HYTELNET at **http://www.cc.ukans.edu/hytelnet_html/US011.html**, or directly by typing **telnet://161.98.1.68** and pressing Enter.

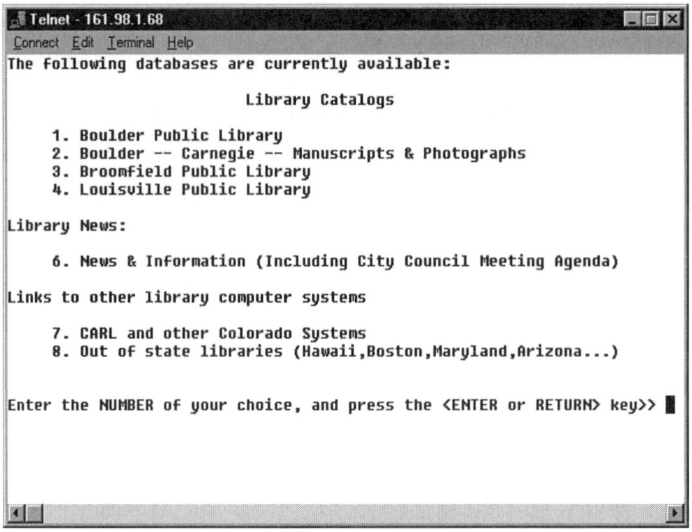
Telnet - 161.98.1.68
Connect Edit Terminal Help
The following databases are currently available:
Library Catalogs
1. Boulder Public Library
2. Boulder -- Carnegie -- Manuscripts & Photographs
3. Broomfield Public Library
4. Louisville Public Library
Library News:
6. News & Information (Including City Council Meeting Agenda)
Links to other library computer systems
7. CARL and other Colorado Systems
8. Out of state libraries (Hawaii,Boston,Maryland,Arizona...)
Enter the NUMBER of your choice, and press the <ENTER or RETURN> key>>

Fig. 14.4
Using CARL, an online library catalog, through Microsoft Telnet.

If you want to keep a record of your session, choose Terminal, Start Logging. When the Open Log File dialog box opens, enter a file name and select a directory, and then choose OK. From that point on (until you close the session or choose Terminal, Stop Logging), all the text that appears on the screen will be placed in the log file. You can also copy text from the session; drag the mouse pointer across the text (or choose Edit, Select All), and then choose Edit, Copy. When you've finished with your session, close the window, or choose Connect, Disconnect.

Telnet can be slow—*very* slow—sometimes. On occasion, you may type something, and not see what you have typed for several seconds or even several minutes. It depends on the amount of network traffic going that way, the number of people working on that machine at that time, and the amount of traffic on your service provider's computer. If you find a particular task to be too slow, you should probably come back later. If it's always slow at that Telnet site, maybe you can find another site with the same services.

Another way to start Telnet

As you've already seen, you don't have to start a Telnet session from the Web browser; you can start the program directly by running the TELNET.EXE file in the Windows directory. This time, however, Windows Telnet won't connect to a Telnet site—it doesn't know which one to use.

However, you'll discover that Telnet has a little history list. You can connect to a site you used earlier by opening the Connect menu and choosing one of the previous sessions listed at the bottom of the menu. You can also choose Connect, Remote System, and select a host from the Host Name dropdown list box (or type a host into the Host Name box), then click on the Connect button.

IBM mainframe Telnet sites

Some Telnet sites are on IBM mainframes running "3270" software. You can connect to these sites using the **tn3270://** URL. This works just like the telnet:// URL; in fact, Windows Telnet will open and connect to the tn3270 site.

In 3270 mode you usually type something at a prompt and press **Enter** or a function key (a *PF key* in 3270-speak). If you connect to a 3270 site, look around for instructions about working at that site.

TIP **For more tips about using Telnet, go to HYTELNET (http://www.cc.ukans.edu/hytelnet_html/START.TXT.html)**, and click on the *Telnet tips* and *Telnet/TN3270 escape keys* links.

15 Reading Newsgroups from the Web

In this chapter:

- **Opening newsgroups from Internet Explorer**
- **What is the newsgroup hierarchy system?**
- **Reading newsgroup messages**
- **Where have the messages gone?**
- **Responding to messages, and starting your own conversations**
- **Grabbing sounds and pictures from newsgroups**

There are thousands of discussion groups—called newsgroups—on the Internet. And you can get to them through Internet Explorer . . . .

Here's another Internet tool that you may be able to launch from Explorer—the newsgroups. Newsgroups are discussion groups. Pick a subject, visit the group, read people's messages, respond, start your own "threads" or "conversations," and so on. There are tens of thousands of Internet newsgroups spread around the world, on every conceivable subject.

Now, you can't get to all these newsgroups through your service provider. Most Internet newsgroups are of local interest only, and are not distributed throughout the world. But thousands are, through a system known as **UseNet**. Each online service has to decide which of these UseNet newsgroups it wants to subscribe to. Service providers typically provide from 3,000 or 4,000 groups to around 10,000 or 12,000. Enough to keep a chronic insomniac *very* busy.

> ***Plain English, please!***
>
> The Internet uses the word "news" ambiguously. Often, when you see a reference to news somewhere on the Internet, it refers to the messages left in newsgroups (not, as most real people would imagine, journalists' reports on current affairs). Newsgroups are, in most cases, discussion groups, though there are some newsgroups that contain real news—real journalism—stories.

What's this got to do with Internet Explorer?

This book is about Internet Explorer, so we're not really concerned with finding a newsgroup about a particular subject. If you want to use a newsgroup, use your newsgroup program. For instance, if you are an MSN member, use the Go word **Internet** to go to the Internet Center forum. (To use an MSN Go word from MSN Central, choose Edit, Go to, Other Location, type the word, and press Enter.) You'll find icons there that lead you to lists of thousands of newsgroups.

Where does Internet Explorer come in, then? Now and again you'll find Web documents that contain links to newsgroups. For instance, just last night I was showing the Web to a friend who's a songwriter. We went to Yahoo (see chapter 8), and followed the hierarchy down to Entertainment:Music: Usenet. (You can go directly to this document with this URL: **http://www.yahoo.com/Entertainment/Music/Usenet/**.) This document provides links to information about dozens of music-related newsgroups: a variety of alt.music newsgroups (alt.music.prince, alt.music.producer, and so on), rec.music.info, rec.music.marketplace, rec.music.misc, and rec.music.reviews. You'll find information about each newsgroup—a short description and the e-mail address of the person running the group—and a link to the group. When you click on the link—a **news:** link—Internet Explorer will launch the MSN newsgroup program, and load the newsgroup (see fig. 15.1).

TIP **Another good search site that references newsgroups is the new** Jump City (http://www.jumpcity.com/). You can select a subject, and you'll find a list of related Web sites and newsgroups.

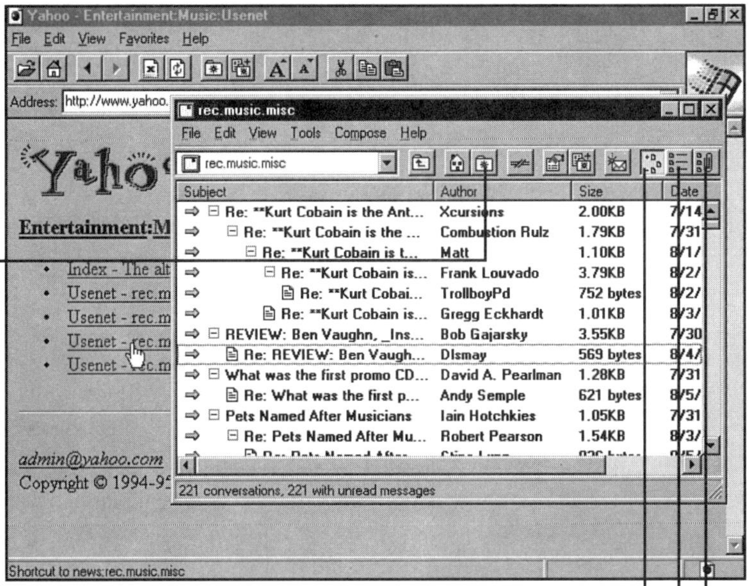

Fig. 15.1
If you have the right software, you can launch the newsgroup program from the Web.

Q&A ***Why didn't Explorer launch my newsgroup program and load the newsgroup?***

There are three possible reasons. First, you are not an MSN member, or don't have a compatible newsgroup program installed (see "But I don't have MSN!", below). Or perhaps your service provider (MSN, if you are an MSN member), doesn't subscribe to that particular newsgroup. These **news:** links call your service provider's newsgroup system and ask for the group. If it's not on your service provider's system, you won't get it.

Finally, if you are working with MSN, you may have chosen a group you do not have access to. MSN keeps the alt. groups off-limits to everyone (because they tend to be a little naughty). To get access you must apply by filling out a form. Go to the Internet Center forum for more information.

There is another way to open a newsgroup. You can type **news:** followed by the newsgroup name into the Address box and press Enter. For instance, you can type **news:alt.aliens.visitors** to get to that group. (Note that the news: URL does *not* have the two forward slashes after the colon.)

But I don't have MSN!

Ah, that's a shame. Because right now you can only use a link to a newsgroup if you are an MSN member. Internet Explorer has been set up to use the MSN newsgroup/BBS program, and if you don't have that installed correctly (and you don't, if you are not an MSN member), you'll get an error message.

That's not to say that pretty soon you won't find other newsgroup programs that will be Internet Explorer compatible. Software publishers may release such programs soon. But at the time of writing there were none available, so you're out of luck. I suggest that if you run across a **news**: link to a newsgroup you want to view, you copy the newsgroup name and open your newsgroup program and load the group from there.

The newsgroup hierarchies

Before we look at how to work in a newsgroup, let's quickly learn about the newsgroup hierarchies. Newsgroup names use a hierarchical naming system. The first name is the top level. For instance, in *soc.couples.intercultural* the *soc.* bit is the top level. Below that are sublevels. There are many sublevels within the *soc.* level, just one of which is *couples*. Then, within the *couples* level are newsgroups, and perhaps more sublevels—one group below the couples level is called *intercultural*. Thus the full name of this newsgroup is *soc.couples.intercultural*. The top-level UseNet groups are shown in the following table.

Top level	Subject matter
comp	Computer-related subjects
news	Information about newsgroups themselves, including software used to read newsgroup messages and information about finding and using newsgroups
rec	Recreational topics—hobbies, sports, the arts, and so on
sci	Science; discussions about research in the "hard" sciences—physics, chemistry, and so on—as well as some social sciences
soc	A wide range of social issues, such as discussions about different types of societies and subcultures, as well as sociopolitical subjects
talk	Debate about politics, religion, and anything else that's controversial
misc	Stuff. Looking for jobs, selling things, a forum for paramedics. You know, *stuff*

Not all newsgroups are true UseNet groups. Many are local groups, although they may be distributed internationally—through UseNet (don't worry about it, it doesn't matter). Such newsgroups are known as **Alternative Newsgroups Hierarchies**. So there are other top-level groups, as shown in the following table.

Top level	Subject matter
alt	"Alternative" subjects; often subjects that many people would consider "inappropriate," pornographic, or just weird. Can also be simply interesting stuff, but the newsgroup has been created in an "unauthorized" manner to save time and hassle
bionet	Biological subjects
bit	A variety of newsgroups from the BITNET network

continues

Top level	Subject matter
biz	Business subjects, including advertisements
clari	Clarinet's newsgroups from "official" and commercial sources—mainly UPI news stories and various syndicated columns
courts	Related to law and lawyers
de	Various German-language newsgroups
fj	Various Japanese-language newsgroups
gnu	The Free Software Foundation's newsgroups
hepnet	Discussions about high-energy and nuclear physics
ieee	The Institute of Electrical and Electronics Engineers' newsgroups
info	A collection of mailing lists formed into newsgroups at the University of Illinois
k12	Discussions about K–12 education
relcom	Russian-language newsgroups, mainly distributed in the former Soviet Union
vmsnet	Subjects of interest to VAX/VMS computer users

Now and again you'll see other groups, too, often local newsgroups from particular countries, towns, universities, and so on.

" ***Plain English, please!***

It's sometimes said that alt. stands for anarchists, lunatics, and terrorists. (Said by whom? By me, though I freely admit I stole this little quip—I wish I could remember from where.) The alt. groups can be very strange; they're also some of the most popular groups on the Internet. **"**

Working in the newsgroups

Let's see how to work in the newsgroups. I'm going to describe the MSN newsgroup program; that's the program that most Internet Explorer users will be using. In fact, as you've just seen, that's the *only* newsgroup program that Explorer users *can* work with for the moment. If things change and by the time you read this another Explorer-compatible newsgroup program has been released, you'll still be able to figure out much of what is going on from the following description. The specific commands may be different, but the concepts should be the same.

TIP **Go to http://www.w3.org/hypertext/DataSources/News/Groups/Overview.html** to find a large list of newsgroups, with links that will open the groups.

The newsgroup window is exactly the same as the MSN BBS windows; you can see an example in figure 15.1. If you are used to working in MSN's BBS windows, though, you should be aware that there are some things you can't do. You can't use all the fancy fonts and message formatting—the Internet newsgroup system is based on ASCII text. Nor can you insert OLE (Object Linking and Embedding, a Windows data-sharing system) objects or files into your messages (but see "Pictures (and sounds and more) from words," later in this chapter).

TIP **When you view BBS messages, text wraps from line to line, as in a** word processor. When viewing newsgroups, however, this doesn't happen, because each line is, in effect, a separate paragraph. Expand the window size to remove the jagged edge from the right side of the text.

Viewing the messages

When you open the newsgroup, a list of messages appears on-screen. At the bottom of the window, in the status bar, you see something like *8 conversations, with 8 unread messages*. This *should* mean that there are eight different message threads (I'll explain that in a moment), and within those threads there are eight different messages. However, at the time of writing the unread messages portion wasn't working properly; you might have 11 unread messages, for instance.

So what's a **conversation** or **thread**? When you post a message to a newsgroup by choosing Compose, New Message, you aren't replying to anyone. You've just created a thread, or what the MSN newsgroup program refers to as a conversation. Then, a few hours later, someone else reads your message and replies. The message, because it's a reply, is part of the conversation you began. A few minutes later, someone else sends a message to the newsgroup—this time, it's not a reply, but a new message. This is the beginning of another thread or conversation.

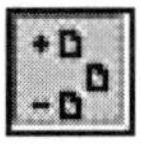

There are three ways to view messages. The default is the Conversation View. This is the view that you can see in figure 15.1. If your messages don't look like this, click the Conversation View toolbar icon, or choose View, Conversation.

In this view, all messages are grouped together in the conversations—pretty logical, eh? You can see a conversation by looking for the little plus (+) and minus (–) signs in the left column. Click the + sign to expand the conversation—MSN will show the first "level" of responses in the conversation. (If you hold the Shift key while you click the + icon, you expand all levels of the conversation.) Click the – sign to "collapse" a conversation, to remove all the listings below the first in a conversation. You can also type **+** and – to expand and collapse conversations.

In figure 15.1 you can see a newsgroup with multiple "layers" of responses in a conversation. Why are these layers ragged, though? Why, for instance, is the fifth message indented to the right, then the sixth indented to the left? Each message is indented to the right from the message to which it is a response. Thus the fifth message is a response to the fourth, but the sixth message—although it was sent after the fifth—is a response to the third.

There's a command that lets you expand all the conversations in a newsgroup without clicking each + sign. Simply choose View, Expand All Conversations. To collapse all the conversations at once, choose View, Collapse All Conversations.

Using the list and file views

Before we go on, let's quickly look at the other two types of View. First, there's the List View. Click the List View toolbar button, or choose View, List. You see that the newsgroup messages are no longer grouped by conversation. Each message in the newsgroup is shown on a line by itself—there's no indentation of messages, no conversations to expand. How are the messages ordered, then? According to the option chosen on the menu that appears when you choose View, Arrange Messages. You can place the messages in chronological order (oldest first), by size (smallest first), or alphabetically by author or subject. Simply click a column heading to sort the messages: click Author to sort by author name, Size to sort by size, and so on.

There's also a File View, but you can ignore this. It's intended for use in the MSN BBSes, not newsgroups. If you select this view in the newsgroup, all the messages are removed from the window.

Where have all the messages gone?

The first time you open a newsgroup, you see all the messages from that newsgroup currently held by your service provider (in this case MSN, of course). How long a message stays in the newsgroup depends on how busy that newsgroup is and how much hard-disk space the service provider wants to allow for the newsgroup messages—eventually messages are removed.

You don't necessarily see all the messages held by the newsgroup, though. You will when you first enter the newsgroup. But when you return to the newsgroup in a later MSN session, you'll see all the messages held by the newsgroup *except* those that have been marked as Read. (Actually, to be more specific, you will see messages that have been marked as Read if they are part of a conversation that includes one or more messages marked as Unread.)

Why didn't I just say "messages that you haven't read?" Because there's a slight difference. MSN has no way of knowing which messages you've read—it can't see what you are doing. Instead it has a way of marking messages that it thinks you've read. And it provides you with a way to mark messages as Read even if you haven't read them (in effect, providing a way for you to tell it that you don't want to see the messages).

Marking your messages as Read

When you open a message, MSN automatically marks the message as Read. You can also mark messages several other ways:

- Click a message and choose Tools, Mark Message as Read.
- Click a message and choose Tools, Mark Conversation as Read—all the messages in that conversation are marked as Read.
- Choose Tools, Mark All Messages as Read. Every message in the newsgroup window is marked as Read.

How can you tell if a message has been marked as Read? Messages shown in the newsgroup window with bold text are Unread, the ones that *aren't* bold have been marked as Read. Also, notice the gray arrow icon in the left column. This means that the conversation contains an Unread message (even if the first message in the conversation has been Read).

Why bother marking messages as Read? To tell MSN that you don't want to see them when you come back to the newsgroup in a later session. For instance, you might get a couple of messages into a conversation and realize it's gibberish. Choose Tools, Mark Conversation as Read, and you don't see the rest of the messages the next time you open the newsgroup window. Or maybe you quickly read all the message Subject lines and find that nothing interests you—mark them *all* as Read so you see only new messages the next time.

Q&A ***I read a few messages, then logged off. Now I realize that I need to read them again. How can I get them back?***

Go to the newsgroup window and choose Tools, Show All Messages. This tells MSN to display all the newsgroup messages, even ones you've read before. Of course, if the message you want to see is no longer held by MSN, you're out of luck. Note also that if you select this command in one session, it will be on the next time you open the newsgroup—so remember to turn it off before you leave. (In some newsgroups using this command may display hundreds of messages and take a *very* long time.)

Notice that there are even commands for marking messages as Unread. Perhaps you've read a message, but want to make sure it appears the next time you open the newsgroup; click the message and then choose Tools, Mark Message as Unread (or Tools, Mark Conversation as Unread if you want to save the entire conversation). There's no Mark All Messages as Unread, though; if you want to do this choose Edit, Select All, then choose Tools, Mark Conversation as Unread.

TIP **You'll find that there are lots of menu commands in the news-**group window that are not appropriate for newsgroups. For instance, View, Refresh is unlikely to do anything. These commands are intended for use in the MSN BBSes.

Reading messages

You can probably figure out how to read a message without my help—just double-click it, of course. Here are all the ways you can open a newsgroup message.

- Double-click the message.
- Click once on the message, and then press Enter.
- Right click a message and choose Open.
- Click a message and choose File, Open.

You can select multiple messages (hold down the Ctrl key while you click each one), then use one of the last three methods.

Once you've read the message, click the X button in the top right corner to close the window. Let's take a look at the newsgroup message window, the window that appears when you read a message. You can see an example in figure 15.2.

Fig. 15.2
You can read, scroll through, and save a newsgroup message.

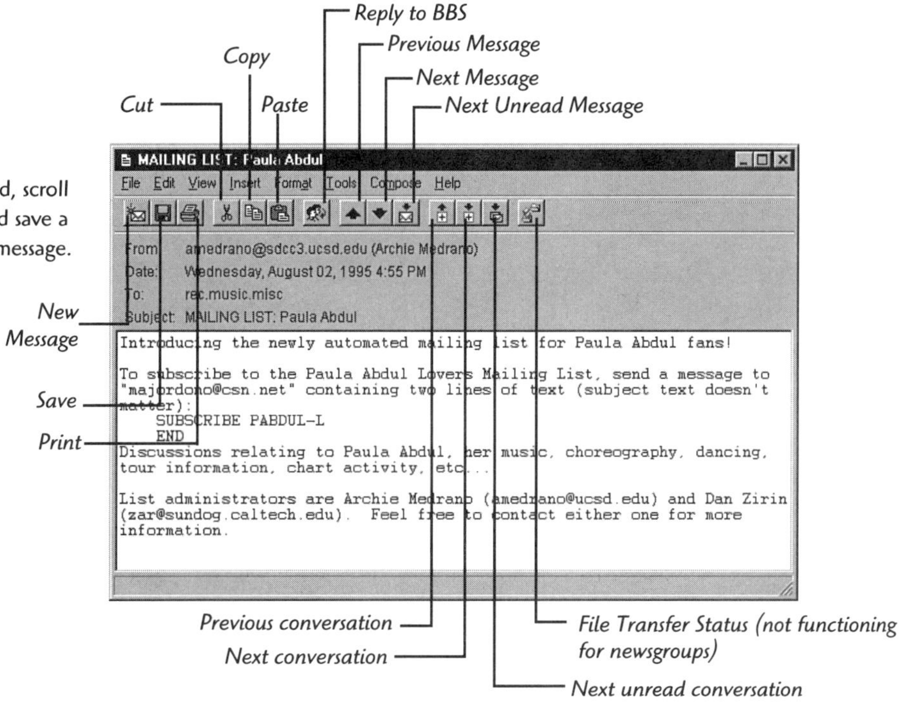

You can move around in the message using the scroll bar and the keyboard (use Page Up, Page Down, Ctrl+Home, and Ctrl+End). You can also highlight text and save to the Windows Clipboard using the Cut and Copy toolbar buttons and the Edit menu.

Moving between messages

You don't need to close a message window before opening the next message. You can use one of the toolbar buttons or menu commands to move directly to another message.

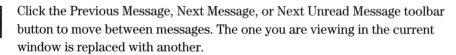

Click the Previous Message, Next Message, or Next Unread Message toolbar button to move between messages. The one you are viewing in the current window is replaced with another.

If you decide that you don't want to read any more messages in the current conversation, you can skip all the other messages by clicking the Previous Conversation, Next Conversation, or Next Unread Conversation buttons.

If you prefer, use the equivalent commands in the View menu, or use the keyboard commands to quickly jump between messages (you can find these in the View menu, too).

Saving and printing messages

If you run across a message that you feel may be useful later, you should probably save it or print it. Simply marking it as Unread isn't good enough, because messages are eventually dropped by the newsgroup, so sooner or later it simply won't be available.

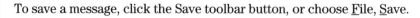

To save a message, click the Save toolbar button, or choose File, Save.

To print a message, click the Print toolbar button to send the message directly to the printer. Or choose File, Print; you'll see the normal Windows 95 Print dialog box, which lets you choose a printer, select the number of copies, and so on. You can also choose the File, Print Setup command to choose a printer.

Of course you can also highlight the text and copy it (press Ctrl+C), then paste it into another Windows application.

How do I send and respond to messages?

There are several ways to send messages, or to respond to messages. Use one of these techniques:

- To send a message that isn't a response—that is, to start a new conversation—choose Compose, New Message, or click the New Message toolbar button.

- To reply to someone's message, open the message and choose Compose, Reply to BBS, or click the Reply to BBS toolbar button. (Yes, I know this is a newsgroup, not a BBS—but as I mentioned, this is the MSN BBS program.)
- To reply to someone privately (send a message that *doesn't* appear in the newsgroup), choose Compose, Reply by E-mail.
- To send a copy of the message to someone else, choose Compose, Forward by E-mail.

If you select one of the E-mail options, you'll see Microsoft Exchange's New Message window. Otherwise, you'll see the newsgroup New Message window.

Using the New Message window

You can see an example of the New Message window in figure 15.3. To send a message, follow these steps:

1. Enter a message title into the Subject text box.
2. Then press the Tab key and begin entering your message.
3. When you've finished, click the Send toolbar button, or choose File, Post Message.
4. Away it goes.

   You don't see the message appear in the newsgroup window, though. Thanks to the way that newsgroup messages are distributed, you—and the other people reading the newsgroup—won't see the message turn up in the newsgroup for a day, maybe several days.

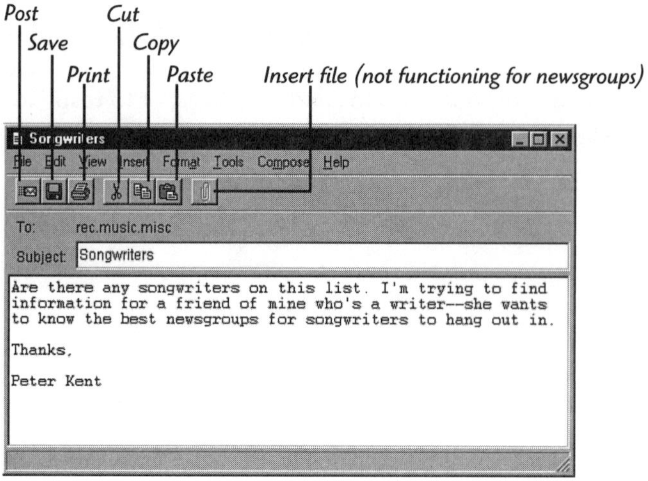

Fig. 15.3
An example of the New message Window

What's this gibberish message? ROT13

Now and again, especially in the more contentious newsgroups, you'll run into messages that seem to be gibberish. Everything's messed up, each word seems to be a jumbled mix of characters, almost as if the message has been encrypted. It has.

What you are seeing is **ROT13**, a very simple substitution cipher (one in which a character is substituted for another). It's actually very easy to read. ROT13 means rotated 13. In other words, each character in the alphabet has been replaced by the character 13 places further along. Instead of A you see N, instead of B you see O, instead of C you see P, and so on. Got it? So to read the message, all you need to do is substitute the correct characters. Easy. (Or *Rnfl*, I should say.)

For those of you in a hurry, there is an easier way. Choose Tools, ROT13 Encode/Decode, and like magic the message changes into real words (see fig. 15.4).

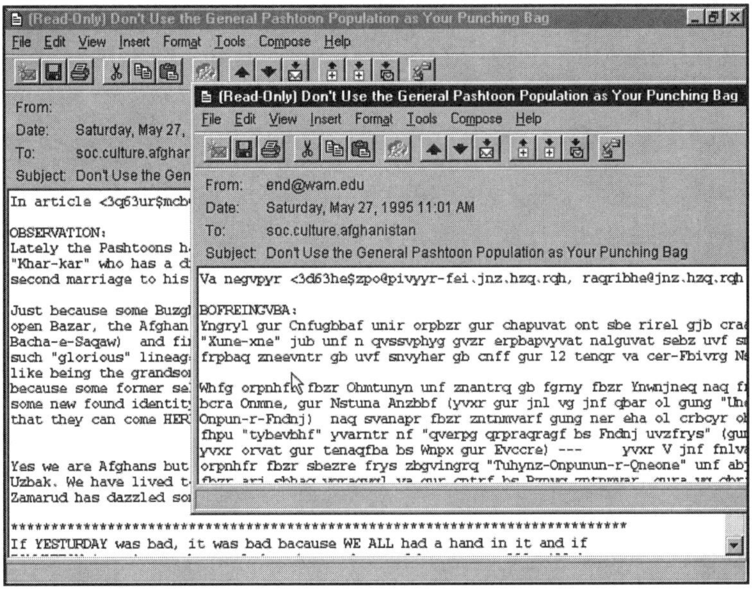

Fig. 15.4
An example of a ROT13 message, with the decoded version behind it.

So what's the point? Why encode a message with a system that is so ridiculously easy to break? People don't ROT13 messages as a security measure, in order to make them unreadable to all but those with the "secret key." After all, anyone with a decent newsgroup reader has the key. No, ROT13ing (if you'll excuse my use of the term as a verb) is a way of saying "if you read this message, you may be offended, so if you are easily offended, *don't read it!*" ROT13 messages are often crude, lewd, or just plain rude. Offensive. Nasty. Converting a message into ROT13 forces readers to decide whether or not they want to risk being offended. And if they do, then that's their problem.

I suspect the use of ROT13 is dying out as the Internet grows. Many new users know nothing about ROT13 because many new newsgroup programs don't let you read or create ROT13 messages.

Pictures (and sounds and more) from words

The newsgroups are simple ASCII text messages. You can't place any character into a message that is not in the standard ASCII character set. So if you want to send a computer file in a newsgroup message—maybe you want to send a picture, sound, or word processing document—you must convert it to ASCII.

You can do this using something called **Uuencode**. Here's how this system works. First, you take the file you want to send and convert it—Uuencode it—to ASCII text. Then you place the text into the message and send it off to the newsgroup. Now, the person reading the message sees a huge jumble of text (see fig. 15.5). If the reader wants to download it from the message, he must save the message in a text file (or, in some cases, place it in the Windows Clipboard), and then **Uudecode** it—convert it from ASCII to its original format. Sound complicated? It's really not, once you know what you're doing.

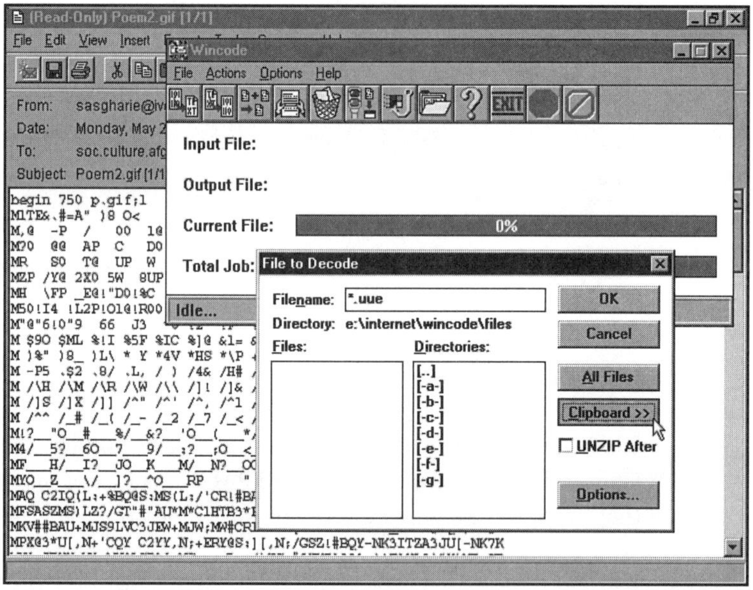

Fig. 15.5
Wincode helps you convert Uuencoded computer files in newsgroup messages back to their original formats. You can see the Uuencoded text in the newsgroup message window.

Perhaps MSN will eventually build Uuencode and Uudecode directly into the New Message and newsgroup windows (some other Internet newsreaders already have these capabilities). For now, however, you'll need to use a special utility. If you have Norton Navigator, the add-on utility collection from Symantec, you already have a Uuencode/decode utility, in Norton File Manager; choose File, Uuencode/decode. You can also use a freeware utility that you can find on the Internet—Wincode. You can find it at **ftp://ftp.cica.indiana.edu/pub/pc/win3/util/**. This site is very busy, and you may not be able to get through. You can also try searching for it using Archie (see chapter 13). Download and unzip Wincode. Read the README.TXT file for information on setting it up.

Grabbing that file

Let's start by grabbing a file from a newsgroup message. This can be a picture, sound, or anything else that can be placed in a computer file. For instance, in the **soc.culture.afghanistan** newsgroup, I found a Uuencoded picture of an Arabic poem. Here's what I did:

1. I opened the message and chose Edit, Select All to highlight the entire message.
2. I chose Edit, Copy, to copy the text to the Clipboard.
3. I opened Wincode and chose File, Decode.
4. In Wincode's File to Decode dialog box I clicked the Clipboard button—Wincode proceeded to decode the text that was in the Clipboard.
5. I saw a message saying *Error 045: Illegal DOS input filename.* This means that the file name given in the Uuencoded text is not correct (and if you look at the top of the message in figure 15.5 you can see that the file name on the first line of the message text is, for some reason, p.gif).
6. I chose OK in this message box, and Wincode displayed a text box into which I typed a new name.
7. I chose OK, and Wincode decoded the picture, placing it in the FILES subdirectory.

TIP **I've found that Wincode's Clipboard system doesn't always work.** If you have problems, save the message text in a file, select the file in Wincode's File to Decode dialog box, and choose OK.

Many Uuencoded files are split into several messages; you might see Subject lines that say something like `Picture.gif 1/3`, `Picture.gif 2/3`, or `Picture.gif 3/3`, for instance. This means that each message contains a portion of the Uuencoded file. In such a case, you would save each message (choose File, Save) in a separate text file. Wincode can pick up each message in sequence while it decodes—see the Wincode instructions for more information.

Part IV: At Work on the Web

16 E-mail, Finger, Chat, and More

In this chapter:

- **Using the mailto: URL**
- **Searching WAIS through the Web (through Gopher)**
- **What's Finger, and how do I use it?**
- **Chatting through the Web?**
- **How do I search for people?—Whois and X.500**
- **Online games**

We haven't finished yet—there are more Internet services available through Internet Explorer . . . .

We've looked at the major "non-Web" services that Explorer can help you with—Gopher, FTP and Archie, Telnet, and newsgroups. But there's more! You can send e-mail from your browser (well, launch your e-mail program, anyway), use the **finger** command, chat online, and use the WAIS database system.

Using the mailto: URL

The **mailto:** URL is used to launch an e-mail program, so you can send an Internet e-mail message. (Note, by the way, that this URL does *not* have the two slashes—//—after the colon.)

There are two ways to use a mailto: URL. You'll often find **mailto:** links at the bottom of Web documents; you'll see a link that says something like "click here to send e-mail to the author," or perhaps see the author's e-mail address. When you click on the link your e-mail program will open, and the new-message window will appear. (You may first see a dialog box that asks which profile you want to use; see your Microsoft Exchange documentation for information about profiles.) Your new message will be addressed to the e-mail address inside the mailto: link. Type a Subject, type your message, and send it.

Which e-mail program will open? Internet Explorer is set up to work with Microsoft Exchange, the Windows 95 messaging system. If you installed Exchange, along with the Internet e-mail service, then Exchange will open when you use a mailto: URL. (It may take a while—it's a little slow—but hang on and it will appear.)

If you haven't installed Exchange, the mailto: URL won't work, *unless* you've installed another, compatible e-mail program. At the time of writing Exchange was the *only* compatible program, though other companies may release Explorer-compatible e-mail programs eventually.

The other way to use the mailto: URL is to type it in the Address box, followed by an e-mail address, and press Enter, just as you would with an http:// or gopher:// URL. For instance, you might type **mailto:robinhood@sherwood.forest.com** and press Enter. This provides a quick way to open your e-mail system. You often see e-mail addresses in Web documents that have *not* been placed inside mailto: links. You can quickly copy the e-mail address to the Clipboard, type **mailto:** into the Address book, press Ctrl+V to paste the address after mailto:, and press Enter.

WAIS Database Searches

WAIS means Wide Area Information Server, and is a system that's been used for some time to allow Internet users to access information on hundreds of databases around the world.

The WAIS servers are one of the most infrequently used tools on the Internet, partly because the WAIS interface is rather confusing. You can get to the WAIS servers in several ways, in theory anyway. Many Gopher servers have links to WAIS servers—use Jughead or Veronica to find them. This is the easiest way to use a WAIS server, and in many cases the *only* way. Most browsers, Internet Explorer included, don't have direct WAIS support (though there is a **wais://** URL, Explorer can't use it).

When you find a WAIS entry at a Gopher site, you'll use it in a similar way to using Jughead or Veronica. Simply click on the link, and enter the search string into the dialog box or form that appears.

You'll find other WAIS-related links; links to information about how to work with WAIS, to lists of WAIS servers, and so on. The **gopher://gopher-gw.micro.umn.edu/11/WAISes/Everything** URL, for instance, will display a list of WAIS servers. Click on a link to search that server.

TIP **If you really want to use WAIS, you're probably better off finding a** WAIS program for Windows. You can use EINet WinWAIS (try **ftp://ftp.einet.net/einet/pc**) or WAIS for WINDOWS (also known as WinWAIS, from **ftp://ridgisd.er.usgs.gov/pub/wais/**).

Perhaps WAIS support will be added to Internet Explorer later. If so, you'll want to go to **http://www.w3.org/hypertext/Products/WAIS/Overview.html**. From here you can get to lists of WAIS servers, as well as a searchable index. Some of the links are **wais://** links, which you can't use now, but once Explorer can use the **wais://** URL, will take you right into the WAIS system.

Finger

The UNIX *finger* command lets you find information about someone's Internet account. If you typed **finger username@hostname** at a UNIX prompt and press Enter, you would see information about that person's real name, whether they are logged on, and so on. And, more importantly, you'll see the contents of their *.plan* file.

So finger is used to distribute information. And you can use finger from the Web, with a finger "gateway." The document at **http://www-bprc.mps.ohio-state.edu/cgi-bin/finger.pl** contains a form into which you can type anyone's email address and finger them. If you are lucky (it doesn't work with all addresses), you'll get back a document containing the finger information (see fig. 16.1).

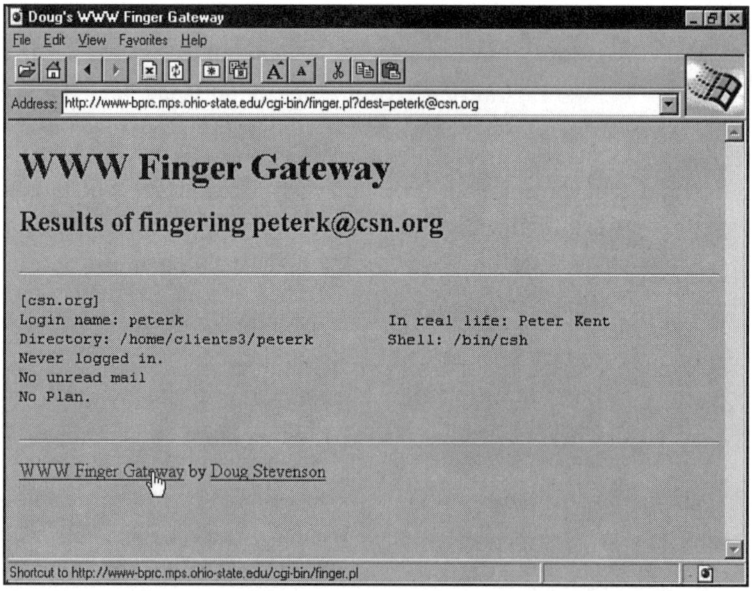

Fig. 16.1
I "fingered" pkent@csn.org, and got this message back, showing me his real name, and that this person has never logged in, has no unread e-mail, and no .plan file.

The sort of information you can get back depends on how the machine you are "fingering" has been set up. Some provide a lot of information, some just a little. Some computers even show you all the names of the people that match what you entered. For instance, if you fingered kent@csn.org you'd get a list of all the people with accounts on that computer whose real names and account names contain *kent*.

TIP **For more finger "gateways," search Yahoo (see chapter 8) for the** word finger, or go to **http://www.yahoo.com/Computers_and_Internet/Internet/World_Wide_Web/Gateways/Finger_Gateways/**.

If you go to **http://www.jou.ufl.edu/commres/jlist/JL_05.htm** you'll go to the Finger list in the Journalism List Web document. This contains links that will get finger information from a variety of sources, on a variety of subjects: auroral activity, NASA's daily news, a hurricane forecast, earthquake information, and all sorts of other, wonderful information. This information is stored in the account .plan files; when you finger the account (by clicking on a link), the contents of the .plan are sent to you. See figure 16.2 for an example.

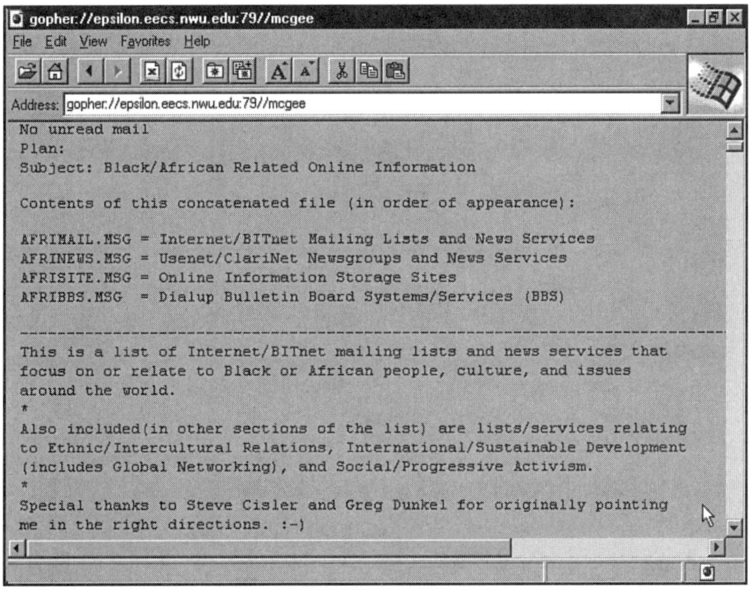

Fig. 16.2
Clicking on a link at **http://www.jou.ufl.edu/commres/jlist/JL_05.htm** used finger to retrieve this text document from someone's .plan file.

Chatting online

Chat is a service that isn't well developed on the Web, but now and again you may run into some kind of chat system. For instance, at **http://www.rock.net/webchat/rwchat.html** you'll find the RockWeb chat system. You type a message into a form and press Enter. Your "view" of the chat is then updated, so you can see your message (see fig. 16.3). If you know a bit of HTML (see chapter 17), you can even include HTML tags in your message, so you can use bold, italics, underlines, and so on—even include a link to somewhere. In other words, someone reading your message could click on the link in your message to go somewhere else. (If you are going to do this fancy stuff you'll probably want to prepare it beforehand in a word processor, copy it to the Clipboard, and paste it into the chat.)

Plain English, please!

A **chat** system is one that allows people to hold "conversations" in "real time." You type a message, and others can read it almost immediately, and respond to you.

If you want to be really geeky, you can tell the system to display a picture next to your name each time you "say" something in the conversation. You'll have to provide the picture, though, and enter a URL pointing to the picture on a system somewhere. (From what I've seen, very few people are using the fancy features that are available in this chat—mostly it's just plain old text.)

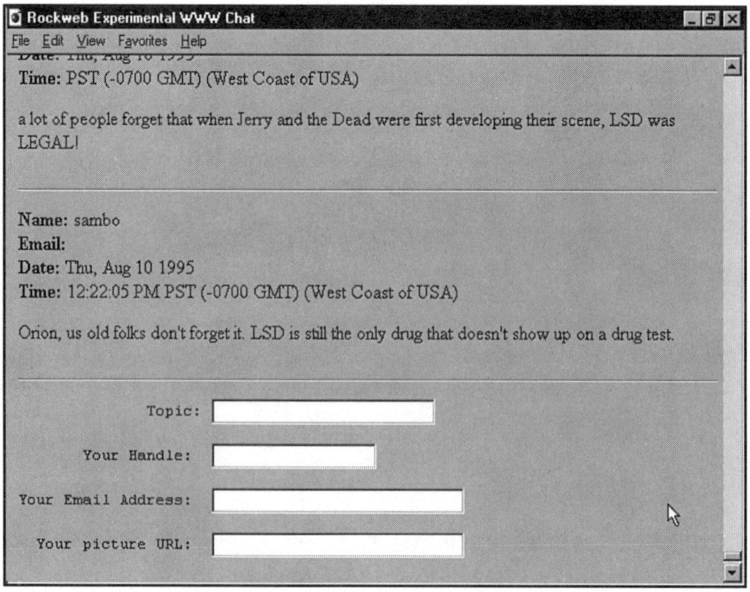

Fig. 16.3
RockWeb is a simple chat system with sophisticated (optional) features.

Whois and X.500

Whois is a system that lets you search for other Internet users. It's been around a long time, well before the Web was ever thought of. There's no direct way to use Whois from a Web browser, so you have to find a site with some kind of Whois interface. Try, for instance, **gopher://sipb.mit.edu/1B%3aInternet%20whois%20servers**. You'll find links to Whois servers around the world, mainly at universities. When you click on a link to one of the servers, you'll see a simple form into which you can type a name. Press Enter, and the server may, if you're lucky, search for that name.

Note, however, that these servers do not provide access to an Internet-wide directory. There is no such thing. Rather, they let you search a particular institution's directory. If you have a friend at the University of Canterbury, for instance, you can search the university's database for that person's information.

There's another system, X.500, which you can get through to at **gopher://go500gw.itd.umich.edu:7777/1** or **telnet://paradise.ulcc.ac.uk/**. With this system you will select a country or organization, then select from a list of areas or organizations, and so on. Eventually you'll get to a form into which you can type the name you want to search for.

Games reach the Web

Games have been very popular on the Internet for a long time. What, after all, were computers invented for? For passing the time while you could be working, of course. Until recently most games were text based; for example, in the MUDs (Multiple User Dimensions or Multiple User Dungeons) you would type instructions on the screen. You would type **left**, **right**, and so on, to tell the game program which way you wanted to move.

Now these games are reaching the Web. For instance, in figure 16.4 you can see the S.P.Q.R. game (**http://www.pathfinder.com/twep/rome/**), which is a role playing game (similar to a MUD), but in which you can actually see where you are going. Click on a part of the picture to go to another area of Rome (that's where the game is set). This game doesn't have the level of interaction that MUD aficionados will probably demand—you can't interact with other players—but I'm sure that's coming soon.

Fig. 16.4 Traveling through ancient Rome, in the S.P.Q.R. game.

TIP **To find a list of games on the Web, go to http://www.cs.cmu.edu/afs/andrew/org/kgb/www/zarf/games.html.**

The chess freaks among you may want to try some of the Web chess pages. These are linked to programs that allow you to play chess with other players, and which update a Web page to show each person's move. You can see an example of this in figure 16.5, a game that you can reach by going to **http://www.willamette.edu/~tjones/chessmain.html**.

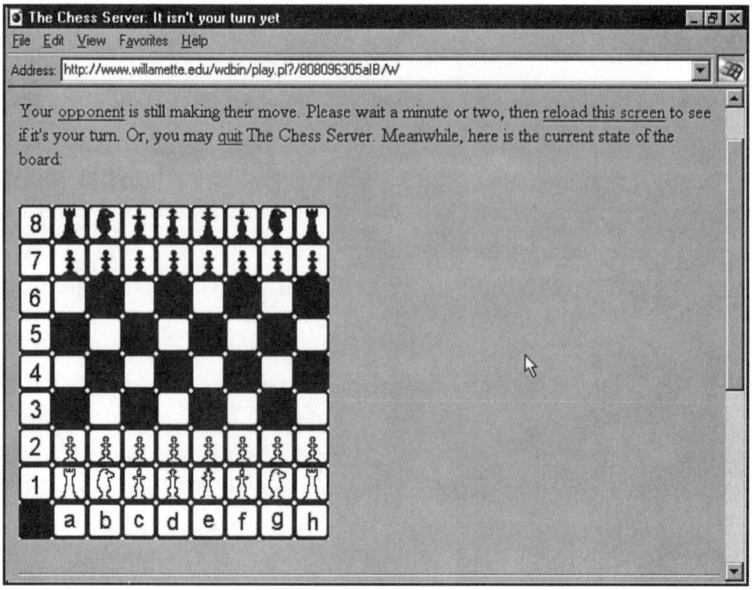

Fig. 16.5 Playing chess through the Web.

17

Create Your Own Home Page

In this chapter:

- **Why create your own Web pages?**
- **The basic HTML tags**
- **Setting your home (or start) page**
- **Links to other Web documents**
- **Creating a multi-document system**
- **Grabbing links and URLs from Web documents**

Feeling creative? You can learn how to create your own Web pages in less than an hour. . . . .

Publishing on the Web is surprisingly easy, and the first step to publishing should probably be creating your own home page. It's a great way to get a feel for how HTML works, and you'll produce something you can use, too.

What is a home page? Here's a quick refresher:

- It's the page that appears when you open Internet Explorer.
- It's the page that appears when you click on the Open Start Page toolbar button or choose File, Open Start Page.

As I've mentioned earlier in this book, there's currently some ambiguity about the term home page. The term *home page* has come to mean two things. The original meaning is the page that appears when you open your browser or use the Home command. The new meaning is a page that you have published on the Web, a page that others on the Web can view (as in "the Rolling Stones' home page"). Because of this confusion, the Explorer programmers chose to use the term *start page* instead of *home page* to refer to the page that appears when you open your browser. Whenever I use the term home page, I mean the one that opens when you open your browser.

Why bother with Web publishing?

Why bother creating your own Web pages? There are two reasons; so you can customize your own home (start) page, and so you can publish on the Web. While many people may not want to bother publishing their thoughts/ideas/inspiration/poetry/fiction/rantings on the Web, many may wish to customize the page that first appears when they open their Web browsers, so that's where we'll start.

Why create your own home (start) page, then? For these reasons:

- On the Internet, one size doesn't fit all. Everyone uses the Internet in a different way. The page provided by Microsoft may be okay to start with, but it won't have all the links you want, and may contain plenty that you don't want. For instance, maybe you prefer to use Yahoo to Lycos; why have a link to search systems that you don't use from your home page (see chapter 8)?

- The History and Favorites lists are very handy, but if you are going to use certain items from these lists frequently, wouldn't it be more convenient if you had them on your home page?
- Why not customize your home page with links across the Internet to where you want to go? Or have a home page, plus a series of documents on your hard drive linked to that home page: one document for work, one for music, one for newsgroups, one for whatever else. Then you can have links from the home page to those separate documents. Hey, let's try that!

First, the basics

You're about to learn about HTML, but don't be concerned that we are getting into very complicated stuff. HTML is remarkably simple. You'll have to pay attention, but don't expect to be blinded by science.

Remember that HTML files are simple ASCII text files, right? ASCII means American Standard Code for Information Interchange. This is a standard system used by computers to recognize text. An ASCII text file comprises the letters of the alphabet, the punctuation characters, the numbers, and a few special characters. The nice thing about ASCII is that it's recognized by thousands of programs and many different types of computers.

HTML files are ASCII files that have been specially designed to be read by Web browsers. These files use the same characters as any other ASCII file, but they use a special convention that all Web browsers "know" about. That convention is this: "if you see anything in brackets like these `< >`, you know that it's a special code." So Web browsers, when they are rendering the HTML document into normal text, look for these brackets and examine the text inside them to look for instructions.

> **Plain English, please!**
>
> *Rendering* is the term used to describe the action of looking at the HTML codes, formatting the text in the ASCII file according to the instructions held in the codes, stripping the codes out of the text, and displaying the resulting text in the browser.

Well, let's create an HTML file—you'll see how easy it really is. Start by opening Notepad. You can get to it by opening the Start menu and choosing

Programs, Accessories, Notepad. Now, enter this text; you can replace the text with other stuff, but don't change the textbetween the brackets (< >):

```
<TITLE>My Home Page</TITLE>
<H1>My Very Own Home Page</H1>

<H2>Really Important Stuff</H2>
These are WWW pages I use a lot. <P>

<H2>Not So Important Stuff</H2>
These are WWW pages I use now and again. <P>

<H3>Not Important At All Stuff</H3>
These are WWW pages I use to waste time. <P>
```

What are these codes?

<TITLE> </TITLE> The text between these tags is the title of the document. You won't see the text in the document itself. Rather, it's an identifier used by browsers, the text that appears in Explorer's title bar when the document is displayed, and the name used in the History and Favorites lists.

<H1> </H> The heading level. You can have up to six different levels. We've used levels 1, 2, and 3.

TIP **Don't worry about the case of the tags. You can type title or** TITLE, or Title, or TItlE, or TiTIE or whatever takes your fancy

<P> This denotes the end of a paragraph. Simply typing a carriage return in your HTML file will *not* create a new paragraph in the final document as it's displayed in the browser. You must put in the <P> tag. Without the tag, you will find that lines run into each other.

Notice that, in most cases, tags are paired. There's an opening and a closing tag, and the closing tag is the same as the opening tag with the exception of the forward slash after the left angle bracket, <H> and </H>, for instance. The <P> tag is an exception; there's only one, and it appears after the paragraph.

Now, choose File, Save. (If you decided to use a word processor rather than Notepad, make sure you save the file as a text-only file.) Save it using the .HTML extension rather than .TXT, even though it's still plain text. For example, don't call it HOME.TXT; call it HOME.HTML. It doesn't much matter where you save the file, though you may want to put it into the \Program Files\Plus!\microsoft internet\ directory.

Now, open Explorer, and choose File, Open. Click on the Open File button, and use the Open File dialog box to open your HOME.HTML file. What do you see? A formatted WWW document (see fig. 17.1). It's rubbish, of course, but you can see how easy it was to create. (If you are using a word processor rather than Notepad, you may not be able to open the file in Explorer until you've closed it in the word processor.)

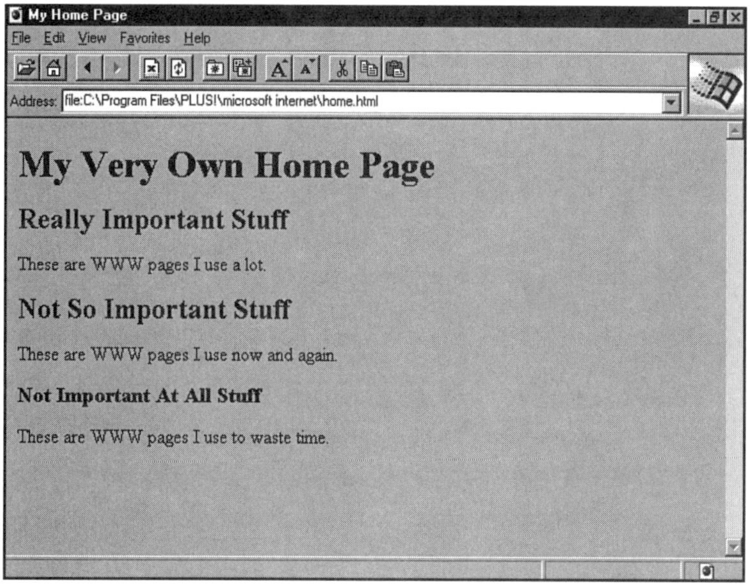

Fig. 17.1
It took me less than five minutes to create this simple (okay, *very* simple) home page.

Now we're going to get fancy. Let's add an **anchor**, a link to another document. Here's a handy link, one to the GLOBHIST.HTM file. This file contains links to all the documents recorded in the History list (see chapter 6).

> ### *Plain English, please!*
> The <A HREF="url"> tags used to create links are often known as *anchors*; for this reason, many people refer to the links themselves in the Web documents as anchors.

This document is in the History directory. Add this line to your home page:

```
<A HREF="file:C:\Program Files\PLUS!\microsoft
internet\history\globhist.htm">The History List</A><BR>
```

TIP **Notice that the GLOBHIST.HTM file has the three-character** (HTM) extension, not the HTML extension.

What's the <BR> tag at the end? That's similar to a paragraph break; it's actually a line break, and you can use it when you want to create a smaller space between lines than is created by the <P> link.

TIP **Want several blank lines? Just run several <BR> tags together** (as in

); there's no need to put them on separate lines.

Here's what that line looks like once it's inside my HOME.HTML file:

```
<H2>Really Important Stuff</H2>
These are WWW pages I use a lot. <P>
<A HREF="file:C:\Program Files\PLUS!\microsoft
internet\history\globhist.htm">The History List</A><BR>
```

When you've added the line, choose File, Save in Notepad to save the changes. Then go to Explorer and click on the Refresh button. You'll see the link appear in your document. Click on the link, and Explorer will open the History list. Handy, eh? (And if it *doesn't* open the list? Check to see that you've entered the information correctly.)

Setting the home (start) page

When you've finished, you need to set the document up as your home page. In Explorer, choose View, Options. When the Options dialog box opens, click on the Start Page tab, then on the Use Current button. Now, the next time you start your browser, you'll see your very own home page. Simple, eh?

Adding links to the Web at large

The link we added to our home page was to a file on your hard disk. If you want to add a link to a page on the Web itself, you'll use a slightly different format. Let's look a little more closely at the way links are created. Here's the link we looked at earlier:

```
<A HREF="file:C:\Program Files\PLUS!\microsoft
internet\history\globhist.htm">The History List</A>
```

A link contains these components:

Component	Purpose
<A HREF="	This indicates the beginning of the link.
URL type	In our example, the URL type is file:, indicating that the page is a file on your hard disk. When you want to link to a page on the Web, though, you'll use http://.
path	The path to the file. In our example the path is C:\Program Files\PLUS!\microsoft internet\history\globhist.htm. When linking to a document on the Web, the path will start with the name of the host computer containing the file.
">	This comes after the path.
Link text	The link text (the History list, in our example), is what you see in the browser. You click on the text to activate the link.
</A>	This indicates the end of the link.

Here's an example of a link to a document on the Web:

```
<A HREF="http://www.yahoo.com/">Yahoo</A><BR>
```

This one takes you to the Yahoo site (see chapter 8). As you can see, the basic structure is the same. The main differences are that we've used an **http://** URL instead of a **file:** URL, and the path includes only the host name of the computer that runs Yahoo. (In some cases you'll enter a path and filename, in this case it's not necessary.)

Creating multiple documents

You may want to create a hierarchy of documents; have a document that appears when you open, with a table of contents linked to several other documents. In each of those documents, you could then have links related to a particular subject.

Let's say you want to set up a document for the music sites you are interested in. We'll call it RNR.HTML. Create that document in the same way as the first one and put it in the same directory. We can then create a link from your home page to the Rock n' Roll document, like this:

```
<A HREF="RNR.HTML">Rock n' Roll</A><BR>
```

Is **RNR.HTML** a URL? There's no path to the document. Well, yes. It's a *relative* URL. I'll explain *relative* and *absolute* URLs in chapter 18. But for now, all you need to know is that this link means "look for the RNR.HTM file." Where? Well, it doesn't say, so the only place the browser *can* look is in the same directory as the original file. (Which is fine, because you are going to place the RNR.HTM file in the same directory, right?)

This is really simple, isn't it? You create a home page (called HOME.HTM) with links to any number of other documents in the same directory. One for Rock n' Roll, one for art, one for music, one for conspiracy theories, one for whatever sort of information you are interested in and can find on the Web. Then, you fill those documents up with more links to all those interesting sites.

TIP **Though you plan to use your own home page, you may still want** to return to Explorer's original home page now and again. Use this tag to create a link to that home page:

```
<A HREF="http://www.home.msn.com/">Microsoft Home Page</
A><BR>
```

About paragraphs

Web browsers don't deal with paragraphs in the same way that word processors do. If the browser finds several spaces—including blank lines—it will compress all the space into a single paragraph, unless it sees the <P> or a <BR> tag somewhere. When it finds the <P> ,it ends the paragraph and starts a new one on the next line. (Actually, browsers vary; some will end the paragraph, leave a blank line, and then start a new paragraph.)

There are various versions of HTML in use, though, and in more recent versions <P> is actually a tag denoting the *beginning* of a paragraph, and there *is* an ending </P>. However, in simple documents you can omit the </P> because each time the browser sees the <P>, it starts a new paragraph—so it has to end the previous one, right?

Also, remember the <BR> tag I showed you earlier. You'll often find that when you use the <P> tag you get a space between lines that is much larger than you really want. Use <BR> instead of <P>, and you'll get a much smaller space.

Faster link creation

There are shortcuts to creating links. Who wants to type all those URLs, after all? Explorer provides a few ways to grab URLs and links.

- Copy a URL from the Address text box.
- Right click on an entry in the Favorites or History window, and choose Properties. Then click on the Internet Shortcut tab, and press Ctrl+C to copy the URL.
- Open an entry from the Favorites or History window in Notepad; these are simple text files, with a URL inside the file, like this:

  ```
  [InternetShortcut]
  URL=http://soundwire.com/cgi-bin/charge/samples/
  Felix.mp2
  ```

  (You can open an entry by opening Notepad, choosing File, Open, finding the History directory, and choosing All Files from the Files of Type drop-down list box. Then double-click on the one you want to open.)
- Open the GLOBHIST.HTM file in a word processor. You'll find actual tags you can take, not just the URL. Note, however, that you'll have to remove the *name=* portion of the URL, which is used to tell Explorer which file to pull from the cache. For instance, if you grab *<a href="http://soundwire.com/" name="808527065">Sound Wire's Home Page.url</a>*, you'll have to remove *name="808527065"* (and the space preceding *name=*).
- You can grab tags directly from other people's documents. Right click in a blank area of the document and choose View Source. When the HTML document opens in Notepad, you can copy the tags.
- Right click on a link in a document and choose Copy Shortcut. I'm not really sure whether this is intended to copy just the URL, or the entire tag (`<A HREF`, etc.), because this feature doesn't currently work. It should work in later versions of Explorer.

Q&A When I look at an entry's properties in the Favorites or History window, I find that there's no Internet Shortcut tab. Why?

There are a couple of reasons. First, your Internet software may not be set up correctly. Windows 95 has a problem configuring this stuff correctly if you've tried out several different configurations. The solution is to remove the Microsoft Plus! Internet Jumpstart Kit, remove Microsoft Network, and reinstall. The other reason is...well, I don't know. Just a bug. Now and again you'll find that the tab simply isn't there. Try again, or try another entry.

18 More Advanced Authoring

In this chapter:

- Different browsers display pages differently
- Adding pictures to Web pages
- Relative and absolute links
- Links within documents
- <PRE> and </PRE> tags, and more
- Creating lists

Did the last chapter whet your appetite for more? Here are a few more ways to enhance your online documents. . . . . .

Perhaps you've realized by now just how easy it is to create Web documents. Sure, it's as hard as you want to make it; if you want to create forms, for instance, you'll have to look elsewhere for information on how to do it. But with just a few simple tags, you can set up a decent Web site of your own. In this chapter we'll learn about a few more advanced techniques that you'll want to master before you place your information on the Web.

Q&A ***Once I've created my Web pages, where do I put them?***

I don't yet know if MSN will allow its members to place their pages on the Web, but there's a very good chance that they will (other online services are doing so). If you are not with MSN, check with your service provider. Many allow people to set up Web pages for little or no cost. For instance, I have a simple Web site (**http://www.usa.net/cipa**) that costs nothing, as long as I limit it to less than 1MB of disk space.

Different browsers see different things

We're going to learn how to define parts of your document as different styles: headers, addresses, lists, and so on. You may have an idea of what each style is (based on what your browser does, or how you have configured your browser), but remember that other people's browsers will do different things.

For instance, here's an interesting tag pair, the <BLOCKQUOTE> and </BLOCKQUOTE> tags. The text between these tags is defined as a *quote*. What does that mean? Whatever the browser wants it to mean. Most browsers will automatically indent the text a few spaces (that's what Explorer does), and they generally don't let users modify the indentation. However, some browsers allow users to change the text. For example, using the InternetWorks browser, you can change the <BLOCKQUOTE> text to be any font on your system.

So remember, in many cases, you are providing text with a style name, but the way it will actually appear depends on the browser. So you may, in some cases, want to select tags that will *force* the browser to use a particular typeface, rather than leave it up to the browser's (or user's) choice. For instance, I'll explain a little later how to force a browser to use italic or bold text.

Creating your web page

You've already learned the basics of creating Web pages, in chapter 17. If you haven't read that chapter, go back, because you'll need that knowledge in this chapter.

Now, we first need to create some kind of main document, the page that Web browsers will see when they visit your site. That is the document in which you will channel people where you want them to go. You'll publicize the URL for that document and get other documents around the Web to link to that main document.

Here's what I have at the top of the first document at my CIPA site—the Colorado Independent Publisher's Association site, at **http://www.usa.net/cipa**:

```
<TITLE>Colorado Independent Publisher's Association</TITLE>
<H1>Colorado Independent Publisher's Association</H1>
<IMG SRC = "cipalogo.gif" ><P>
<HR>
```

I start with the `<TITLE>` and `</TITLE>` tags. The text between these is the document title. It's not seen in the document when viewing it in a browser—it's a reference, the name of the document, which is placed in Explorer's toolbar while viewing it.

Next, we have the `<H1>` and `</H1>` tags. These are Heading 1 tags, and I generally use the same text as the TITLE text, so the heading at the top of the document is the same as the heading that will appear in a browser's history list or hotlist (Favorites list, in Explorer parlance). Next we have the `<IMG SRC = "cipalogo.gif" >` line, followed by a `<P>`. This line puts the CIPA logo just below the heading—we'll come back to this in a moment. Finally, I end with `<HR>`. This is a divider line (a horizontal rule) across the screen, a good way to break up portions of the document. Below this line, I've added some introductory text about the CIPA site. So, figure 18.1 shows what you'll actually see when viewing the document.

Fig. 18.1
The CIPA Web site.

Adding pictures to your web pages

What's the first thing you notice at Web sites these days? Some kind of picture—a logo, someone's face, a landscape, or whatever. These pictures are *inline images*, and they can be one of three kinds: .GIF files (Graphics Interchange Format), .XBM files (an X Window System graphics format), or .JPG files (a compressed image format). The .JPG format is probably the preferred, as it takes up less space and can be transferred more quickly. But it's also a more recent format; while most of the new browsers work with it, earlier ones can't display these images. (I created this CIPA site when browsers generally couldn't work with .JPG files, and I haven't got around to converting from .GIF to .JPG.)

Where are you going to get these images? Lots of Windows graphics programs can create .GIF and .JPG files, these days.

The easiest way to deal with an inline image is to put it in the same directory as the document, and then use a *relative* URL to point to it, like this:

```
<IMG SRC="url">
```

(What's IMG SRC? Nothing technical—just *Image Source*.) Here's what I actually put in the document:

```
<IMG SRC = "cipalogo.gif" ><P>
```

The text cipalogo.gif is the picture I'm using, and I've added a <P> tag to break the paragraph up, so this will sit on a line by itself. Now, what about turning a graphic into a link so that when the user clicks on the graphic, it takes him somewhere? Easy; place the entire graphic entry, tags and all, inside a link:

```
<A HREF = "contact.htm"><IMG SRC = "cipalogo.gif"></A><P>
```

Notice that I placed the text <IMG SRC = "cipalogo.gif"> where a link's text would normally go; the picture is the link. When the reader clicks on this picture, the CONTACT.HTM file appears.

You can place an image on a line with text and then determine the position of the text relative to the picture. For instance, if you have a tag like this:

```
<IMG ALIGN=TOP SRC = "filename" ><P>
```

you'll get the text aligned with the top of the image. If you use ALIGN=BOTTOM, the text is at the bottom of the image, and if you use ALIGN=MIDDLE the text is in the middle of the image. This doesn't work well with very large images, such as the CIPA logo, but can work well for images that are relatively small. (With large images, you end up with loads of space above or below the text that's on the same line.)

TIP **Want to find some icons you can use in your documents? Go to an** *icon server*: a Web site from which you can download icons or even link your documents across the Web to a particular icon. Try these:

http://www.bsdi.com/icons
http://www-ns.rutgers.edu/doc-images
http://www.di.unipi.it/iconbrowser/icons.html
http://www.cit.gu.edu.au/~anthony/icons/

What does a user see if he doesn't have a graphics browser, or if he has turned inline images off? Well, he'll see one of two things. He'll either see what the browser automatically displays when it can't display an image, or he'll see the text *you* want him to see. Browsers often display a small logo, or some text, such as [IMAGE] for instance, if they're not displaying inline images. But you can use the ALT= parameter to display something else. For instance, if I use this:

```
<IMG SRC="cipalogo.gif" ALT="CIPA_Logo"><P>
```

the user will see the word "CIPA_Logo" in place of the actual logo. (Put the text in quotation marks, and don't put any spaces inside; you can use an underscore character in place of the space.)

Actually, while this works okay with early Web browsers, some more recent browsers won't use this, *unless* you also define the size of the image. For instance,

```
<IMG border=0 width=460 height=55 SRC="filename"
ALT="text"><P>
```

This tells the browser how large the image should be, in **pixels**; the browser will leave a box that large if inline images have been turned off, so there's enough room to display the alternative text. (No box, no text.)

> **Plain English, please!**
>
> A **pixel** is the smallest element on your screen, the "dots" that are used to create the pictures you see. For instance, if you are using VGA mode, your screen is 640 pixels wide and 480 pixels tall. How do you know how large your image is? Some graphics programs can tell you (there's often a command that displays image information).

We've already looked at linking to other documents in chapter 17. Here's what I originally added to the main CIPA page (if you visit this site you'll see that I've modified things, but this is how I started):

```
<A HREF = "book.htm">Click here for a list of Book Titles</
A><BR>
<A HREF = "subject.htm">Click here for a list of Subjects</
A><BR>
<A HREF = "publish.htm">Click here for a list of Publishers</
A><P>
<A HREF = "contact.htm">Click here for information about
joining or contacting CIPA</A><P>
<A HREF = "members.htm">Click here for information for CIPA
members</A><P>
If you are interested in joining an organization for small
publishers, but don't live in Colorado, <A HREF =
"pma.htm">click here</A><P>
<A HREF = "1sttime.htm">For the First Time Publisher...</
A><P>
<HR>
```

As you can see, I have several links to other documents. In fact, this site (like most Web sites) is a series of interlinked documents. For example:

```
<A HREF = "book.htm">Click here for a list of Book Titles</
A><P>
```

This line will appear as the text *Click here for a list of Book Titles*. That text is a link to the BOOK.HTM document. This is a relative URL, meaning "look for BOOK.HTM in the same directory as the current document." Within that document are a series of links to other documents, each about a particular book, and *those* documents have links to other documents containing information about publishers and ordering.

At the bottom of this list of links is another <HR> tag; again, this puts a line across the screen. (By the way, I later turned this list into a *bulleted* list—we'll look at this later.)

TIP **When I first created this site, I was working in Windows 3.1, so I** was using the .HTM extension rather than .HTML. I'd recommend that you use .HTML, though, if you plan to put your documents on your service provider's server. The server will recognize .HTM automatically, but may require extra configuration to recognize .HTML.

Relative versus absolute links

Let's come back to the issue of *relative* and *absolute* links. I'm using relative links here. I can do so safely because all these documents are going to be grouped together—in the same directory—so the links will always work. In fact, it's better that I do so because I don't know the name of the directory the files will be placed in when I've finished; I'm creating these files at home on my PC, but eventually they'll sit on my service provider's system somewhere. If I used absolute addresses, I'd have to know for sure where the files would be when I finally place them on that system.

Sometimes, of course, you *have* to use absolute addresses. If I want to create a link from this document to a document elsewhere in the world (perhaps to a Web site created by another small-publisher's association), I'd have to give the absolute URL. I'd use `http://this.web.site.com/this_directory/thisfile.htm` or whatever.

If you are creating Web documents that are probably going to be copied by people back to their computers, then you'll have to use absolute addresses. For instance, if you copy the CIPA main page back to your hard disk, the

URLs will no longer make sense because they refer to files on a different computer. If I'd used an absolute address, this wouldn't be a problem—wherever the file is, the links make sense.

Now, about those URLs. A URL is, you'll remember, a *Uniform Resource Locator*. It's an address to a file somewhere else on the Web. We've looked at the **http://** URLs so far. These are pointers to files on a Web server, but the Web lets you link to much more than just Web documents. You can also link to Gophers, FTP sites, newsgroups, and more (see chapters 12 to 16). So there are other forms of URLs, ones that tell the browser the sort of resource it's going to. There's `gopher://host.name/`, for instance. This points to a Gopher server. There's `file://host.name/directory/filename`, which points to a particular file on a particular machine, perhaps an FTP site. And there's `ftp://host.name/directory/filename`, which also points to an FTP site. These allow you to easily link to Gopher and FTP sites, and to add files to your Web site that the readers can download. Use these URLs in the same way you create an **http://** link.

Links within documents

What happens if you want to create a link that jumps from one part of a document to another? That is, when your reader clicks on the link, you want to take the reader to a point further down (or maybe higher up) in the same document, not a different document.

No problem. First, you have to set a `<A NAME= >` tag. For instance, let's look at the Travel and Learn document at the CIPA site, which contains a sample book chapter. In that chapter is a list of companies that have archaeology, history, and dinosaur programs. In the actual paper book, the list sits on a page preceding the information about each company, and you have to flip through the pages to find the one you want. In the Web document, why not let the user click on the one he wants to find out about and go directly there?

One of those companies is called Archaeological Tours. I set this tag on the line immediately preceding the heading for that company:

```
<A NAME = ARC>
```

This acts as a sort of bookmark. Then, I created the link earlier in the document:

```
<A HREF = "#Arc">Archaeological Tours</A> <P>
```

This is just like a normal, document-to-document link, *except* that instead of placing a filename into the link, I use the # sign followed by the name of the `<A NAME = >` tag. Now, when my readers click on the words *Archaeological Tours*, they go straight to that section.

Forcing the browser to keep the format

As you've seen, browsers ignore spaces and line breaks. They are only interested in the tags. Take a look at this example:

```
<C1>Blah blah blah, blahdey blah, blah blah blah. Blah blah
blah, blahdey blah, blah blah blah. Blah blah blah, blahdey
blah, blah blah blah. Blah blah blah, blahdey blah, blah blah
blah.
```

And now this example:

```
Blah blah blah, blahdey blah,        blah blah blah. Blah
blah blah, blahdey blah, blah blah blah.       Blah blah
blah, blahdey blah, blah blah blah.

Blah blah blah, blahdey blah, blah blah blah.
```

These actually display exactly the same thing, because your Web browser won't use the extra spaces and blank lines—it moves everything together. There *is* a way to force browsers to use the extra spaces and lines (and other items, such as indents). Use the `<PRE>` and `</PRE>` tags (the *preform* tags). The following figure shows what the second example looks like in a browser, first without the `<PRE>` and `</PRE>` tags, and then with them.

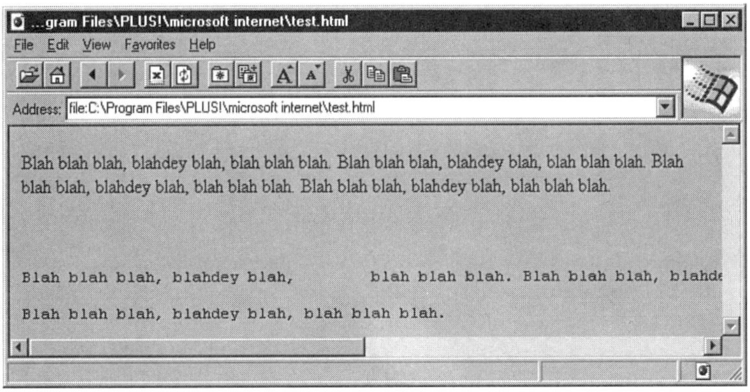

Fig. 18.2
The "preformed" text retains its spaces and extra lines.

You'll notice also that the text has run off the screen (it's not being "wrapped" onto the next line); the browser is only starting a new line when a new line begins in the HTML document. Also, notice that the text in the preformed text is Courier. Most browsers use a Sans Serif font for preformed text, though a Roman font for normal body text. These tags are often used to show program listings, and a Sans Serif font is commonly used in documentation for such listings.

That's a drawback, of course, that will limit the use you can put these tags to. You can't just create your HTML files in a word processor; format them anyway you want, use the preform tags, and expect them to look good!

The mailto: tag

Remember in chapter 16 we discussed the mailto: URL? When a user clicks on a mailto: link, up pops his e-mail program, with an e-mail address already inserted.

Creating one of these tags is very simple. You'll use a line like this in the HTML document:

```
To email the author of this Web document, <a href =
"mailto:pkent@lab-press.com">click here: pkent@lab-
press.com</a>
```

You've created a link, just as we've seen before. The only difference is that you've used the mailto: URL—**`mailto:pkent@lab-press.com`**. In effect mailto: tells the browser to open the e-mail program, while pkent@lab-press.com is the address that is to be used in the message.

More HTML codes

There's plenty more that we haven't covered, enough to fill a large book (many of which you'll find at your local bookstore!).

For instance, how about placing addresses on the left side of the page in italics, without blank lines between each line of the address. Here's how you can do that:

```
<H5><A NAME = Arc></A>ARCHAEOLOGICAL TOURS</H5>
<I>271 Madison Avenue/Suite 904<br>
```

```
New York NY 10016<br>
Phone: (212)986-3054<br>
Contact: Linda Feinstone</I><P>
```

The first line is an H5 heading (this is the name of the company). Each line of the address is placed on a separate line, with a <BR> tag to force a line break. That way, browsers that leave blank lines after <P> tags won't break up this address.

To make the text italic, place it between <I> and </I> tags. A browser will display everything between those tags as italic. But there's an <ADDRESS> and </ADDRESS> tag set; why couldn't you use that? Well, these are not really for street addresses. Rather, they are intended for a single line of information about a document's author, such as the e-mail address, and different browsers treat these tags in very different ways; it is safer to set it using italics and a line break, to be sure how it would look.

More text styles

There are other text formatting tags, such as <B> and </B> (bold); <U> and </U> (underlined); <TT> and </TT> ("typewriter-style" font); and <STRONG> and </STRONG> (emphasis). There are *loads* of these, but you'll find that some browsers simply don't use them, or simply won't do what you think they should. Should the <STRONG> and </STRONG> tags display the text as bold or italic? It's probably bold. What about <EM> and </EM> tags (more emphasis tags)? Probably italics, but who knows for sure? If you want to make sure the text is bold or italics, don't use these tags; use the <B></B> and <I></I> sets, instead.

Creating lists

There are several tags you can use if you'd like to like to place lists of items:

Type of list	Tags to use
Unnumbered (Bulleted) Lists	Place a <UL> tag at the top of the list, and </UL> after the last entry. Place <LI> before each item in the list. When a browser displays the list, each item will be preceded by a bullet.

continues

Type of list	Tags to use
Numbered (or Ordered) Lists	Use the <OL> and </OL> tags to create a list with numbers before each item. (The numbers are added automatically for you.) Place <LI> before each item in the list.
Definition Lists	Start the list with <DL>, and end it with </DL>. Place <DT> before each definition term and <DD> before each definition. This creates a list of terms followed by their definitions.

TIP **When creating lists, there's no need for a <P> or <BR> after each** line in the list. Each item automatically appears on a separate line. And the `<LI>`, `<DT>`, and `<DD>` tags are single tags; they have no corresponding `</>` tag and are placed before the text they are formatting.

Where next?

I've told you about just a few HTML features. It's enough for you to start creating a pretty good little Web site, but as you get further into things, you may find that you want to try something more complicated.

There are about a gazillion books on the subject now, but you can find loads of information online, too. Try these Web documents:

- A Beginner's Guide to HTML:

  http://www.ncsa.uiuc.edu/SDG/Software/Mosaic/Docs/d2-htmlinfo.html

- HTML Quick Reference:

  http://kuhttp.cc.ukans.edu/lynx_help/HTML_quick.html

- How to Write HTML Files:

  http://www.ucc.ie/info/net/htmldoc.html

- Introduction to HTML:

  http://melmac.harris-atd.com/about_html.html

- The Official HTML Specification:

  http://www.w3.org/hypertext/WWW/MarkUp/MarkUp.html

- CERN's Style Guide for Online Hypertext:

  http://www.w3.org/hypertext/WWW/Provider/Style/Introduction.html

- Fill-out Forms Overview:

  http://www.ncsa.uiuc.edu/SDG/Software/Mosaic/Docs/fill-out-forms/overview.html

TIP **If you really get into Web authoring, a quick and easy way to** learn is to learn from others. Find a site you like, right-click on the background, and choose View Source to see how the author put everything together. (Of course some things, such as form creation, won't be clear to you until you read a good book on HTML.)

19

Web Sampler

In this chapter:

- **Online banking with First Virtual, NetCash, and ecash**
- **Shopping online, buying cars**
- **Babes on the Web**
- **Information and software from Microsoft**
- **Really bad stuff on the Web**
- **Lots more**

Here are a few examples of what you'll find on the Web, just to get you started. . . . .

The World Wide Web is relatively easy to search. See chapter 8 for information about finding subjects that interest you. In this chapter, though, I'm going to give you a little sampler, an idea of what you'll find and what you can do.

When I began the book, I'd almost decided not to include this sampler. "If they want something, they can quickly find it with the tools I've shown them," I thought. But during the time I was writing this book, I was interviewed by Karen Steele of the WALE 990 radio station in Providence, Rhode Island. She told me how *useful* these samplers can be, as a way for whetting one's appetite, and giving an idea of what's possible. Well, I've got some space left. I'm not going to fill half the book with pretty pictures, but I'll show you some of the things I've found while cruising around the Web (in no particular order).

TIP **Here's a good way to find interesting sites. When you visit a site,** look for links to other sites. Many Web authors include their "favorite links," and if you have a few hours to spare you can travel all over the world and find loads of interesting things, just by checking out other people's recommendations.

First Virtual

http://firstvirtual.com/

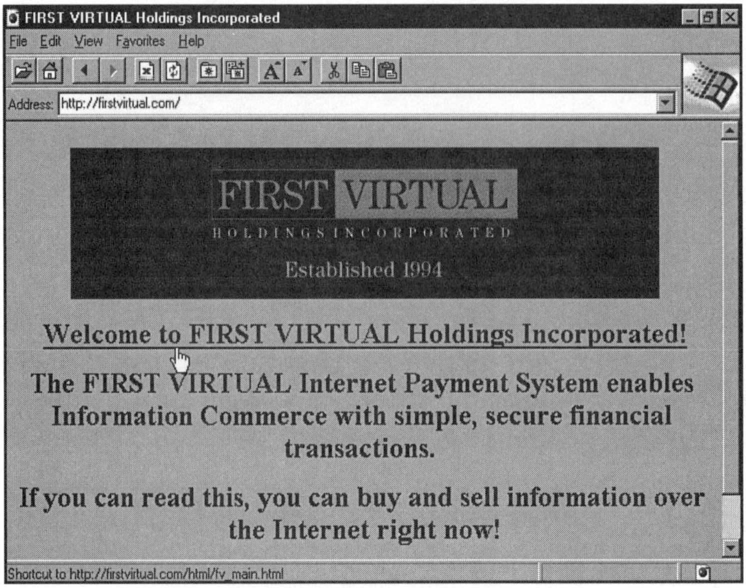

If you plan to do any shopping on the Internet, you'll probably want to open a First Virtual account. The only charge is a $2 application fee (though you must reapply each time your credit card expires). What's the advantage of a First Virtual account? Safety. If you don't want to risk transmitting your credit-card number across the Internet, you can use your First Virtual account number instead. Store owners then bill First Virtual, which then bills your credit card.

NetCash

http://www.teleport.com/~netcash/ncquick.html

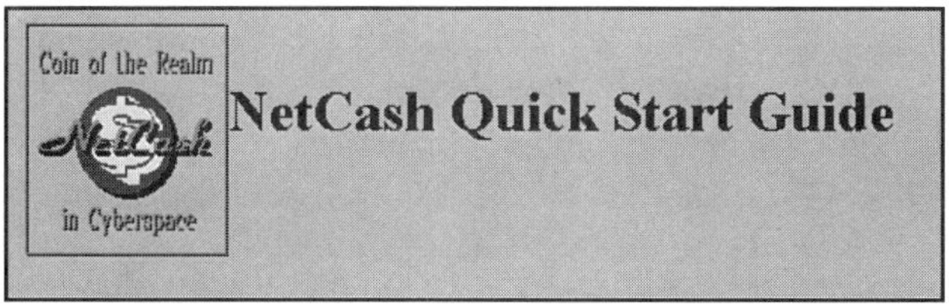

Here's another form of online money—NetCash. You apply for an account via e-mail. Then, each time you want money, you ask for a coupon (which is really a serial number representing a sum of money). To buy, you give the merchant the number.

ecash

http://www.digicash.com/ecash/

Yet another form of online money (this one's often known as DigiCash—after the company that developed it—or CyberCash). This one uses a special program. You use this program to get money from the "bank" (which takes it from your checking account). When you click on an ecash link at a Web site, the program pops up and asks if you want to give the store the money. (At the time of writing there was an ecash free trial going on. Sign up, and you get $100 of Cyberbucks, which you can spend on the Web; one site is selling 10-cent snippets of music, for instance!)

Microsoft Windows 95

http://www.windows.microsoft.com/

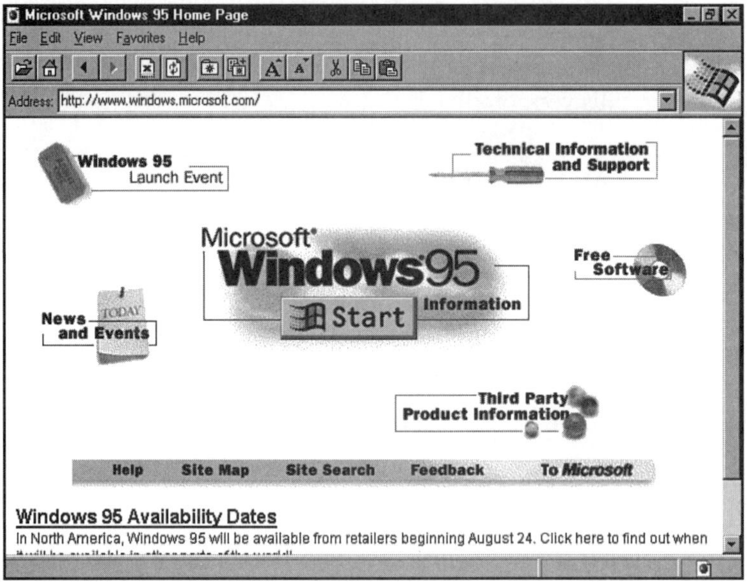

This is a good place to find useful information about Windows 95, and even free software—utilities that will make working in Windows 95 a little easier.

Auto-By-Tel

http://shopping2000.com/shopping2000/auto-by-te/index.html

Looking for a new car? Try Auto-By-Tel. You can fill in a form with information about yourself and the car you want to buy, and you'll get a price quote back.

Shopping2000

http://shopping2000.com/shopping2000/

You'll find an online shopping mall here; flowers, software, insurance, vacations, books, clothing, and plenty more. Products from small companies, and large well-known firms such as Hanes, Lens Express, NordicTrack, Sears, and Teleflora are offered.

Microsoft KnowledgeBase

http://www.microsoft.com/KB/

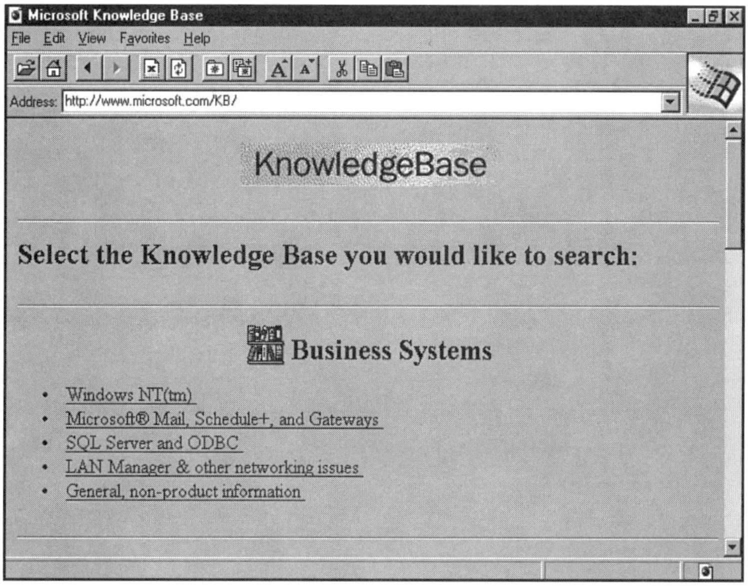

If you need technical support from Microsoft, but don't want to wait on hold or pay some ridiculous fee, check out the KnowledgeBase. This is the same information used by Microsoft's tech. support people.

NPR Online

http://www.npr.org/

Did you catch the tail end of an interesting National Public Radio story during your commute home? You can go to the NPR site and download the story so you can listen to it at your leisure. You can also search for the text transcripts of stories, and order online if you don't mind sending your credit-card number through e-mail. (Maybe they'll use First Virtual soon.)

Leonardo da Vinci Museum

http://cellini.leonardo.net/museum/main.html

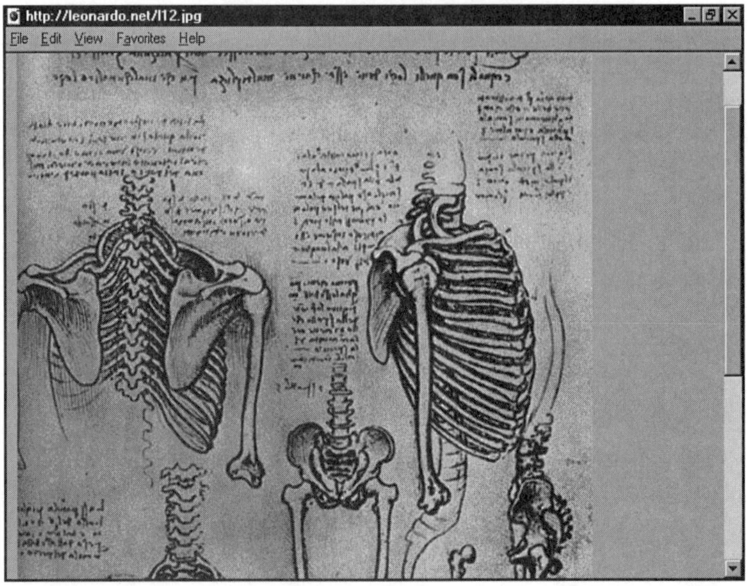

Leo's paintings, sketches, and designs, along with a short biography.

Internet Underground Music Archive

http://www.iuma.com/

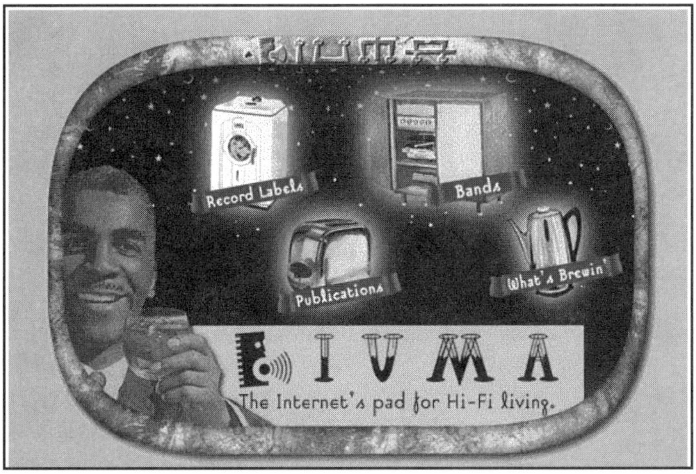

Lots of bands and music online.

Babes on the Web

http://www.tyrell.net/~robtoups/BABE.html

This one's caused quite a cyberstir. As the author of this site, Rob Toups, writes, the scandal has "caused me to move to New York City, found me nude in WIRED magazine, written about on every continent on the earth, been discussed as a seminar for cyberspace lawyers, had the guys at EFF send me glowing e-mail, on the radio to 150 stations, potential guest for David Letterman…and let me thumb my nose at all those critics that said they were 'GONNA SHUT ME DOWN!'."

This Web site provides links to other Web pages created by women. How are those Web pages chosen? "By the personal photos of the author from the neck up. What is above the neck? That's for you to decide." It seems that the author cruises the Web looking for photographs of "babes" in their Web pages. He then rates those babes using the *Toupsie Scale*, and adds a link from his page to theirs. It should be noted that some of the babes who have been rated are very upset, while others have asked to be rated and clearly *like* the exposure. Pictures range from respectable portraits, to, well, not quite so respectable portraits. Distasteful? Tacky? Sexist? Or just plain fun? You decide. I'll leave you with a few more words from Mr. Toups:

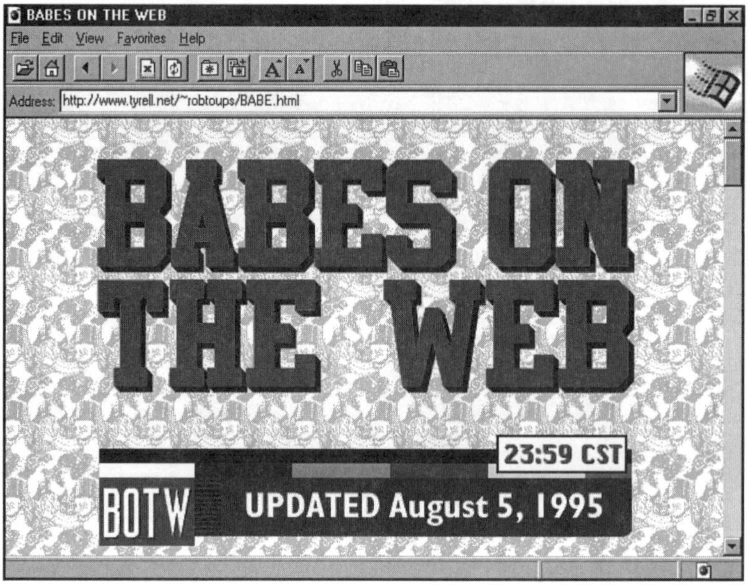

"Rumor has it that 'BABES ON THE WEB' is the favorite World Wide Web site of the current President of the United States, William Jefferson Clinton. Though the author of 'BABES OF THE WEB' is not a political supporter of President Clinton, the author is impressed with his choice of extramarital Babes."

The Worst of the Web

http://turnpike.net/metro/mirsky/Worst.html

Want to see the very worst stuff available on the Web? Check out this page. You'll find links to all sorts of cyberubbish. Actually you may not agree that the pages are so bad, but you will find some weird stuff, such as the *Home Appliance Shooting* page, *Screwing over your local McDonald's*, and *GUILTY OR NOT GUILTY? (an OJ site)*.

Phrantic's Public Housing Project

http://phrantic.com/phrantic/phpwhy.html

Want to set up your own Web page, but can't find a home for it? Phrantic will find a place for you. "PPhP is a collection of generous people on the 'net willing to share their webspace with you. If you would like a homepage of your own, you've come to the right place!"

Sandra's Clip Art Server

http://www.cs.yale.edu/HTML/YALE/CS/HyPlans/loosemore-sandra/clipart.html

If you need clip art, this is the place to see. You'll find links to sites containing thousands of images just waiting to be downloaded.

The Rock and Roll Digital Gallery

http://www.hooked.net/julianne/

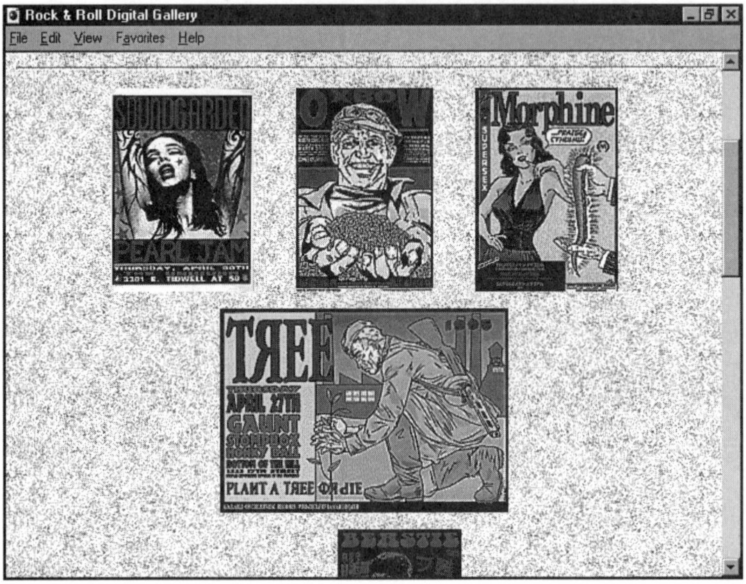

This site contains Rock and Roll poster art. You can download the posters, view the Rock and Roll Digital Gallery (which changes its exhibit frequently), and even grab a rock and roll screen saver.

BookWire

http://www.bookwire.com/

This site contains the Publisher's Weekly best-seller lists (current and past), information about interesting new books, and links to book publishers, book sellers, electronic texts, and online libraries on the Internet.

50 Greatest Conspiracies of All Time

http://www.webcom.com/~conspire/

This site promotes the book of the same name. You'll find sample chapters, chapters not included in the book, and links to other strange sites. This is an excellent, extremely well-designed site. It came in number 3 in a recent rating of Web sites by The Point. Speaking of which…

The Point

http://www.pointcom.com/

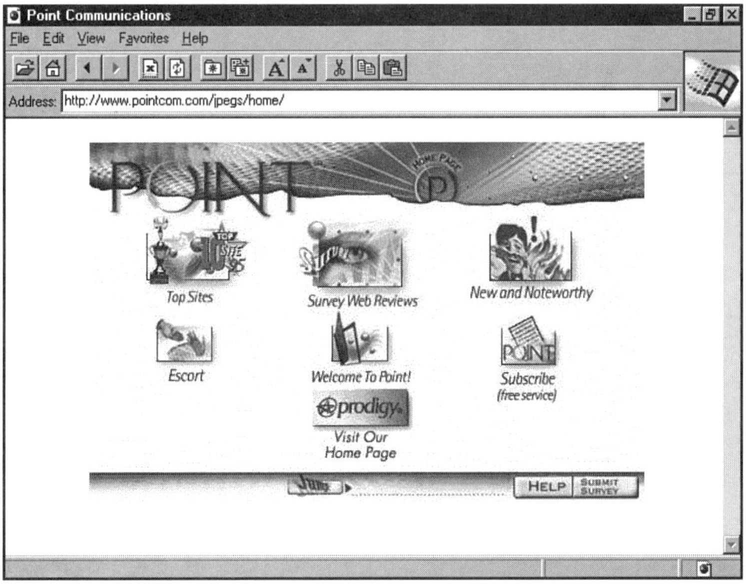

This site rates Web sites. They spend their time searching for the best sites around, so you can find the really neat stuff quickly.

Gigaplex

http://www.gigaplex.com/wow/

I'm getting lazy now. Here's another one I found at the Point. The Gigaplex is information about film, TV, books, food, shopping, golf, theater, yes—even Yoga. It's "a whopping 600-plus page Webmagazine devoted to arts & entertainment! [with] 20 megabytes of text and graphics, plus 80 megabytes of audio and video clips."

First Millennial Foundation

http://www.csn.net/~mtsavage/

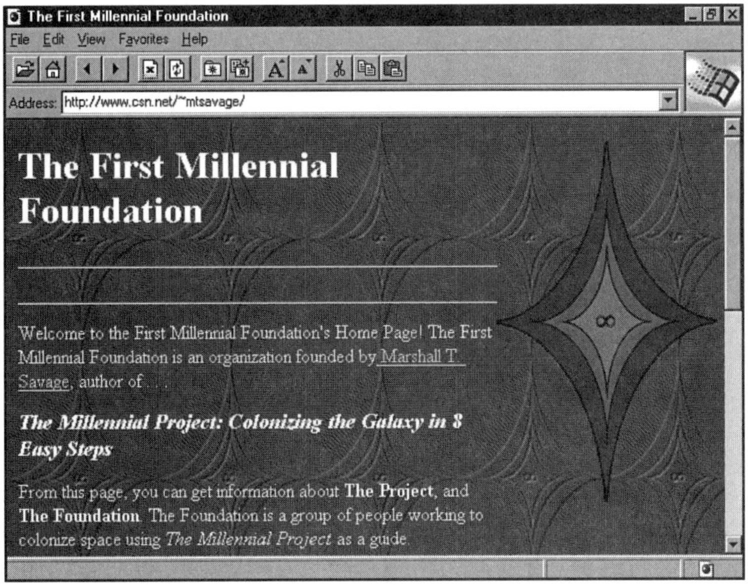

If you've read the book *The Millennieal Project: Colonizing the Galaxy in 8 Easy Steps*, you'll know what this site is all about. If you haven't read the book, you may think these guys are nuts. "The Foundation is a group of people working to colonize space using The Millennial Project as a guide." I've read the book (it's excellent), and I'm not prepared to ridicule them. It sounds like author Marshall T. Savage really knows what he's talking about. (No, I'm not a member.)

The Oceania Project

http://www.oceania.org/

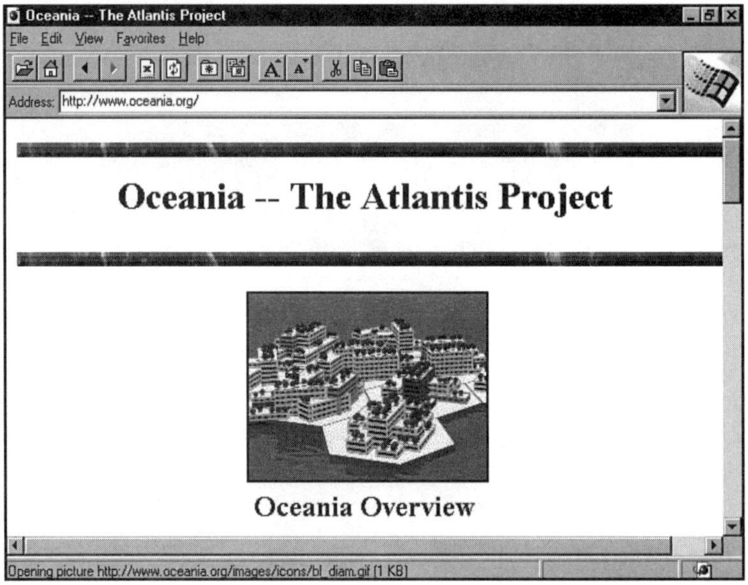

The authors of this site plan to start their own country. Most of the world's habitable land is already taken, so they're going to build their own country from the ground—well, the sea—up. They want to create the world's first sea colony. It will be built by Sea Structures, Inc.; visit this site if you want to know exactly how.

The Internal Revenue Service

http://www.ustreas.gov/treasury/bureaus/irs/irs.html

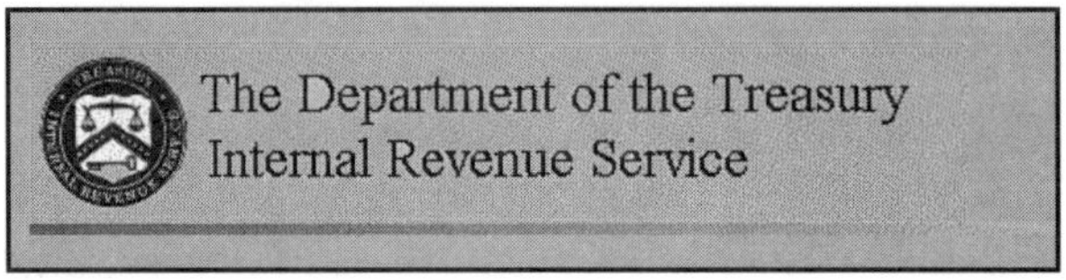

Late filing your taxes? Forgot to get one last form? You can get it here.

National Materials Exchange

http://www.earthcycle.com/g/p/earthcycle/

Got any industrial materials or waste you need to get rid of? Don't we all. Well, check out this Web site for information about how to deal with it. It's not a pretty site (hence no picture), but it is a good idea, and it's also a National Information Infrastructure (NII) awards winner.

OncoLink

http://cancer.med.upenn.edu/

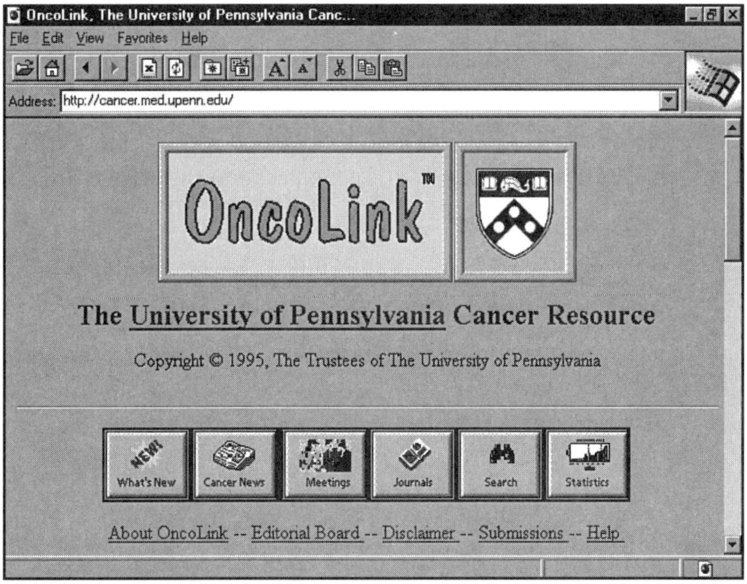

This one was a finalist for the NII awards. It provides everything you ever needed to know about cancer; news, meetings, journals, statistics, text, pictures, sounds, and video. There's a searchable index, too.

HotWired

http://www.hotwired.com/

The online version of the journal of the cyberage. You have to register, but there's no cost to do so (at least at the moment).

Part V: Appendixes

A

Installing Explorer on Non-MSN Systems

In this appendix:

- **Downloading Internet Explorer**
- **Connecting to an Internet service provider**
- **Creating a login script**
- **How do I set up a SLIP connection?**
- **How do I dial *without* a login script?**

So you want to install Internet Explorer to work with a service provider other than Microsoft Network. Here's what it takes . . . .

In this appendix I'm going to explain how to find Internet Explorer online, and how to install it for use with another service provider. I'll also explain what you need to do to if you are an MSN subscriber but want to use Internet Explorer with another service provider.

Yes, it's a long appendix. Yes, there are a lot of steps involved. It's nothing tremendously complicated, though. In fact you may even be lucky and breeze right through in a few minutes. Setting up a TCP/IP connection is not always simple. If you know what it took to install a Windows TCP/IP connection a couple of years ago, you'll discover that we've come a long way (though not quite as far as I'd like)! Just take your time and read carefully, and it'll work out okay, I promise!

Downloading from the Internet and online services

In chapter 3, I explained that you can download Internet Explorer from MSN, or you can install it from the Microsoft Plus! pack. But it's also available (for free) from the Internet and a variety of online services. If you already have Internet access, you can get the software from **http://www.windows.microsoft.com/windows/ie/ie.htm**. (If this URL no longer works, go to the Internet Explorer home page at **http://www.home.msn.com/** and dig around.) You'll also be able to download it from this Web site: **http://www.windows.microsoft.com**. And from this ftp site: **ftp://ftp.microsoft.com/PerOpSys/Win_News**. You also can find it on these online services:

- CompuServe: GO WINNEWS
- Prodigy: JUMP WINNEWS
- America Online: keyword WINNEWS
- GEnie: MOVE TO PAGE 95

You'll download an executable file (currently MSIE10.exe). Run this file, and the software will be installed on your hard disk. Reboot Windows, then double-click on the Internet icon that the installation program placed on your Windows desktop. The Internet Setup Wizard will start. I'll explain that in detail in a few moments.

Microsoft says that this executable file contains the Internet Jumpstart kit (which is also in the Microsoft Plus! pack). But, at the time of writing at least, this executable lacks some of the features of the Plus! pack's Jumpstart kit. You won't get Dial-Up Scripting, and you won't get the software needed to set up a SLIP connection. However, if you have Windows 95 on a CD, you'll find these programs in the ADMIN\APPTOOLS\DSCRIPT directory on the CD. Read the DSCRIPT.TXT file for installation instructions. Then follow the instructions in this appendix for creating a login script and, if necessary, setting up a SLIP connection.

If you *don't* have the CD version of Windows 95, you won't find these applications on your floppy disks. However, they should be available online, at **http://www.windows.microsoft.com/windows/software/admintools.htm** and the other locations I've just noted. (Look for links and categories such as these: the *Windows 95 CD-ROM Extras*, *Administration Tools*, *Dial-Up SLIP and Scripting Support*.)

Gathering information

Before you can install your software you must gather some information from your service provider. (Do you have a service provider? If not, see chapter 1, "What is the Internet?" to find out how to get one.)

TIP **The standard Microsoft Windows 95 TCP/IP stack only works on** PPP (Point-to-Point Protocol) connections. However, once you've installed Microsoft Plus! you'll find that you can also use a SLIP (Serial Line Internet Protocol) connection. The PPP protocol is preferred; it's faster and more stable. If your service provider can't give you a PPP connection, though, you'll be able to use SLIP. The instructions in this appendix begin by assuming that you are setting up a PPP connection. For information about SLIP, see "How can I use SLIP?" later in this appendix.

The first thing you should ask is this: *Do you have some kind of setup program that will set up my Windows 95 Dial-Up Networking software to connect to your system?* The answer will probably be *no*, especially in the first few months after Windows 95 is released. Perhaps eventually some service providers will offer such a service.

The next question—assuming you got a *no* to the first one—is this: *Do you have some kind of instruction sheet that tells me what to do?* Some service providers already have written instructions that explain what information you should enter into which dialog box. I'm going to help you with that to some degree, but I can't know the particulars—the actual names and numbers—that must be entered.

The next question is this: *Do you have a script file for the Windows 95 Dial-Up Scripting tool?* In the first few weeks after the release of Windows 95, most service providers won't know what you are talking about, so here's what you tell them. *The Dial-Up Scripting tool lets you associate a login script with a particular service provider, to help the Dial-Up Networking program connect to that service provider. The script file is an .SCP file.* You'll learn all about this later in this appendix (see "Creating a login script"). If you are lucky your service provider *will* have a script file; it will save you a lot of trouble. (If not, and if you go to the trouble of creating one, why not donate it to your service provider so they can pass it on to other users?)

You have a few more questions to ask. You need to know all the following information:

Information	Description
User name	The name assigned to your account; your account name, user name, account ID, login name, or whatever your service provider calls it.
Password	The password you use to access your account.
Phone number	The telephone number your modem has to dial in order to connect to your service provider.
IP address	This is the Internet Protocol address, and it identifies your computer once connected to the Internet. Ask your service provider if they "dynamically (or automatically) assign" a number; that means their software tells your software what number to use when it connects, so it may vary each time. If the number is *not* dynamically assigned, ask them what numbers you must enter for the **IP Address** and the **Subnet Mask**. With PPP, the IP address is normally assigned automatically, so you are not given a number.

Information	Description
DNS Server Address	Ask which number you must enter for your Domain Name Service server. This number identifies a computer that is used to help your software find resources on the Internet. The DNS system is a sort of giant directory in which each DNS server contains a portion of the information needed to route transmissions across the Internet. Ask your service provider if they have an **Alternate DNS Server Address**, too. Many only have one address, but some will provide two or more.
Domain name	You need your service provider's domain name, something like usa.net or mcp.com. This identifies your service provider's computer to the rest of the Internet.
Domain suffix	Ask if you have to enter a domain suffix, and if so exactly what you should enter. For instance, a domain suffix may be something like this: ns1.usa.net. (Strictly speaking the ns1 bit is the suffix, while the usa.net bit is the domain; however, you'll enter the entire suffix and domain together.)
Gateway	Ask if you need to enter a gateway number. A gateway links one network to another. It's quite possible that you won't have to enter a gateway number (it's more likely to be used when setting up Internet access from a LAN), but some service providers may provide such a number.
Your e-mail address	The address you give to other people so they can send e-mail to you: robinhood@sherwood-forest.com, for instance.
Internet mail server	The address of your mail server. For instance, mine is mail.usa.net.
SLIP or CSLIP	If you have a SLIP connection rather than a PPP connection, ask if the service provider uses SLIP or CSLIP. CSLIP is a variation of SLIP (Compressed SLIP) that is quite common. If your service provider can provide you with a PPP account, though (and most can, these days), get a PPP account and forget about this SLIP stuff.
How do I log on?	You must have instructions about how to log onto the service provider's system. For instance, many systems require that you type a command (ppp, for instance) and press Enter to begin running the PPP protocol.

Once you've got all the information you need, you are ready to install the software.

Installing from Microsoft Plus!

To install the Internet software, including Internet Explorer, from Microsoft Plus!, follow these instructions:

1. Place the Microsoft Plus! CD into your CD-Rom drive (or the first disk in the set in your floppy disk drive).
2. Click on the taskbar's Start button to open the Start menu.
3. Choose Settings, Control Panel.
4. Double-click on the Add/Remove Programs icon.
5. In the dialog box that opens, click on the Install button.
6. In the dialog box that opens, click on Next. Windows 95 will begin looking at the disks in your floppy disk and CD-Rom drives for SETUP and INSTALL programs.
7. When Windows 95 finds a SETUP or INSTALL program, it displays the Run Program dialog box. Look closely at the drive on which it says it found the program, because it may find the wrong one. For instance, if you have a CD-Rom drive with the Microsoft Plus! disc, but forgot that you left a program disk in your floppy disk drive, it may find the program on the floppy disk first.

   If the program shown is not the SETUP.EXE program on the Microsoft Plus! disk, click on Browse to open a typical Windows 95 Browse box, then find the program on the correct disk and double-click on it.
8. When you have the correct program displayed in the Run Program dialog box, click on Finish and Windows 95 runs the Setup program.
9. When the first message box appears, click on Continue.
10. In the dialog box that follows, type your name and organization name, then click on OK. Click on OK again in the next dialog box, to confirm your name and organization.

11 Click on OK in the Product Number dialog box.

12 A dialog box showing you where the Microsoft Plus! files will be placed opens; click on OK.

13 When given the choice between a Typical and Custom installation, click on Custom.

14 The next dialog box to open will show you a list of the products available in Microsoft Plus! Choose the ones you want. Make sure that the Internet Jumpstart Kit is selected. Then click on Continue.

15 The Setup program begins copying the files to your hard disk. What happens next depends on the items you chose to install. (We'll assume that you are only installing the Internet Jumpstart Kit.)

16 The Internet Setup Wizard opens, as you can see in figure A.1.

Fig. A.1
The Internet Setup Wizard will help you enter the correct settings for your TCP/IP connection.

17 Click on Next. The Wizard shows you two options: click on the option button labeled **I already have an account with a different service provider**, then click on Next.

18 The Wizard now lets you enter the name of your service provider (see fig. A.2). Type the name, then click on Next.

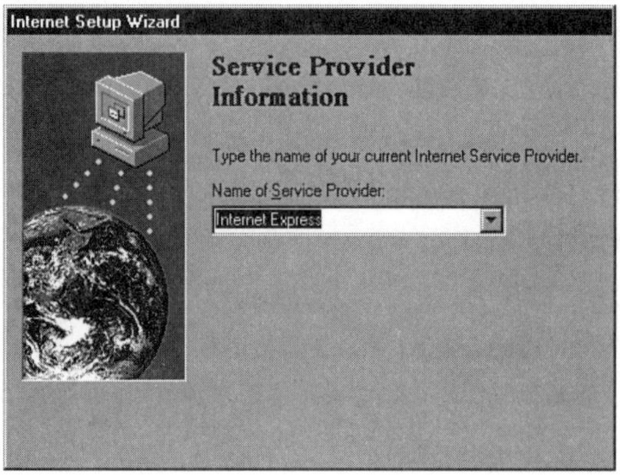

Fig. A.2
Type the name of your service provider.

19 Now you have to enter the telephone number you must dial to connect to your service provider (see fig. A.3). In a few cases it may be necessary to select, from the **Country code** dropdown list box, the country that must be dialed to contact your service provider.

There's another check box, **Bring up terminal window after dialing**. This opens a special window in which you can see the text being transmitted between your service provider's computer and your computer during the login procedure. You can then type your user name and password into this terminal window to log in. But I'm going to show you how to create a login script that will do all this automatically, so leave this check box cleared.

Click on Next.

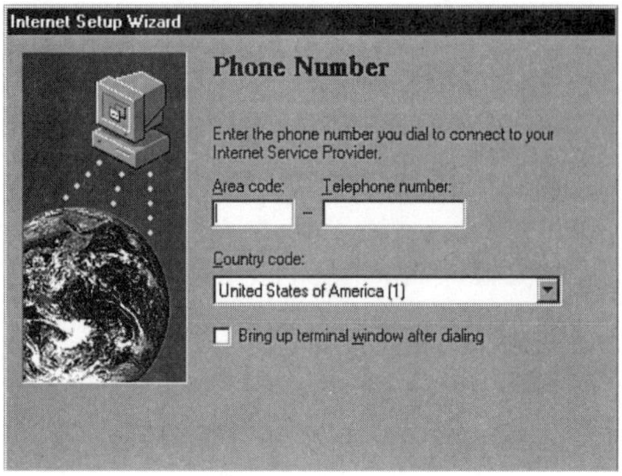

Fig. A.3
Enter your service provider's telephone number—the one you dial when connecting to the Internet.

20 Enter the **User name** (also known as account name, User ID, and so on) that identifies your account with this service provider, and the **Password** that you use. (See fig. A.4.) Make sure you type the password very carefully, because the Setup program displays asterisks while you type (so nobody can look over your shoulder at the screen and see your account password). Then click on Next.

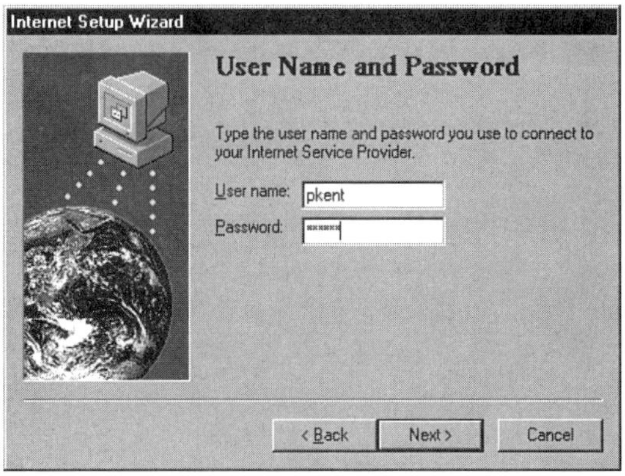

Fig. A.4
Type the User name and Password that you use to access your account.

21 The next dialog box asks you how your IP (Internet Protocol) address is assigned (see figure A.5). It's probably assigned dynamically (automatically), in which case you should select the first option button. If your service provider told you to enter **IP Address** and **Subnet Mask** numbers, click on the second option button and enter those numbers. An example of an IP address is: 192.156.196.1 Make sure you enter the periods between the numbers. Then click on Next.

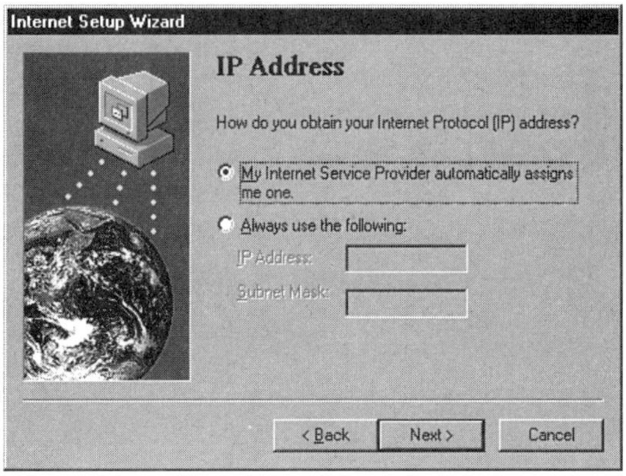

Fig. A.5
Tell the Setup program how your IP address is assigned.

22 Now you have to provide the IP address of at least one DNS server—two servers if your service provider gave you more than one number. (See fig. A.6.) Then click on Next.

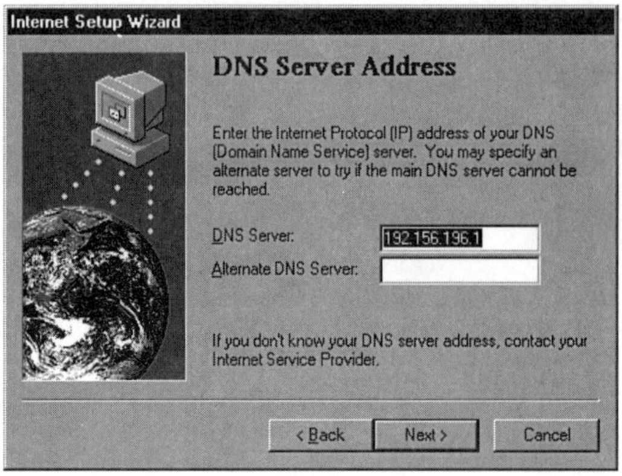

Fig. A.6
Enter the DNS server address from your service provider.

23 The next dialog box asks if you want to use e-mail. I'm not getting into e-mail much in this book, but if you are setting up a TCP/IP stack you'll probably want to use the connection to collect your e-mail messages. You may already have an e-mail program you use; if not, you may want to use Microsoft Exchange, which is on your Windows 95 setup disk or disk set. Click on the **Use Internet Mail** check box, then enter your e-mail address and the name of your mail server. See figure A.7 for an example.

Fig. A.7
Now enter your e-mail address and mail-server name.

24 The next dialog box asks you which "profile" you want to use for Microsoft Exchange (I'm assuming you have MS Exchange installed.) You should leave the settings in this dialog box alone, unless you understand everything about profiles. (You can always change the settings later; you can find out about them from your Windows 95 documentation. *Using Microsoft Network* also has a detailed description of MS Exchange and its profiles.) Click on Next.

Fig. A.8
You can generally leave these settings as they are.

25 The next dialog box tells you that you've finished the Internet setup. (You probably haven't—I'll explain why in a moment.) Click on Finish.

26 You'll see a dialog box telling you that you must restart your computer. Click on Restart Windows.

Once you are back in Windows you can quickly check your settings, to see whether they work. Open the Start menu and then choose Programs, Accessories, Dial-Up Networking. The Dial-Up Networking folder will open, and inside it you'll find an icon representing the Internet connection you've just created. Double-click on the icon and the Connect To dialog box opens. Click on Connect, and the program dials into your service provider.

TIP **Right-click on the icon that represents your Internet connection** in the Dial-Up Networking folder, and choose Create Shortcut from the pop-up menu. This will place a shortcut on your desktop, so you can quickly start an Internet session by double-clicking on the shortcut.

Did you get all the way through to a message that says *Connected at nn,nnn bps*? (The *nn,nnn* is the speed of your modem; *28,800*, for instance.) Or did you get a message telling you that "*Dial-Up Networking could not negotiate a compatible set of network protocols*," or something similar? You probably got the second of these messages, and you didn't manage to get all the way through. Why? Because you don't have a **login script**.

TIP

Bug Alert! At the time of writing, once you had received the "Dial-Up Networking could not negotiate a compatible set of network protocols," message, Dial-Up Networking would simply quit bothering to try to connect. In other words, even if you set up everything correctly, and wrote a good login script, Dial-Up Networking still wouldn't connect properly if it has already had a bad session. The only way around the problem was to restart Windows 95 and try again.

By the time you read this the problem may be fixed...or it may not. If you write a login script and test it (see "Testing the script," later in this appendix), and if the test seems to indicate that the script is *good*, yet Dial-Up Networking still shows the same "*Dial-Up Networking could not negotiate...*" message, try restarting Windows 95 and testing the script again.

Creating a login script

Microsoft's Dial-Up Networking program is supposed to dial into your service provider, make a connection, then establish the TCP/IP connection. The problem is, each service provider works a little differently. With some you just have to dial in and provide your user name and password, and away you go—you're connected and the TCP/IP software is running. But many, perhaps most, service providers don't do this.

For instance, when connecting to my service provider their computer prompts for my user name, and then my password. But then it sends a short message. When this message is received, there are three options. I can type **c** and press Enter; that takes me into my **shell** account, a simple menu-system that can be used by any serial-communications program. Or I can type **slip** and press Enter, and start a SLIP (Serial Line Internet Protocol) connection. Or I can type **ppp** and press Enter, and start a PPP (Point-to-Point Protocol) connection.

So how does Dial-Up Networking know all this? It doesn't. So I had to tell it how to handle this—and you will, too, if you found that you couldn't connect. I had to create a **login script**, a text file with a set of instructions that tell Dial-Up Networking what it will see and what to do.

Remember I told you earlier to ask your service provider if they have a login script file that will work with Windows 95's Dial-Up Networking program. If your service provider *does* have such a script file, all you need to do is place a copy in the \Program Files\Plus! directory, and skip to "Assigning the script file," later in this appendix. If they *don't* have a script file, you'll have to create one; read on.

TIP **If your service provider wrote the script file using the transmit** $PASSWORD and transmit $USERID commands, as described below, there's no need to change anything in the script. However, if the service provider used the transmit *username* or transmit *password* commands, where *username* and *password* are the actual User name and password, rather than system variables, you'll have to replace the *username* and *password* with your User name and password, or with the $PASSWORD or $USERID system variables. Ask your service provider if you need to modify the script in any way.

Watching a login procedure

The first thing you should do is log in to your service provider using a simple serial-communications program. Something like CrossTalk, Qmodem, or whatever your favorite program is. If you don't have a favorite, you can use the new HyperTerminal program, the one that comes with Windows 95. (If you didn't install it, choose Start, Settings, Control Panel. Double-click on the Add/Remove Programs icon, then click on the Windows Setup tab. You'll find HyperTerminal in the Communications category.)

TIP **If your service provider gave you clear and accurate instructions** on how to log in, you can skip this step, and create the login script from those instructions. If the script doesn't work, though, you'll probably need to come back and follow this procedure, to find the correct login sequence.

Follow these instructions:

1. Open the Start menu, and choose Programs, Accessories, HyperTerminal. The HyperTerminal folder will open.

2 Double-click on the Hypertrm.exe icon, and HyperTerminal starts. You'll see the Connection Description dialog box.

3 Type the name of your service provider, then click on OK. You'll see the Phone Number dialog box.

4 Enter the phone number that your modem has to dial to connect to your service provider, then click on OK. You'll see the Connect dialog box.

5 Click on Dial, and HyperTerminal begins dialing into your service provider.

6 When you connect, do everything that your service provider told you you'd have to do to make your connection; when prompted, enter your username and password, and any other commands that are necessary to make your connection.

7 When you get all the way logged onto the system, copy all the text that appeared in the window during the session to the Clipboard (choose Edit, Select All, then choose Edit, Copy), and paste it into a word processor or Notepad.

8 Close the HyperTerminal window.

So what did you get? Take a look at the text saved from my sample session (I've bolded the text that I had to type):

```
Checking authorization, Please wait...
Connected to port #33[Denver-1]

Welcome to the INTERNET EXPRESS Network

CUSTOMER SERVICE: 800-592-1240  or  719-592-1240.
Normal hours are Mon-Fri 7:30AM-10:00PM, Sat and Sun 8:00AM-
10:00PM.
24 Hour Live Operator Support for service interruptions.

Username: pkent
Password: (my password)

Permission granted
Type "c" followed by <RETURN> to continue ppp
Switching to PPP.
~ }#À!}!}!} }4}"}&} } } } }%}&DX=Ö}'}"}(}"ƒø~~ }#À!}!}"}
}4}"}&} } } } }%}&1_„I}
'}"}(}"êT~~ }#À!}!}#} }4}"}&} } } } }%}&ÍÂRO}'}"}(}"+_~~
}#À!}!}$} }4}"}&} } } }
```

```
 }%}&h_]$}'}"}(}"}+ ~~ }#À!}!}%} }4}"}&} } } }
}%}&3S}#Û}'}"}(}""_~~ }#À!}!}&} }
4}"}&} } } } }%}&Òª Å‰}'}"}(}"'Ë~~ }#À!}!}'} }4}"}&} } } }
}%}&}0}?ò{}'}"}(}"}%}/
~~ }#À!}!}(} }4}"}&} } } } }%}&Ú(q)}'}"}(}"b¦~~ }#À!}!}))}
}4}"}&} } } } }%}&‰}3}
,ô}'}"}(}"'R~~ }#À!}!}*} }4}"}&} } } } }%}&}0CÄ}'}"}(}"_ª~~
}#À!}!}+} }4}"}&} }
```

What can you tell from this?

- When I see the *Username:* prompt, I have to type **pkent** (my account name), and then press Enter.
- When I see the *Password:* prompt, I have to type my password and then press Enter.
- When I see the *Type "c" followed by <RETURN> to continue* prompt, I have to type **ppp** and press Enter. (No, I don't need to press c, though that's what the prompt says. The c is used to start my "shell" account.)

What's all that garbage at the bottom? Well, when I typed `ppp` and pressed Enter, my service provider's computer began the PPP session. PPP is a form of TCP/IP, but HyperTerminal is not a TCP/IP program; it has no idea what the information it is receiving means. That's okay, because at this point I know that I've got all the information I need—the service provider's computer sent the message *Switching to PPP*, so I must have done something right.

Now, if you can't get through to your service provider's system in this manner, you need to call your service provider and find out why. I'm going to assume that you've been able to find the information you need, and are now ready to write the script file.

Writing the script file

Open Notepad—open the Start menu and then choose Programs, Accessories, Notepad. Now type your login script. What login script, you ask? Here's mine as an example:

```
proc main
waitfor "username:"
transmit $USERID
transmit "^M"
waitfor "password:"
```

```
transmit $PASSWORD
transmit "^M"
waitfor "continue"
transmit "ppp^M"
endproc
```

This is a really simple script, but it works. Here's what it all means:

```
proc main
```

This must appear at the top of the script. It just means "this is the top of the script," okay?

```
waitfor "username:"
```

Remember we saw that when I logged on to my service provider's system I had to wait for the prompt `Username:`? Well this line tells Dial-Up Networking to wait until it sees that prompt. Note that I typed `username:`, not `Username:`. The case you use doesn't matter.

```
transmit $USERID
```

When Dial-Up Networking sees the `Username:` prompt, it moves to the next line in the script. This line tells Dial-Up Networking to type my user name. `$USERID` means "look at the user name entered during setup, and type that." Remember, you entered your User name in the Internet Setup Wizard.

TIP **Some readers may be creating an Internet connection from** scratch, not using the Internet Setup Wizard. (You may be using the instructions "Converting from MSN to another service provider," later in this appendix.) If so, don't worry about the User name and password right now. Use the `transmit $USERID` and `transmit $PASSWORD` commands. You'll enter the User name and password later, just before you dial into your service provider.

```
transmit "^M"
```

This line means "press Enter." (`"^M"` represents the Enter key—note that it is enclosed in quotation marks.)

```
waitfor "password:"
```

Now we are waiting for the `Password:` prompt.

```
transmit $PASSWORD
```

Once Dial-Up Networking has seen the `Password:` prompt, it sends my password. Again, `$PASSWORD` means "use the password entered into the Internet Setup Wizard."

```
transmit "^M"
```

Again, this means "press Enter."

```
waitfor "continue"
```

Now we are waiting for the `continue` prompt (remember, the full prompt was `Type "c" followed by <RETURN> to continue`).

```
transmit "ppp^M"
```

Once it's seen the `continue` prompt, Dial-Up Networking will type `ppp` and press Enter. This time the `^M` is added directly after the text that is being typed, because we've entered the text directly, rather than by using a *system variable*. (`$USERID` and `$PASSWORD` are system variables, and as such are treated differently.) There's no need for a separate line for the `^M` command. Note, though, that the text `ppp` and the `^M` are enclosed by quotation marks.

```
endproc
```

That's it, we've finished. The `endproc` command tells Dial-Up Networking that the script has finished, and that it can start the PPP protocol.

There's a lot more to writing scripts, if you really want to get into it. You should find a file called SCRIPT.DOC, which you can open in WordPad, in the \Program Files\Plus! directory. This describes the scripting language, though it's by no means easy to figure out; it helps if you have some computer-geek experience.

There are a couple of commands you may want to use. For instance, you can add `until 10` to your `waitfor` commands, like this:

```
waitfor "password:" until 10
```

This tells Dial-Up Networking to wait 10 seconds (You could use `until 5`, `until 20`, or whatever you want). If the prompt doesn't appear within that time, Dial-Up Networking will give up.

There's also a `set ipaddr getip` command that is used to retrieve your IP command if your service provider's computer sends that information to your computer during login. (For more information on this command you can also see "How can I use SLIP?" later in this appendix.)

Most login scripts will probably be fairly simple, like mine. Use mine as an example and substitute the correct information. If you need more, refer to the SCRIPT.DOC file. You'll also find sample .SCP files in the \Program Files\Accessories\ directory—you may be able to modify one of these. If you can't figure it all out, ask your service provider for more help. After all, the service provider only has to write a script once, and can then use it for all their subscribers who want to use their Windows 95 software to connect. (And if your service provider won't help? Find another!)

When you have finished your script, save it in the \Program Files\Accessories\ directory, using the .SCP extension. For instance, you might call it SCRIPT.SCP.

TIP **I told you to open Notepad to create this file, because Notepad** saves ASCII text files. If you decided to create this in a word processor, make sure you save the file in the ASCII format.

Assigning the script file

Once you've created your script file, you need to associate it with the Dial-Up Networking configuration you created. Here's how:

1. Open the Start menu and choose Programs, Accessories, Dial-Up Scripting Tool. You'll see the dialog box in figure A.9.
2. In the **Connections** list box, click on the connection that you created earlier in this appendix. (It may be the only one there, of course. My illustration shows The Microsoft Network, because I also created an MSN Internet connection.)
3. Click on Browse, to open a typical Browse dialog box. Find the script file you created (SCRIPT.SCP, for instance), and double-click on it to place it into the **File name** text box in the Dial-Up Scripting Tool dialog box.

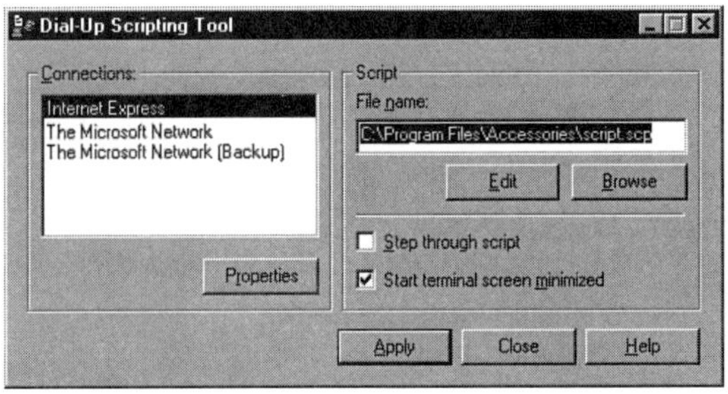

Fig. A.9
The Dial-Up Scripting Tool lets you tell Dial-Up Networking how to connect to your service provider.

4 Click on the **Step through script** check box.

5 Click on the Apply button.

Testing the script

Now we are ready to test the script, to make sure it works. We selected the **Step through script** check box just now because this tells Dial-Up Networking to let us view what's going on, step by step. Follow this procedure:

1 If you have created a desktop shortcut to the Dial-Up Networking Connection earlier, double-click on the shortcut. Otherwise, open the Start menu, and choose Programs, Accessories, Dial-Up Networking. Then double-click on the connection icon in the Dial-Up Networking folder.

2 In the Connect To dialog box, enter your User name and Password, and click on Connect. The Dial-Up Networking program begins dialing. When your modem connects to your service provider, you'll see the dialog boxes in fig. A.10.

TIP **Notice the Save Password check box. If you click on this, Windows** 95 should save your password for future sessions, so that you don't have to enter it each time. However, this feature is a little flakey. If you have set up separate user profiles for Windows 95, it will save this password. (See your Windows 95 documentation for information about user profiles.) If you haven't, Windows probably won't save the password (though I've been informed by Microsoft personnel that it should), so you'll have to enter it each time you log on. You could also place it in your script if you wish, though you probably shouldn't do so if your computer can be used by other people.

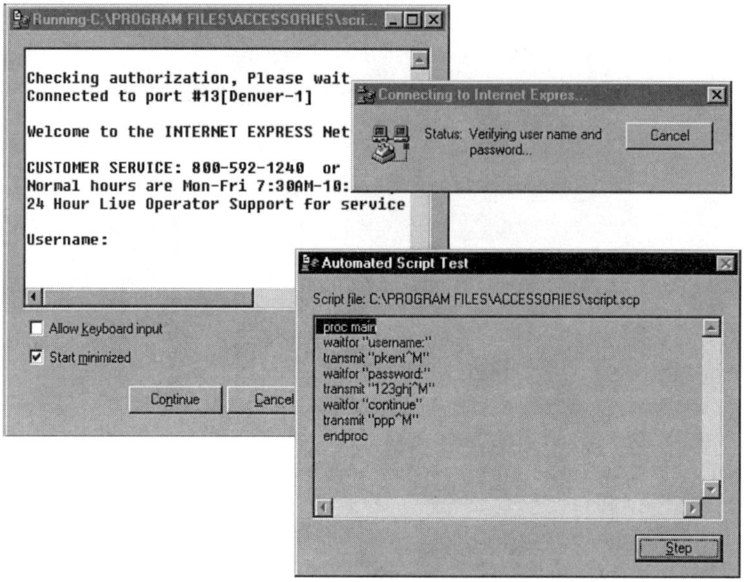

Fig. A.10
Move these windows into position quickly, so you can see what's going on.

3 These windows may be positioned rather awkwardly; you may not be able to see what's going on very well. I suggest you move them into the positions shown in figure A.10, but do so quickly; if you take too long, your service provider's computer will give up waiting for you and disconnect your modem.

4 Click on the Step button in the Automated Script Test window to move through the script, step by step. Each time you click on the button, the highlight in the window moves to the next line in the script.

TIP **You may see a message telling you that you have a *syntax* error in** your script. Cancel the session and take a look at the script—click on the Edit button in the Dial-Up Scripting Tool dialog box. You may find a spelling error, or a missing ", for instance.

5 Watch the effect in the Running-*scriptname* window, where you can see the login session in effect. Each time you click while the highlight is on a `transmit` command, for instance, Dial-Up Networking should "type" the text that appears after `transmit`. You'll be able to see that happening in the window.

6. When you click the Step button while the highlight is on the `endproc` command, both windows will close, and Dial-Up Networking will begin running the PPP protocol. In a few seconds you should see the message *Connected at nn,nnn bps* in the little Connected To dialog box (see fig. A.11).

7. Click on the Disconnect button to end the session.

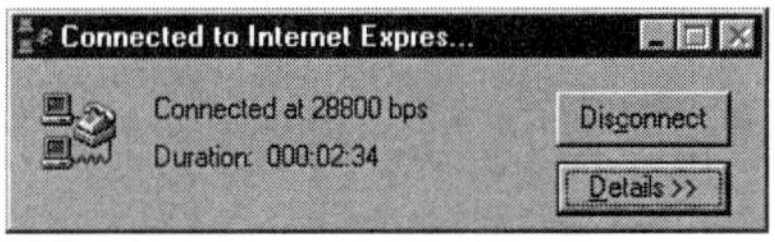

Fig. A.11
You've done it! You're connected to your service provider.

Did everything work correctly? If not, go back and try again. Watch the session very carefully, and try to figure out where things went wrong:

- Did you spell something incorrectly, thereby using a `transmit` command to send the wrong information?
- Did a spelling mistake after a `waitfor` command tell Dial-Up Networking to wait for the wrong information?
- Have you used the `^M` in the correct places to press Enter?
- Have you missed any quotation marks?

Look at your script carefully, watch the session carefully, and you should be able to see where you are going wrong.

And remember to talk with your service provider. Send them a copy of your login script, so they can tell you where you are going wrong.

TIP **If you are having problems, you may want to try logging on** manually. That is, you will see your service provider's prompts and will have to type the responses. See "Preparing for a manual login," later in this chapter.

Finishing off

Once you've got your script working correctly, return to the Dial-Up Scripting Tool dialog box. Click on the connection you just tested, then *clear* the **Step through script** check box. Click on Apply, and then click on Close.

Now try connecting to your service provider again. This time Dial-Up Networking should be able to connect without your assistance. However, note that just because Dial-Up Networking tells you that your connection has been made, it doesn't mean that the connection is working correctly. Here's a quick way to test the connection.

Choose Start, Programs, MS-DOS Prompt. When the MS-DOS window opens, type `ping` followed by an Internet host name. Try `ping usa.net`, `ping ftp.microsoft.com`, `ping ftp.mcp.com`, `ping www.mcp.com`, `ping csn.org`, `ping gopher.sara.nl`, or any other Internet host name you've come across. Try pinging your service provider's host name. If one of these doesn't work, try another (it may be that the host you tried is not operating at the moment). If your connection is working correctly, you should see something like this:

```
C:\WIN95>ping csn.org
Pinging csn.org [199.117.27.21] with 32 bytes of data:
Reply from 199.117.27.21: bytes=32 time=232ms TTL=239
Reply from 199.117.27.21: bytes=32 time=239ms TTL=239
Reply from 199.117.27.21: bytes=32 time=237ms TTL=239
Reply from 199.117.27.21: bytes=32 time=236ms TTL=239
```

Ping is a command that sends a message to a host, and asks it to respond. It's a way to confirm that you can communicate with a host. And if you can communicate with a host, your TCP/IP connection is working correctly!

It didn't work!

The procedure we've just looked at will probably be enough to get your connection working. However, this TCP/IP thing is very complicated, with lots of variations, and you may find that you *can't* get your connection running this way. You may need to enter more configuration information. Follow this procedure:

1. Choose Start, Settings, Control Panel.
2. When the Control Panel opens, double-click on the Network icon.
3. In the Network dialog box, click on the TCP/IP entry and then click on Properties.
4. If your service provider told you that the IP address would be assigned dynamically or automatically, leave Obtain IP Address Automatically

selected. If you were given an IP address, click on Specify An IP Address, then type the number into the IP Address box. If you were given a Subnet Mask number, enter that too.

5 Click on the Gateway tab at the top of the dialog box. You probably won't need to enter anything in here. However, if your service provider told you to do so, type a gateway number into the New Gateway text box and then click on the Add button.

6 Click on the DNS Configuration tab.

7 You'll almost certainly have to select Enable DNS. Most service providers provide one or more DNS numbers that you need to enter.

8 Enter a Host and Domain. The Host is your computer name. It doesn't matter what you put here for our purposes; I suggest you just enter your account name. In the Domain text box enter your service provider's host name.

9 Type the primary DNS server number given to you by your service provider, into the text box below DNS Server Search Order, then click on the Add button. This places the number into the list box. Add any others given to you in the same way.

10 You *may* have to enter something into the Domain Suffix Search Order. This is the domain name preceded by some other letters and/or numbers. Type what your service provider told you to enter into the text box, then click on Add.

11 There are several more tabs in this dialog box; WINS Configuration, Bindings, and Advanced. Most of this stuff is related to setting up a TCP/IP network, which I'm not covering in this book (I'll leave that up to your system administrator). Only change things in these areas if told to do so by your service provider or system administrator.

12 Click on OK to finish the TCP/IP setup.

13 Click on OK in the Network dialog box. You'll see a message box telling you that you must restart your computer. Click on Yes.

Now try connecting to your service provider again.

How can I use SLIP?

If you have to use a SLIP connection, rather than a PPP connection, you have a few more steps to run through. The SLIP software comes with the Internet Jumpstart Kit, which is part of Microsoft Plus! So begin at "Installing from Microsoft Plus!" earlier in this appendix.

Install the Internet Jumpstart Kit, and let the Internet Setup Wizard set up your Internet connection. When the Wizard has finished setting up the connection, follow this procedure:

1. Open the Start menu and choose Programs, Accessories, Dial-Up Networking.
2. In the Dial-Up Networking dialog box, right-click on the new connection icon, and choose Properties.
3. In the dialog box that appears, click on Server Type. You'll see the dialog box in figure A.12.

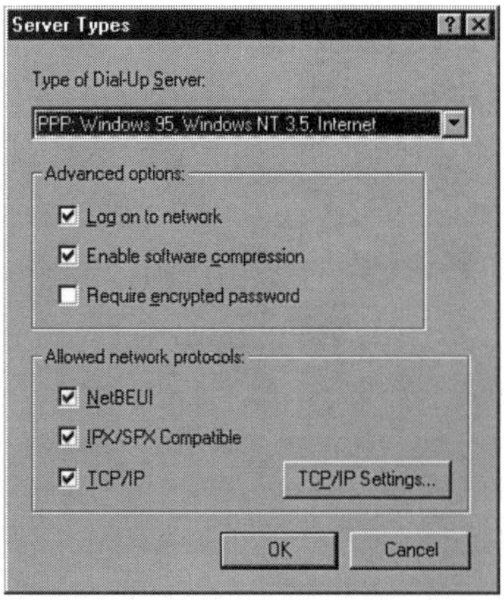

Fig. A.12
The Server Types dialog box lets you select the type of connection you want to make.

4. Open the **Type of Dial-Up Server** dropdown list box, then select **Slip: Unix Connection or CSLIP: Unix Connection with IP Header Compression**, depending on which form of SLIP your service provider uses. (The choice may be yours, if your service provider has both forms. If so, choose CSLIP.)

5 Click on TCP/IP Settings. The dialog box in figure A.13 opens. This dialog box shows you the IP address and DNS server information that you entered into the Wizard earlier. That information can be changed here later, if necessary. Leave the other information alone, unless your service provider tells you to enter something here.

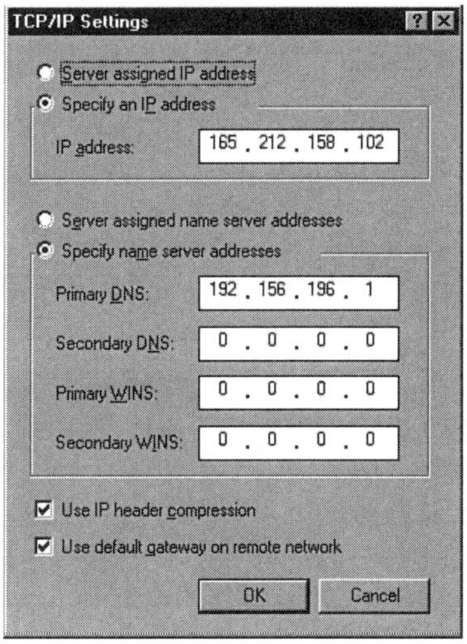

Fig. A.13
The TCP/IP Settings dialog box shows your IP address and the DNS server address.

6 Click on OK to close this dialog box, then click on OK again to close the Server Types dialog box.

7 Create a login script, as described earlier (start at the section title "Watching a login procedure," then follow the instructions under "Writing the script file" and "Assigning the script file." Then test your script and connection (see "Testing the script").

Note that there are a couple of ways to handle the IP address assigned to your SLIP account. You can tell the Wizard which IP address to use (or enter the IP address into the TCP/IP Settings dialog box later—see fig. A.13). Or you can add a line to your script to tell Dial-Up Networking to "grab" the IP number from your service provider.

For instance, here's what happens when I dial into my service provider's system and log on using SLIP:

```
Type "c" followed by <RETURN> to continue slip
Annex address is 165.212.158.10. Your address is
165.212.158.117
```

The second number on the last line is my IP address; my service provider's system assigns it to me automatically. In fact this number changes. I *may* get the same number the next time I connect, but I probably won't.

So I've added the following line to my SLIP login script, to tell Dial-Up Networking to use this second number:

```
set ipaddr getip 2
```

The `2` at the end refers to the position of the number on the line. If I'd used a `1`, Dial-Up Networking would grab the first number on the line, `165.212.158.10` (which is wrong, of course, as this is the address of the Annex, the computer I'm connecting to).

Converting from MSN to another service provider

If you installed your Internet-access software while an MSN member, it's set up to work with MSN—it won't work for other service providers. You need to make a few changes.

If you got your Internet software online from MSN, rather than by installing the Internet Jumpstart Kit from Microsoft Plus!, you will not have installed the software needed to set up a SLIP connection, and you won't have the Dial-Up Scripting Tool. These are both included in Microsoft Plus! You can also get them from the Windows 95 CD, or by downloading them; see "Downloading from the Internet and online services," earlier in this appendix.

TIP **If you are converting from MSN to another Internet service** provider, you'll also need to change the auto-dial feature (the feature used by Internet Explorer to "call" Dial-Up Networking when it needs to retrieve a document from the Web). See "Setting up the auto-dial feature" in chapter 4 for more information.

Creating an Internet connection "from scratch"

Here's a summary of how you can create an Internet connection without using Microsoft Plus!'s Internet Setup Wizard.

The first thing you should do is call your service provider and ask the first few questions listed under "Gathering information," earlier in this appendix. With luck, your service provider will have a program that you can run to set up your connection software, or perhaps a set of written instructions and a login script. If not, you've got plenty of work to do. Follow these instructions:

1. Gather all the information you'll need to set up a connection to your service provider. (See "Gathering information," earlier in this appendix.)
2. Open the Start menu and choose Programs, Accessories, Dial-Up Networking.
3. In the Dial-Up Networking dialog box, double-click on the Make New Connection dialog box.
4. In the Make New Connection dialog box, type the name of your service provider and select the modem you want to use. Then click on Next.
5. Enter the telephone number your modem must dial to connect to your service provider. Then click on Next.
6. Click on Finish. The dialog box closes.
7. Open the Dial-Up Scripting Tool, create a log-in script, and assign the script to your new connection. (For details, see "Creating a login script," earlier in this appendix. If you are setting up a SLIP connection, you should also read the information about scripts under "How can I use SLIP?" earlier in this appendix.)

   If you don't have Microsoft Plus! or the Windows 95 CD—so you don't have the Dial-Up Scripting Tool—either forget about using a script and log in manually (I'll explain how under "Connecting to your service provider," in a moment), or download the software (see "Downloading from the Internet and online services," earlier in this chapter).

8 In the Dial-Up Networking folder, right-click on the icon representing the connection you have created, and choose Properties.

9 Click on the Server Type button. The Server Types dialog box (fig. A.12) opens.

10 Make sure the correct **Type of Dial-Up Server** has been selected, depending on the system your service provider has set up for you: PPP, SLIP, or CSLIP.

11 Click on the TCP/IP Settings button to open the TCP/IP Settings dialog box (see fig. A.13).

12 If your service provider told you that your IP address is assigned automatically, make sure the **Server assigned IP address** check box is selected. If your service provider told you to use a particular IP address, click on **Specify an IP address** and type the number into the **IP address** box.

13 Click on the **Specify name server addresses** option button and enter the DNS address given to you by your service provider into the **Primary DNS** box. If you were given a second number, enter it into the **Secondary DNS** box.

14 Leave the other items in this dialog box alone unless you were told to change them by your service provider.

15 Click on OK to close the dialog box, then click on OK twice more to return to the Dial-Up Networking dialog box.

Preparing for a manual login

If you don't have the Dial-Up Scripting Tool you'll have to log in to your service provider manually. It's also useful to be able to do this for troubleshooting purposes. That is, if you are having trouble connecting using a script, you may want to try logging on manually to see if you can get through that way. Follow this procedure to prepare for this:

1 In the Dial-Up Networking folder, right-click on the icon representing the connection you have created, and choose Properties.

2 Click on the Configure button. The modem Properties dialog box opens.

3 Click on the **Options** tab.

4 Click on the **Bring up terminal window after dialing** check box.

5 Click on OK twice to return to the Dial-Up Networking folder.

Connecting to your service provider

Now you are ready to connect to your service provider. Follow these steps:

1 In the Dial-Up Networking folder, double-click on the icon representing the connection you have just created. That connection's Connect To dialog box opens (see fig. A.14).

Fig. A.14
Enter the correct User name and Password into the Connect To dialog box.

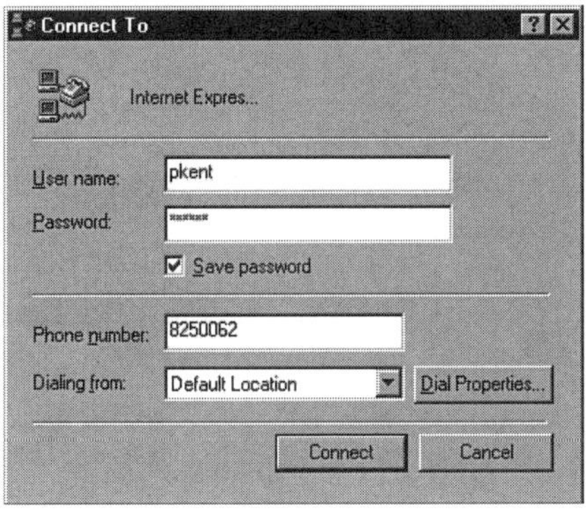

2 Type your **User name** and **Password**. (If you are going to log in manually, you can ignore these text boxes.)

3 Notice the **Save password** check box. Click on this if you want Dial-Up Networking to save the password for you, so you don't have to enter it each time. (Again, ignore these if you are logging in manually.)

4 Click on Connect, and Dial-Up Networking begins to dial into your service provider. If you created a login script, with luck you'll be connected successfully. If not, read the information under "Testing the script" and "Finishing off" earlier in this appendix. This will explain how to test your login script.

CAUTION **The User name and password that you've just entered are not saved** until part way through the connection procedure. Strange, but true. This means that if you don't get all the way through the procedure, you may find that when you return to this dialog box you have to re-enter the information.

5 If you haven't created a login script, and selected the **Bring up terminal window after dialing** check box in the modem's Properties dialog box, you'll have to login manually. You'll see the Post-Dial Terminal Screen, as shown in figure A.15.

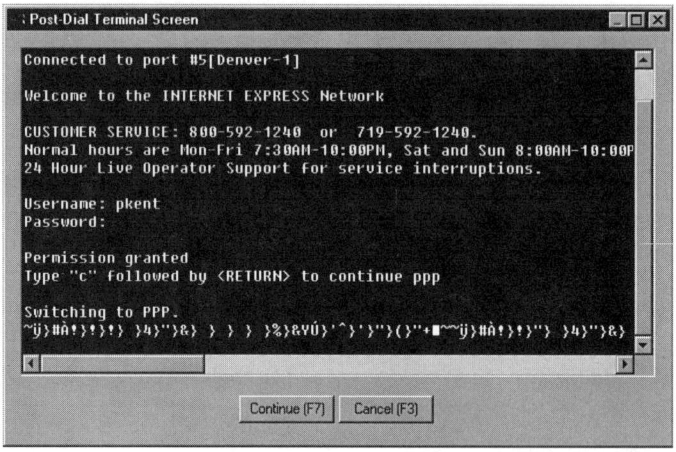

Fig. A.15
The Post-Dial Terminal Screen is where you'll type your login commands.

6 You can quickly maximize this window if necessary, by clicking on the X button in the top right of the window.

7 Type the login commands into this window. You can see from this example that I typed my User name, my password, and the `ppp` command.

8 When your service provider's computer begins the PPP or SLIP protocol, click on the Continue button, or press F7. The Post-Dial Terminal Screen will close, and your session should begin.

Still got problems? Remember to ask your service provider for help! Setting up these things is complicated, and there are many different variations. You must get everything just right for it to work. You should also refer to "It didn't work!," earlier in this appendix.

Action Index

Background information

continues

Installing the program

Navigating the Web

Working in Web pages

History, favorites, shortcuts

Customizing the program

continues

Finding Web pages that interest you

Saving what you find

Working with Viewers

continues

Non-Web Internet services

continues

Creating Web pages

continues

Index

F

I

J-K

O

P-Q

R

V

X–Y–Z

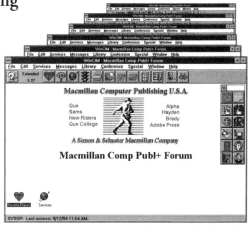

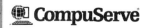